Home Inspection EXAM PREP

Carson Dunlop
& Associates

Dearborn™
Home Inspection

President: Roy Lipner
Publisher: Evan M. Butterfield
Senior Development Editor: Laurie McGuire
Content Consultant: Alan Carson
Managing Editor, Production: Daniel Frey
Quality Assurance Editor: David Shaw
Creative Director: Lucy Jenkins

Published by Dearborn™ Real Estate Education
a Division of Dearborn Financial Publishing, Inc.®
a Kaplan Professional Company®

30 South Wacker Drive
Chicago, IL 60606-7481
www.dearbornRE.com

Printed in the United States of America.

04   05   06   10   9   8   7   6   5   4   3   2   1

CONTENTS

INTRODUCTION   v
   How to Use this Book   v
   Exam Preparation Tips   v

PART A: DIAGNOSTIC TEST   1
   Diagnostic Test Questions   2
   Diagnostic Test Results   5

PART B: PRACTICE QUESTIONS   7
  1. Exterior Systems   8
   Practice Questions   8
   Answers and Explanations   18
  2. Structural Systems   22
   Practice Questions   22
   Answers and Explanations   34
  3. Roofing Systems   39
   Practice Questions   39
   Answers and Explanations   49
  4. Electrical Systems   53
   Practice Questions   53
   Answers and Explanations   63
  5. Heating and Cooling Systems   68
   Practice Questions   68
   Answers and Explanations   88

  6. Insulation and Ventilation Systems   96
   Practice Questions   96
   Answers and Explanations   100
  7. Plumbing Systems   102
   Practice Questions   102
   Answers and Explanations   117
  8. Interior Systems   123
   Practice Questions   123
   Answers and Explanations   130
  9. Fireplace and Chimney Systems   133
   Practice Questions   133
   Answers and Explanations   141
 10. Reporting and Professional Practice   144
   Practice Questions   144
   Answers and Explanations   149
 11. Appliances   151
   Practice Questions   151
   Answers and Explanations   153

PART C: SAMPLE EXAM   155
   Sample Exam Questions   156
   Sample Exam Answers and Explanations   173

INTRODUCTION

An increasing number of state licensing bodies and professional organizations require home inspectors to pass a written examination to prove their competency. Perhaps the best known of these exams is the National Home Inspection Exam (NHIE), which is used in many states and by the American Society of Home Inspectors® (ASHI). Some states and other professional organizations have developed their own exams for licensing or certification of home inspectors.

Regardless of the specific test, preparing for and taking a formal home inspection exam can be a stressful proposition. This book is designed to help you approach your exam with confidence and improve your ability to pass on the first try.

HOW TO USE THIS BOOK

Home Inspection Exam Prep consists of three major parts:

Part A: Diagnostic Test—This brief test will help you determine which topic areas you're strongest in and which areas you need to concentrate on improving. Use the diagnostic test to help organize your review for the exam and prioritize the practice problems on which you will focus.

Part B: Practice Problems—This part contains nearly 1,400 questions organized by house systems, reporting and professional practice, and appliances. Some of the questions focus on a strictly technical understanding of the system or component, and others test your understanding of inspection methods and reporting techniques for specific conditions.

You can select a cross-section of problems from each topic, focus on particular topics, or, for the most rigorous exam preparation, practice with all the problems. Solutions and explanations are provided to help you understand the correct answer for each problem.

Part C: Sample Exam—This exam contains the same number of questions (200) and the full range of topics found in the NHIE. It is also a useful model for other home inspection exams. Use the sample exam to simulate your actual exam experience and test your readiness to pass a real home inspection exam.

EXAM PREPARATION TIPS

In addition to using this book, you should consider several other strategies and issues to help you prepare for your exam:

Standards of Practice and State-Specific Information. In addition to testing technical knowledge of home inspection, some states and professional organizations also require candidates to answer exam questions relating to Standards of Practice (SOPs). Because SOPs vary between states and organizations, this book does not cover this topic. Be sure to study and understand the SOPs for the exam you are taking.

Even if your state uses the NHIE, it may include some additional questions specific to the scope of home inspections or laws governing the profession in your state. For example, some states require home inspectors to inspect home appliances, whereas others do not. Contact your state board for details about examination and licensing requirements. Many have information available via a Web site for your convenience.

Your Specific Exam. To increase your comfort level, you should become familiar with the scope of the exam you'll be taking, such as the number of questions and time limit. The NHIE consists of 200 multiple-choice questions, each with four answer choices. Examinees have four hours to complete the exam. If you are taking a different exam, contact the relevant state board or professional organization for details.

Content Review. Although this book can help you prepare for the experience of taking an exam and identify topic areas where you need more review, it does not provide in-depth content review. For that, be sure to review the reference books, class notes, and other materials you have used in your training and practice. The Examination Board of Professional Home Inspectors, which oversees the development and validation of the NHIE, provides a list of suggested readings to help prepare for it at *http://www.homeinspectionexam.org/suggested_reading.html*.

Good luck!

P A R T

DIAGNOSTIC TEST

This brief test includes three questions on each of the major home systems and on professional practices. In addition, there are two questions on home appliances. The questions are presented in random order.

After answering the questions, use the answer key on the Diagnostic Test Results page to identify the topic areas you may want to focus on first when you prepare for your exam.

DIAGNOSTIC TEST QUESTIONS

1. The purpose of a home inspection is to
   a. provide a client with the cost of improving their property.
   b. provide a client with a list of the property's problems and their causes.
   c. provide a client with information regarding the property conditions at the time of the inspection.
   d. provide the client with conclusions about all of the conditions of the property at the time of the inspection.

2. The minimum slope for asphalt shingles in a conventional (not low-slope) application is
   a. 6-in-12.
   b. 5-in-12.
   c. 4-in-12.
   d. 2-in-12.

3. Cracks due to horizontal forces are usually
   a. diagonal.
   b. accompanied by bowing and bulging.
   c. most pronounced at the edge, and die out toward the middle of the wall.
   d. insignificant.

4. Which statement about nail pops is false?
   a. Longer nails are more likely to pop.
   b. Wetter wood is more likely to have nail popping.
   c. The problem does not show up until someone pushes on the wall.
   d. They can best be corrected by removing the nail.

5. In an atmospheric gas burner, the thermocouple
   a. senses the main flame.
   b. initiates the spark ignition.
   c. prevents flame rollout.
   d. senses the pilot flame.

6. Aluminum branch circuit wiring was commonly used from
   a. 1920 to 1958.
   b. 1965 to 1978.
   c. 1940 to 1958.
   d. 1950 to 1968.

7. Which of the following is *NOT* a form of ignition for a gas burner?
   a. Pilot
   b. Electronic ignition
   c. Piezo-electric ignition
   d. Flint ignition

8. What is the maximum static water pressure you should find in a residential plumbing system?
   a. 50 psi
   b. 60 psi
   c. 70 psi
   d. 80 psi

9. House ventilation can include all of the following *EXCEPT*
   a. venting roofs to flush out warm, moist air.
   b. exhausting stale air.
   c. introducing fresh air.
   d. a way to add moisture to a home in winter.

10. Common problems with any exterior cladding include all of the following *EXCEPT*
    a. water penetration.
    b. too close to window openings.
    c. too close to grade.
    d. planters against the wall.

11. How many heat transfer coils do conventional air-cooled central air conditioning systems have?
    a. None
    b. One
    c. Two
    d. Three

12. Low water pressure on the hot water side of a plumbing system may be related to the water heater because
    a. the water heater adds considerably to the length of the distribution piping system.
    b. sludge may obstruct the dip tube.
    c. the flow of water is slowed because of the volume required to fill the tank.
    d. the baffles or turbulator slow down the passage of the water.

13. Which of the following statements about flue size is *NOT* true?
    a. Wood flues need to be larger than gas flues.
    b. A larger flue is required for a taller chimney.
    c. Undersized flues will tend to backdraft.
    d. Oversized flues will tend to backdraft.

14. Holes and notches in 2-by-4 studs in bearing walls
    a. are not allowed.
    b. must be within 12 inches of the end of the stud.
    c. must be in the middle ⅓ of the stud length.
    d. must leave ⅔ of the stud depth intact.

15. On examining a closed valley on an asphalt shingle roof, it is critical to
    a. ensure that the points have been cut
    b. make sure the valley widens as it extends down the roof.
    c. lift up the shingles at the bottom of the valley to ensure there is roll roofing or a similar underlayment.
    d. make sure the metal valley is not longer than 10 feet.

16. When a split-system air conditioner is operating, the suction line
    a. is the smaller line.
    b. is the warmer, uninsulated line.
    c. is the cooler, insulated line.
    d. is the warmer, insulated line.

17. Which one of the following is a reliable indicator of service amperage?
    a. The size of the service drop wires
    b. The rating of the meter
    c. The size of the service entrance conductors
    d. The rating of the distribution panel

18. In a microwave oven, what is the purpose of the stirrer?
    a. To generate high-frequency radiation
    b. Rotate the food
    c. Ensure the food does not overheat
    d. Disperse the microwaves

19. Apart from the shoulders of the smoke chamber, the maximum recommended offset in a masonry chimney is
    a. 10°.
    b. 20°.
    c. 25°.
    d. 30°.

20. Joists should have an end bearing of at least
    a. 1 inch.
    b. 1½ inches.
    c. 3½ inches.
    d. 6 inches.

21. Which material is *NOT* a vapor barrier?
    a. Polyethylene film
    b. Housewrap
    c. Kraft paper
    d. Vinyl wallpaper

22. The most common exhaust pipe material used for high efficiency furnaces is
    a. PVC.
    b. stainless steel.
    c. aluminum.
    d. Plexvent, Sel-Vent, or Ultravent.

23. Basic tools for a home inspection include all of the following, *EXCEPT*
    a. combustible gas analyzer.
    b. flashlight.
    c. ladder.
    d. measuring tape.

24. Which of the following is *NOT* a common condenser problem?
    a. Excess noise or vibration
    b. Corrosion or mechanical damage
    c. Location restricts intake or outlet air flow
    d. Exposure to direct sunlight

25. The heat exchanger on a hot water boiler can clog on the fire-side from
    a. debris in the boiler water.
    b. poor burner adjustment.
    c. a dripping pressure-relief valve.
    d. circulator failure.

26. The maximum rise for each stair is roughly
    a. 7 inches.
    b. 8 inches.
    c. 9 inches.
    d. 10 inches.

27. The combustible clearance required around the front of a wood-burning fireplace, assuming that all combustibles are flush with the face, is
    a. 2 inches.
    b. 4 inches.
    c. 6 inches.
    d. 10 inches.

28. Grounded and grounding conductors must be connected at
    a. all subpanels.
    b. the service panel only.
    c. all boxes and panels.
    d. all possible locations.

29. Garage door operators may fail to operate for any of the following reasons *EXCEPT*
    a. improper installation.
    b. the auto reverse sensitivity being set too low.
    c. poor door adjustment.
    d. tripping of the GFCI receptacle.

30. Frame deformation of doors and windows is typically caused by
    a. building racking.
    b. overfoaming around the door.
    c. winds over 60 miles/hour.
    d. steel lintels used with vinyl doors.

31. Truss uplift is caused primarily by
    a. differential humidity levels within the attic.
    b. mixing different types of trusses in an attic space.
    c. insufficient attic insulation.
    d. improperly attaching drywall to the ceiling of the top floor.

32. Which single-ply membrane is compatible with asphalt?
    a. PVC
    b. Mod bit
    c. Polystyrene
    d. EPDM

33. If you go to inspect a house and the utilities are off, you should
    a. refuse to do the inspection because the liability is too great.
    b. insist that the agent get the utilities turned before the end of the inspection.
    c. explain the limitations to your client.
    d. reduce your fee.

34. All of the following are clues that insulation may have been added in a flat roof *EXCEPT*
    a. plugged holes in roof coverings or ceilings.
    b. vents added to the roof.
    c. a higher-than-expected roof surface temperature in winter.
    d. a lower ceiling height than expected.

35. Entrances into shower stalls should be a minimum of
    a. 16 inches wide.
    b. 20 inches wide.
    c. 22 inches wide.
    d. 28 inches wide.

DIAGNOSTIC TEST RESULTS

Use the following answer key to check your diagnostic test answers. The italicized text below each answer is a topic area. If you got more than one answer wrong in a particular topic area, you may want to focus on that topic first in the practice problems.

1. **c.** The home inspection is designed to provide clients with a better understanding of the property conditions observed at the time of the inspection.

   Professional Practice and Reporting

2. **c.** The minimum slope for conventional asphalt shingles is 4-in-12. Low-sloped shingles can be applied down to a slope of 2-in-12. There is also a special application that allows conventional shingles to go down to a slope of 2-in-12.

   Roofing Systems

3. **b.** Cracks due to horizontal forces are often horizontal and accompanied by bowing or bulging.

   Structural Systems

4. **d.** Removing the nail is not the best solution to nail pops. The nail can simply be reset and the drywall compound over the nail head can be patched.

   Interior Systems

5. **d.** The thermocouple senses the pilot flame.

   Heating and Cooling Systems

6. **b.** Aluminum branch circuit wiring was commonly used from 1965 to 1978.

   Electrical Systems

7. **d.** There is no such thing as flint ignition on a gas burner.

   Appliances

8. **d.** The maximum static water pressure we should find in a residential plumbing system is 80 psi.

   Plumbing Systems

9. **a.** House ventilation has nothing to do with venting roofs.

   Insulation and Ventilation Systems

10. **b.** Siding being close to window openings is not a problem.

    Exterior Systems

11. **c.** Central air-conditioning systems have two heat transfer coils.

    Heating and Cooling Systems

12. **b.** Sludge obstructing the dip tube on a water heater may result in low water pressure on the hot water side of the plumbing system.

    Plumbing Systems

13. **b.** A larger flue is not required for a taller chimney.

    Fireplace and Chimney Systems

14. **d.** Notches and holes in 2 by 4 studs in bearing walls must leave ⅔ of the stud depth intact. This question is tricky because many people answer **c,** thinking that the holes or notches must be in the middle third of the stud. If it is a notch, though, it can't be in the middle of the stud.

    Structural Systems

15. **c.** When you have a closed valley on an asphalt shingle roof, you want to lift up the shingles at the bottom of the valley to make sure there is roll roofing or some other underlayment.

    Roofing Systems

16. **c.** The suction line is the cooler, insulated line.

    Heating and Cooling Systems

17. **c.** The size of the service entrance conductors is the most reliable indicator of service amperage.

    Electrical Systems

18. **d.** The stirrer is a fan-like device located at the top of the oven.

    Appliances

19. **d.** The maximum recommended offset in a masonry chimney is 30°.

    Fireplace and Chimney Systems

20. **b.** Joists should have an end bearing of at least 1½ inches.

    Exterior Systems

21. **b.** Housewrap is not a vapor barrier. It is only an air barrier.

Insulation and Ventilation Systems

22. **a.** PVC is the most common material.

Plumbing Systems

23. **a.** A combustible gas analyzer is not a standard tool.

Professional Practice and Reporting

24. **d.** It is not a problem to have the condenser exposed to direct sunlight.

Heating and Cooling Systems

25. **b.** The heat exchanger can clog on the fire side because of poor burner adjustment.

Heating and Cooling Systems

26. **b.** The maximum rise for each stair is roughly 8 inches.

Interior Systems

27. **c.** A six-inch combustible clearance is required around the front of the fireplace, assuming that all combustibles are flush with the face.

Fireplace and Chimney Systems

28. **b.** Grounded and grounding conductors must be connected at the service panel only.

Electrical Systems

29. **b.** If the auto-reverse sensitivity is set too low, the auto-reverse mechanism will not be very sensitive at all. This will not prevent the garage door from operating, but will perhaps prevent it from stopping and reversing automatically.

Exterior Systems

30. **b.** Frame deformation of doors and windows is usually caused by overfoaming around the door.

Interior Systems

31. **a.** Truss uplift is caused by differential humidity levels in the attic between the top and bottom cords.

Structural Systems

32. **b.** Mod bit is compatible with asphalt.

Roofing Systems

33. **c.** If the utilities to a home are off, the client should understand the limitations and should decide whether or not to go through with the inspection.

Professional Practice and Reporting

34. **c.** A higher-than-expected roof surface temperature in winter suggests no insulation, rather than insulation having been added.

Insulation and Ventilation Systems

35. **c.** Entrances into shower stalls should be a minimum of 22 inches wide.

Plumbing Systems

PART B

PRACTICE QUESTIONS

The following practice questions are organized by the major home systems and professional practice:

1. Exterior Systems
2. Structural Systems
3. Roofing Systems
4. Electrical Systems
5. Heating and Cooling Systems
6. Insulation and Ventilation Systems
7. Plumbing Systems
8. Interior Systems
9. Fireplace and Chimney Systems
10. Reporting and Professional Practice

In addition, a selection of questions on home appliances is included. If your state or exam requires knowledge of home appliances, be sure to answer these questions as well.

1. EXTERIOR SYSTEMS

Practice Questions

1. Beams should be mechanically fastened to their supporting members.
   a. True
   b. False

2. Most garage floors are not structural.
   a. True
   b. False

3. Bad grading will always cause wet basements.
   a. True
   b. False

4. Asphalt shingles are installed on walls the same way as on roofs.
   a. True
   b. False

5. Asbestos cement shingles should be removed from homes.
   a. True
   b. False

6. A house with integral gutters is more prone to ice damming if it has a steep roof.
   a. True
   b. False

7. Wall cladding materials should be six to eight inches above grade.
   a. True
   b. False

8. Synthetic stucco (EIFS) has good drying potential.
   a. True
   b. False

9. The single-biggest problem with cantilevered decks is excess deflection or bounce.
   a. True
   b. False

10. Plywood is a good material choice for outdoor floors, such as on a porch.
    a. True
    b. False

11. An exterior inspection includes all of the following *EXCEPT*
    a. trim.
    b. driveways.
    c. soffits and fascia.
    d. fences.

12. Which of the following is *FALSE?* Exterior cladding is intended to
    a. protect the structure from water damage.
    b. protect the interior from water damage.
    c. provide reasonable security.
    d. provide insulation.

13. All of the following are siding materials *EXCEPT*
    a. housewrap.
    b. stucco.
    c. steel.
    d. concrete block.

14. Which of the following statements about building paper is *FALSE?*
    a. It is also referred to as sheathing paper.
    b. It protects the wall from water that gets past the siding.
    c. It prevents heat loss.
    d. It is vapor-permeable.

15. Housewraps replace
    a. building paper.
    b. sheathing.
    c. insulation.
    d. siding.

16. Most problems with exterior cladding involve
    a. heat loss.
    b. vapor diffusion.
    c. water penetration.
    d. efflorescence.

17. Wood siding
    a. should be at least four inches above roofing.
    b. should be two inches above grade.
    c. will wick moisture through the end grains.
    d. does not hold paint well.

18. OSB siding
    a. should stop one to two inches above roof surfaces.
    b. should never be used in contact with masonry walls.
    c. is not prone to buckling.
    d. requires weep holes about every 32 inches.

19. Which of the following is the worst case situation?
    a. The top of the foundation wall is 16 inches above grade.
    b. The top of the foundation wall is three inches below grade.
    c. The top of the foundation wall is at grade.
    d. The top three inches of the foundation wall is covered by siding.

20. Raised planters should
    a. only be used with masonry walls.
    b. have waterproof liners.
    c. be kept two inches from exterior walls.
    d. have covers to prevent them filling with water during heavy rains.

21. Vines on exterior walls
    a. are a bigger problem on wood siding than masonry.
    b. help the wall keep dry.
    c. help the inspector, in that their presence indicates a durable wall.
    d. can always be easily removed.

22. Which of the following statements about masonry walls is *FALSE?*
    a. They may or may not be load-bearing.
    b. They usually require a foundation.
    c. They are water-repellant.
    d. They may be damaged by abrasive cleaning.

23. Cracks in brickwork are *NOT LIKELY* to occur because of
    a. freeze/thaw action.
    b. building settlement.
    c. mechanical damage.
    d. repointing.

24. All of the following can cause mortar problems in a masonry wall *EXCEPT*
    a. improper mortar mix.
    b. that temperatures are too cold during application.
    c. applying the mortar to damp bricks.
    d. that mortar joints are too thin.

25. Weep holes in masonry walls
    a. are only provided in solid masonry walls.
    b. drain to the building interior.
    c. require a flashing at the bottom of the wall.
    d. are used instead of a vented rain screen.

26. You are looking at a two-story masonry building. You notice large metal plates on the front and back walls of the home about every four feet across the walls, at approximately the second-story floor level. These are
    a. support brackets for balconies.
    b. support points for porch roofs.
    c. stabilizing a bowed wall.
    d. to increase structural rigidity in earthquake zones.

27. Stucco
    a. is basically cement, aggregate, and water.
    b. uses gypsum as the principal binder.
    c. is applied to a fiberglass mesh lath.
    d. is always installed over rigid insulation.

28. Stucco
    a. is typically installed in a one-coat application.
    b. is typically applied in a two-coat application over wood frame walls.
    c. is typically ⅜-inch-thick over wood frame walls.
    d. will often have a drip screed at the bottom.

29. Common stucco problems include all of the following *EXCEPT*
    a. cracking.
    b. bulging.
    c. crumbling.
    d. no paint.

30. An EIFS assembly may consist of all of the following *EXCEPT*
    a. plywood sheathing.
    b. foam insulation boards.
    c. metal lath.
    d. a ¹⁄₁₆-inch-thick to ¼-inch-thick base coat.

31. Causes of problems with EIFS include all of the following *EXCEPT*
    a. poor drying potential.
    b. installation in warm climates.
    c. lack of a drainage plane.
    d. lack of building paper.

32. A rain screen has all of the following *EXCEPT*
    a. building paper or housewrap.
    b. an air space behind the siding.
    c. an air/vapor barrier directly behind the siding.
    d. a drainage space behind the siding.

33. Which of the following homes is most likely to have concealed damage behind the EIFS? A home
    a. in the southwest United States.
    b. exposed to strong winds.
    c. with a four foot roof overhang.
    d. with fewer-than-average windows.

34. All of the following are common wood siding types *EXCEPT*
    a. flemish bond.
    b. bevel.
    c. board and batten.
    d. tongue and groove.

35. Wood shakes
    a. can only be made of cedar.
    b. are typically 18 to 24 inches long.
    c. can only be hand split and resawn.
    d. should be butted tightly side to side to prevent leakage.

36. Paint may contain all of the following *EXCEPT*
    a. pigments.
    b. binder.
    c. additives.
    d. fire retardants.

37. All of the following statements about plywood are true except one. Which statement is *FALSE*?
    a. Plywood comes in panels up to 4 feet × 10 feet.
    b. Plywood is more dimensionally stable than conventional wood siding.
    c. Plywood sheet siding adds little to the rigidity of a building.
    d. Plywood always has an odd number of layers.

38. OSB siding is
    a. fiber cement.
    b. a type of plywood.
    c. a type of waferboard.
    d. a type of hardboard.

39. Common problems with hardboard include all of the following *EXCEPT*
    a. swelling.
    b. delamination.
    c. buckling.
    d. efflorescence.

40. Inner-Seal siding is
    a. OSB.
    b. hardboard.
    c. fiber cement board.
    d. plywood.

41. All of the following statements about vinyl siding are true except one. Which one is *FALSE*?
    a. The color is on the surface only.
    b. Vinyl siding cannot be easily repainted.
    c. Vines should be kept off of vinyl siding.
    d. Buckled or wavy siding is a common problem.

42. Metal siding
    a. is usually steel.
    b. is usually painted on site.
    c. does not need to be kept eight inches above grade.
    d. is prone to thermal expansion and contraction.

43. Common problems with metal and vinyl siding include all of the following *EXCEPT*
    a. buckling or waviness.
    b. mechanical damage.
    c. metal siding not having been grounded.
    d. nails not having been driven tight.

44. Fiber cement siding
    a. has never contained asbestos.
    b. is prone to rot.
    c. is brittle.
    d. is combustible.

45. The most common problem with fiber cement siding is
    a. mechanical damage.
    b. poor nailing.
    c. inadequate substrate.
    d. improper caulking.

46. Clay tile siding is
    a. quarried.
    b. combustible.
    c. light.
    d. brittle.

47. Asphalt shingles used as siding
    a. are different from roofing shingles.
    b. should be installed with six nails per shingle.
    c. do not require roofing cement.
    d. will last roughly half as long as shingles on a roof.

48. Common problems with asphalt shingles include all of the following *EXCEPT*
    a. missing shingles.
    b. torn shingles.
    c. rotted shingles.
    d. loose tabs.

49. Common soffit and fascia problems include all of the following *EXCEPT*
    a. burn-through due to ultraviolet light.
    b. loose or missing pieces.
    c. rot.
    d. mechanical damage.

50. Common door and window problems include all of the following *EXCEPT*
    a. rot.
    b. damage.
    c. lack of paint or stain.
    d. sills that slope down and away from the window.

51. Common window problems include all of the following *EXCEPT*
    a. frame deformation.
    b. missing or damaged storm windows and screens.
    c. cracked or broken glass.
    d. single glazing.

52. Common problems found with trim, flashings and caulking include all of the following *EXCEPT*
    a. missing flashings or caulking.
    b. kickout flashings on roof/wall intersections.
    c. looseness.
    d. rust or rot.

53. Typical problems with steps and landings include all of the following *EXCEPT*
    a. rise, run, and slope.
    b. settlement.
    c. cantilevered beams.
    d. spalling mortar/masonry units.

54. A maximum rise for steps is commonly
    a. 7 inches.
    b. 8 inches.
    c. 9 inches.
    d. 10 inches.

55. Generally speaking, guardrails are required on
    a. balconies only.
    b. any decks, porches, or balconies 36 inches above grade.
    c. any decks, porches, or balconies 2 feet or 30 inches above grade.
    d. stairs leading to any balcony.

56. Why is a 2×6 on edge considered a poor handrail?
    a. A 2×6 may not be strong enough to support a person's weight.
    b. It can be difficult to grab.
    c. When wet, a 2×6 can become slippery.
    d. The boards tend to shrink as the wood dries, leaving exposed slivers.

57. When inspecting railings, the inspector should do all of the following *EXCEPT*
    a. make reference to the standards set by local authorities.
    b. consider height of surface above grade.
    c. consider guardrail height.
    d. test for adequate securement.

58. Exterior columns typically support all of the following *EXCEPT*
    a. porch floors.
    b. decks.
    c. carports.
    d. patios.

59. Which of the following would *NOT* cause a column to shift?
    a. Frost heave
    b. Improper footings or foundations
    c. Mechanical damage
    d. Rising damp

60. Beams rely on at least _____ inches of bearing:
    a. 2
    b. 3½
    c. 4
    d. 6

61. Common beam problems on porches include all of the following *EXCEPT*
    a. checking.
    b. sag.
    c. poor end support.
    d. wood/soil contact.

62. Joist twisting or warping is commonly caused by
    a. uneven settling.
    b. poor end bearing.
    c. lumber shrinking unevenly as it dries.
    d. higher-than-anticipated loading of the deck.

63. Cedar is *NOT* a good choice for cantilevered balconies because
    a. it is resistant to rot.
    b. it is not very strong.
    c. it cannot be pressure treated.
    d. it is too expensive to be used as a framing member.

64. Sagging joists can be the result of any of the following *EXCEPT*
    a. over-spanned joists.
    b. undersized decking.
    c. sagging beams.
    d. undersized joists.

65. Which of the following statements is *FALSE?*
    a. Cantilevered joists have most of their length inside the house, and up to one-third of their length exposed outside.
    b. Carpet-type PVC roof membranes are not suitable for use on deck surfaces.
    c. Wood skirting around porches and decks should be kept six inches above the soil.
    d. It is a bad idea to visually align a beam with a gutter to check for sag.

66. The cantilevered portion of joists should be no more than
    a. one-third the entire joist length.
    b. one-quarter the entire joist length.
    c. six feet.
    d. four feet for 2 × 8s and six feet for 2 × 10s.

67. Why is carpeting on wood porches considered to be a problem?
    a. It hides the wood from home inspectors.
    b. If not fastened down, it could slip, causing injury.
    c. The carpet can trap water next to the wood, promoting rot.
    d. Ventilation below the porch floor is obstructed.

68. Scanning a porch with your eye at floor level is a good way to check for
    a. rot.
    b. sag.
    c. undersized floorboards.
    d. loose or twisted joists.

69. Which of the following is *NOT* a common problem with wood decks?
    a. Rotting wood
    b. Use of pressure treated lumber
    c. Carpet over wood
    d. Loose steps

70. Where is rot most to occur in deck and porch floors?
    a. On the underside of the floorboards
    b. Where there is the most foot traffic
    c. Near steps, due to the stringer attachments
    d. At horizontal joints with end grain

71. To prevent sagging, 2 × 6 floorboards need support every
    a. 16 inches.
    b. 20 inches.
    c. 24 inches.
    d. 32 inches.

72. Poor materials for porch floors include all of the following *EXCEPT*
    a. plywood.
    b. oriented strandboard (OSB).
    c. hardboard.
    d. cedar.

73. The most likely cause of a porch roof pulling away from a house wall is
    a. insect damage.
    b. settlement, heaving or buckling of columns.
    c. rot.
    d. heavy roofing materials, such as slate, used over an unreinforced roof structure.

74. When inspecting porch roofs, you should be checking for all of the following *EXCEPT*
    a. insulation in the ceiling.
    b. sagging beams.
    c. evidence of water damage on the underside.
    d. rot and loose connection points to the building.

75. Skirting
    a. is found on decks but not on porches.
    b. can obstruct ventilation.
    c. should not have an access door.
    d. should extend down into the soil.

76. Carports
    a. do not have vehicle doors.
    b. typically have cantilevered roof structures.
    c. typically have floor drains.
    d. should not have the same roof covering materials as the house.

77. Combustible insulation exposed in garages
    a. significantly reduces heating costs.
    b. eliminates sound transmission between the house and the garage.
    c. is only required on the ceiling to minimize heat loss.
    d. is a fire hazard.

78. A man door between the house and garage should
    a. be weather-stripped.
    b. always be fire-rated and open into the house.
    c. have a six-inch step up from the house into the garage.
    d. never have a self-closer, because a child may be locked in the garage.

79. A gas-fired, forced-air furnace in a garage should
    a. not have any gas piping in the garage.
    b. not have a standing pilot.
    c. be protected from impact damage by vehicles.
    d. be located well away from the vehicle door to avoid pilot flame blowout by wind.

80. Fireproofing in attached garages
    a. cannot be achieved using masonry block.
    b. never requires a fire rated man door.
    c. may require a one-hour fire rating.
    d. always includes a fireproof ceiling.

81. All of the following statements are true of structural garage floors *EXCEPT*
    a. structural garage floors may need inspection by a specialist.
    b. structural garage floors should not be inspected for design adequacy as part of a home inspection.
    c. cracks in structural garage floors indicate structural failure.
    d. much of the strength in suspended concrete garage floors is derived from the steel reinforcement in the concrete.

82. Elements of a well-constructed garage floor (slab-on-grade type) include all of the following *EXCEPT*
    a. adequate slope toward the vehicle door.
    b. a free-draining granular base below the concrete.
    c. rigid foam insulation under the concrete floor slab.
    d. well-compacted backfill placed in the trenches around the garage foundation.

83. Random, hairline cracks in the concrete garage floor are usually caused by
    a. shrinkage during curing.
    b. heaving.
    c. settlement.
    d. poor drainage.

84. Draping of concrete garage floors is usually caused by
    a. slab settlement at perimeter.
    b. concrete shrinkage.
    c. water absorption and subsequent freezing.
    d. too much water in the concrete mix.

85. The following are common problems with overhead sectional vehicle doors in garages *EXCEPT*
    a. operability.
    b. rot/rust.
    c. counterweights.
    d. automatic-opener problems.

86. A properly operating "auto-reverse" feature should
    a. stop if an obstruction is sensed on the way down.
    b. stop and reverse if an obstruction is sensed on the way up.
    c. stop and reverse if an obstruction is sensed on the way down.
    d. stop when an obstruction is sensed when moving in either direction.

87. An oil furnace in a garage
    a. should not have a buried oil tank.
    b. requires an outdoor combustion air intake.
    c. should be installed at least 18 inches above the floor level.
    d. should have 18-inch clearance from combustibles on all sides.

88. All of the following statements about basement walkouts in freezing climates are true except one. Identify the *FALSE* statement.
    a. Basement walkouts allow greater frost depth around the house.
    b. Lowering house foundations and footings can protect against frost damage around basement walkouts.
    c. Railings should not be provided around the top of basement walkouts for fear of obstructing escape.
    d. Many basement walkouts provide an easy path for water to get into basements.

89. A floor drain at the bottom of a basement walkout
    a. should be tied into the perimeter drainage tile around the house.
    b. must be tested for functional drainage.
    c. can be connected to a French drain or to a floor drain pipe inside the house.
    d. should connect to a minimum four-inches-in-diameter drain pipe.

90. Cracking, leaning, or bowing retaining walls for basement walkouts
    a. are less serious than spalling masonry or concrete, or mortar deterioration.
    b. are easily remedied by reducing the lateral soil pressure through improved grading.
    c. are caused by frost pressure and hydrostatic pressure.
    d. may be caused by free-draining soil conditions.

91. All of the following statements about basement walkouts are true except one. Pick the *FALSE* statement.
    a. Walkouts that were built at the same time as the house are more likely to be problems.
    b. Walkouts built in free-draining soils are less likely to be problems.
    c. Perimeter drainage tile is rarely extended around the walkout and reconnected.
    d. Repairing poorly built walkouts is expensive.

92. Problems with drains for basement walkouts include all of the following *EXCEPT*
    a. missing drains.
    b. undersized drains.
    c. the drain has an outdoor trap in cold climates.
    d. the drain is connected to a house floor drain system.

93. What are the implications of improper lot grading?
    a. Foundation damage
    b. Trees growing too close to the house
    c. Reduced insulation values
    d. Contamination of water supplies

94. A swale is
    a. a flashing.
    b. a connection to a downspout through a parapet wall.
    c. a low retaining wall.
    d. a shallow drainage ditch

95. Plastic grid-type foundation drainage material relies on what other building component for successful performance?
    a. Gutters and downspouts
    b. Foundation insulation
    c. Perimeter drainage tile
    d. Dampproofing with bituminous coatings

96. All of the following are common surface water drainage problems *EXCEPT*
    a. improper ground surface slope.
    b. clogged catch-basins.
    c. basement windows without wells.
    d. porous soil.

97. Drains should be provided outside the vehicle door in garages that are
    a. below grade, where the driveway slopes down toward the garage.
    b. detached.
    c. in wet climates where the garage is attached.
    d. provided with interior drains.

98. The most expensive solution to wet basement problems is typically
    a. improving grading.
    b. repairing gutters and downspouts.
    c. excavating, dampproofing, and adding new drainage tile.
    d. adding basement window wells.

99. Catch-basin problems include all of the following *EXCEPT*
    a. clogged basins.
    b. clogged outlet pipes.
    c. obstructed covers.
    d. outlet pipes with 90-degree elbows facing down.

100. Porous materials around the perimeter of a house, such as gravel, may represent a grading problem because
    a. gravel is too easily disturbed.
    b. homeowners will not accept the appearance of gravel.
    c. the gravel may expand 10 feet down into the ground and wick moisture up through the voids.
    d. the true slope of impervious materials below cannot be determined.

101. Common gutter materials include all of the following *EXCEPT*
    a. galvanized steel.
    b. brass.
    c. aluminum.
    d. copper.

102. Integral gutters are
    a. gutters that are necessary because of the architecture of the house.
    b. gutters that are necessary because of the roof size and slope.
    c. gutters built in to the roofline.
    d. gutters incorporated into the roof gables.

103. Common gutter problems include all of the following *EXCEPT*
    a. lack of flow capacity.
    b. leaking.
    c. connection to two downspouts.
    d. looseness.

104. A common slope for a gutter is
    a. 1 in 25
    b. 1 in 100
    c. 1 in 200
    d. 1 in 300

105. All of the following are common downspout problems *EXCEPT*
    a. missing downspouts.
    b. leakiness.
    c. too few downspouts.
    d. discharge onto the ground.

106. Downspouts running across roof surfaces
    a. may damage the roof.
    b. can cause ice damming problems.
    c. protect the roof from roof or gutter discharge from a higher roof.
    d. are prone to clogging, because they are not vertical.

107. The most common downspout weak spots are
    a. at seams and elbows.
    b. at securement points.
    c. at the bottom.
    d. on aluminum downspouts.

108. The best discharge point for a downspout is
    a. below grade, into a storm sewer.
    b. above grade, six feet from the house.
    c. six inches above grade, adjacent to the house.
    d. three feet above grade, adjacent to the house.

109. All of the following are flat roof drainage systems *EXCEPT*
    a. Yankee gutters.
    b. interior drains.
    c. downspouts.
    d. galvanized-steel gutters.

110. Basement window wells should have drains unless
    a. ABS plastic is used.
    b. the floor of the well is filled with gravel.
    c. the base of the well is 12 inches below the window.
    d. a plastic cover is provided over the well.

111. Common window well materials include all of the following *EXCEPT*
    a. poured concrete.
    b. wood.
    c. masonry.
    d. copper.

112. All of the following are common problems with window wells *EXCEPT*
    a. the floor of the well being 12 inches below the window.
    b. a missing window well.
    c. damaged well walls.
    d. rusted well walls.

113. The floor of a window well should be
    a. poured concrete.
    b. Single-ply roofing membrane.
    c. gravel.
    d. level with the bottom of the window.

114. Problems with window well drains include all of the following *EXCEPT*
    a. missing drains.
    b. disconnected drains.
    c. drains obstructed by debris.
    d. drains that are six inches below the window.

115. The advantages of window well covers include
    a. better ventilation.
    b. use of egress.
    c. reduced heat-loss.
    d. reduced risk of leakage.

116. Sidewalks that are the property of the municipality
    a. do not have to be inspected.
    b. are typically asphalt.
    c. are usually in worse condition than other walkways.
    d. must be at least five feet wide.

117. Common materials for walks and driveways include all of the following *EXCEPT*
    a. concrete.
    b. asphalt.
    c. brick.
    d. cork.

118. All of the following are common problems with walks and driveways *EXCEPT*
    a. cracked surfaces.
    b. uneven surfaces.
    c. control joints.
    d. improper slope.

119. The causes of unevenness in a concrete walkway include all of the following *EXCEPT*
    a. poor installation.
    b. using concrete with entrained air.
    c. heavy vehicle traffic.
    d. tree roots.

120. Two-inch-high steps in walkways
    a. are better than a sloped surface because of drainage issues.
    b. require a railing if there are more than three steps in a row.
    c. may be hard to see.
    d. should have a maximum tread width of 12 inches.

121. The implications of trees or shrubs too close to a house include all of the following *EXCEPT*
    a. excess soil moisture adjacent to the house.
    b. mechanical damage to the house.
    c. reduced drying-potential of siding.
    d. roots blocking or collapsing sewer pipes.

122. Recently disturbed ground may mean all of the following *EXCEPT*
    a. a recent excavation.
    b. repairs to gas, water, or sewer mains.
    c. dampproofing operations.
    d. termite treatment.

123. Common problems with patios include all of the following *EXCEPT*
    a. trip hazards.
    b. a lack of railings.
    c. slopes that drain water toward the house.
    d. uneven surfaces.

124. A terrace is
    a. a raised patio.
    b. a wood deck more than two feet above grade.
    c. a balcony that is too small to walk out on.
    d. a stepped-foundation wall.

125. A vulnerable spot for rust on a steel railing is
    a. the newel post.
    b. the base, where it enters concrete.
    c. the connection between the spindles and the bottom of the railing.
    d. the point at which the railing connects to a house wall.

126. All of the following are types of retaining walls *EXCEPT*
    a. cantilevered.
    b. pile.
    c. tied back.
    d. cavity.

127. The single biggest enemy of retaining walls is
    a. rust.
    b. water.
    c. undersized rebar.
    d. inadequate tie backs.

128. All of the following are common retaining wall problems *EXCEPT*
    a. the use of shoring.
    b. leaning.
    c. rot or insect damage.
    d. lack of drainage system.

129. A ratchet effect on a retaining wall is
    a. a repair method.
    b. another term for gabion.
    c. another term for tie backs.
    d. a mode of failure.

130. Gabion is
    a. a gravity retaining wall.
    b. a cantilevered retaining wall.
    c. a pile-type retaining wall using steel I beams as piles.
    d. a prefabricated retaining wall.

131. The most rot-resistant wood retaining wall would be made using
    a. railway ties impregnated with creosote.
    b. pine.
    c. conventional pressure-treated lumber.
    d. preserved wood foundation pressure treating.

132. Weep holes in retaining walls should be
    a. ½ inch in diameter.
    b. 1 inch in diameter.
    c. 4 inches in diameter.
    d. 6 inches in diameter.

133. Weep holes in retaining walls should typically be spaced no more than
    a. 6 inches apart.
    b. 6 feet apart.
    c. 10 feet apart.
    d. 15 feet apart.

134. Deadmen are
    a. used in gabions.
    b. form the T in a cantilevered retaining wall.
    c. connected to tie backs.
    d. used as footings for shoring.

135. Leaning retaining walls may be the result of any of the following *EXCEPT*
    a. hydrostatic pressure.
    b. frost.
    c. cantilevered construction.
    d. age and weathering.

ANSWERS AND EXPLANATIONS

1. **a.** Beams should be mechanically fastened to their supporting members, not merely resting on the tops of columns or pillars.

2. **a.** Most garage floors are not structural.

3. **b.** Some grading conditions are less-than-ideal but do not result in problems, for example, where sandy soil carries the water away very effectively.

4. **b.** Asphalt shingles are installed differently on walls than on roofs.

5. **b.** Asbestos cement shingles do not need to be removed from homes.

6. **b.** A house with integral gutters is more prone to ice damming if it has a low-slope roof.

7. **a.** To protect the cladding system and the structure from water damage, masonry should be at least six inches above grade and most other sidings should be at least eight inches above grade.

8. **b.** Poor drying potential is one of the main causes of problems with synthetic stucco.

9. **b.** The single-biggest problem with cantilevered decks is maintaining a weather-tight joint where the joists pass through the house wall. These joints typically move as a result of expansion and contraction caused by changes in moisture and temperature.

10. **b.** Plywood, waferboard, and other manufactured wood products generally are not successful in outdoor applications where they are installed horizontally and wetted regularly.

11. **d.** Fences are not included in the exterior inspection.

12. **d.** Exterior cladding does not usually insulate the home.

13. **a.** Housewrap is an air barrier, not a siding material.

14. **c.** Building paper does not prevent heat loss directly.

15. **a.** Housewraps replace building paper.

16. **c.** Most cladding problems involve water penetration.

17. **c.** Wood siding will wick moisture through end grains.

18. **a.** OSB siding should stop an inch or two above a roof surface. It can be used with masonry walls.

19. **b.** Foundation walls below grade are extremely vulnerable.

20. **c.** Planters should be kept two inches away from exterior walls.

21. **a.** Vines are more likely to damage wood siding than masonry.

22. **c.** Masonry walls are not water repellant. Water in a driving rain will go through brick.

23. **d.** Cracks in brickwork do not occur as a result of repointing. Repointing is replacement of the mortar between bricks. It is a repair technique.

24. **c.** Applying the mortar to damp bricks is a recommended practice, not a problem.

25. **c.** Weep holes in masonry walls require a flashing at the bottom of the wall.

26. **c.** These plates are typically holding a bowed wall together. The plates are usually attached to cables or rods that go right through the building.

27. **a.** Stucco is cement, aggregate, and water.

28. **d.** Stucco often has a drip screed at the bottom of the wall.

29. **d.** An absence of paint is not a problem. Stucco doesn't need paint.

30. **c.** EIFS does not use metal lath. It uses all of the other components listed here.

31. **b.** EIFS problems can occur in warm climates or cold climates. The drying potential is more important than the temperature.

32. **c.** Except in very hot, humid climates, you do not want vapor barriers directly behind the siding.

33. **b.** A house exposed to strong winds will be susceptible to moisture penetration by wind-driven rain. The other items in this question are either only for dry climates or details that tend to protect against damage.

34. **a.** Flemish bond is a brick pattern.

35. **b.** Wood shakes typically are 18 to 24 inches long.

36. **d.** Paints do not typically include fire retardants.

37. **c.** Plywood sheets add considerable rigidity to a building.

38. **c.** OSB siding is a type of waferboard.

39. **d.** Efflorescence is not a problem with hardboard.

40. **a.** Inner-Seal siding is OSB.

41. **a.** The color on vinyl siding goes all the way through. Vinyl siding can be repainted. It just means that paint has to be redone every few years.

42. **d.** Metal siding is prone to thermal expansion and contraction.

43. **d.** Nails should not be driven tight with metal and vinyl siding. You need to allow the siding to move under the nails.

44. **c.** Fiber cement siding is brittle.

45. **a.** Mechanical damage is the most common problem with fiber cement siding.

46. **d.** Clay tile siding is brittle.

47. **b.** Six nails per shingle should be used with asphalt shingles installed as siding.

48. **c.** Rotted asphalt shingles are not a common problem.

49. **a.** Burn-through is not a common problem with soffit or fascia.

50. **d.** Sills should slope down away from the window.

51. **d.** Single glazing is not, in itself, a problem with windows.

52. **b.** Kickout flashings are not a problem. They are a good thing.

53. **d.** Cantilevered beams are not a typical problem with steps and landings.

54. **b.** The maximum rise for steps is commonly 8 inches.

55. **c.** Guardrails are needed on decks, porches, or balconies that are two feet or 30 inches above grade, depending on the jurisdiction that you live in. Guardrails are not the same as handrails, which are needed on stairs leading to any balcony.

56. **b.** A 2 × 6 on edge does not make a great handrail because it can be difficult to grab. You can't wrap your hand around it, you can only drape your hand over the top of it.

57. **a.** You shouldn't be making code references, local or otherwise, during an inspection.

58. **d.** Patios typically rest directly on the ground and do not need column support.

59. **d.** Rising damp would not cause a column to shift until the column actually failed. All of the other forces listed can shift columns.

60. **b.** Beams typically require at least 3½ inches of end bearing.

61. **a.** Checking is a normal condition on wood beams and is not usually a problem.

62. **c.** Lumber shrinking unevenly as it dries may result in joist twisting or warping.

63. **b.** Cedar is not a very strong wood.

64. **b.** Undersized decking does not cause joists to sag. The deck boards may sag, but there is no increased load on the joists.

65. **b.** Carpet type PVC roof membranes are suitable for use on deck surfaces.

66. **a.** The cantilevered portion of joists should be no more than one-third of the joist length.

67. **c.** Carpet can trap water next to the wood on the porch, promoting rot.

68. **b.** Scanning along a porch at floor level is a good way to check for sag in the porch.

69. **b.** Pressure treated lumber is acceptable for use on wood decks.

70. **d.** Rot is most likely to occur in deck and porch floors at horizontal joints with end grain.

71. **c.** To prevent sagging, 2 × 6 floorboards should be supported every 24 inches.

72. **d.** Cedar is a good material for a porch floor, although it is not as strong as some other softwoods.

73. **b.** Settlement, heaving, or buckling columns are the most likely cause of a porch roof pulling away from the house wall.

74. **a.** Insulation is not usually an issue with porch roofs because both sides of the porch roof are cold.

75. **b.** Skirting can obstruct ventilation of the area below the porch. The best skirting is a lattice work or some other material that will let air move relatively freely.

76. **a.** Carports typically do not have vehicle doors.

77. **d.** Exposed combustible insulation in garages is a fire hazard.

78. **a.** A man door between the house and garage should be weather stripped.

79. **c.** A garage furnace should be protected from impact damage by vehicles. Steel posts filled with concrete are one common way this is done.

80. **c.** Fireproofing in attached garages may require a one-hour fire rating.

81. **c.** Cracks in structural garage floors do not necessarily indicate structural failure. Much of the strength in the floor system is derived from the steel reinforcement.

82. **c.** Foam insulation is not a necessary element in a well-constructed garage floor slab.

83. **a.** Shrinkage during curing is the most common cause for random, hairline cracks in garage floors.

84. **a.** Draping of concrete floors in garages is usually caused by settlement of the slab around the perimeter. Settlement of the backfill along the foundations is the cause.

85. **c.** Counterweights are not problems on sectional doors. They are typical.

86. **c.** The auto-reverse mechanism on a garage door opener should cause the door to stop and reverse if an obstruction is sensed on the way down.

87. **c.** An oil furnace in a garage should have the burner at least 18 inches above the floor level.

88. **c.** Railings should be provided. Railings will not obstruct an escape route.

89. **c.** The drain can be connected to a French drain or to a floor drain pipe inside the house. It does not need to be a four-inches-in-diameter pipe.

90. **c.** Retaining wall movement on basement walk-outs is typically the result of frost or hydro-static pressure.

91. **a.** Walkouts built at the same time as the house are actually less likely to be problems. Appropriate footing considerations can be made during original construction. After the house is built, appropriate footings are very expensive to create.

92. **d.** Connecting the drain for a basement walkout to the house floor drain pipe above its trap is an acceptable arrangement.

93. **a.** Foundation damage is one of the implications of improper lot grading.

94. **d.** A swale is a shallow drainage ditch.

95. **c.** Foundation drainage material relies on a good perimeter drainage tile system to carry the water away.

96. **c.** Basement windows without wells are not necessarily a grading problem. The basement windows may be above grade level.

97. **a.** Drains should be located outside the garage door if the driveway slopes down toward the garage.

98. **c.** Excavation, dampproofing, and drainage tile is the most expensive wet basement solution.

99. **d.** The outlet pipes should have 90-degree elbows facing down.

100. **d.** Porous materials aren't great because you don't know what the true slope of the impervious materials below may be. The water will flow quickly through the porous materials and get hung up on the impervious materials, which may slope toward or away from the house.

101. **b.** Brass is not a common gutter material.

102. **c.** Integral gutters are built into the roofline of the house.

103. **c.** It's acceptable for gutters to be connected to two downspouts.

104. **c.** A gutter slope of 1 in 200 is typical.

105. **d.** Downspouts that discharge onto the ground are preferable.

106. **c.** Downspouts running across roof surfaces are a good thing. They protect the roof from water runoff from roofs or gutters above.

107. **a.** The most common downspout weak spots are at seams and elbows.

108. **b.** The best discharge point for a downspout is above grade, six feet from the house.

109. **a.** Yankee gutters would not be used on a flat roof.

110. **d.** Basement window wells should have drains, unless a plastic cover is provided over the well.

111. **d.** Copper is not a common window well material.

112. **a.** It's acceptable if the bottom of the well is 12 inches below the window.

113. **c.** The floor of the window well should be gravel (or some other porous material).

114. **d.** A drain that is six inches below the window is a good arrangement in a window well.

115. **d.** Covers on window wells reduce the risk of leakage.

116. **a.** Sidewalks that are the property of the municipality do not have to be inspected.

117. **d.** Cork is not a common material for a walk or a driveway.

118. **c.** Control joints are not a problem in walks and driveways. They are a desirable feature.

119. **b.** Entrained air in concrete is not likely to cause unevenness. This is a method used to control damage due to freezing.

120. **c.** Two-inch-high steps in walkways may be difficult to see. It's usually better to have a few larger steps.

121. **a.** Having trees or shrubs too close to a house doesn't usually create excess moisture in the soil adjacent to the house.

122. **d.** Termite treatment does not usually disturb the exterior ground.

123. **b.** Patios do not usually require railings because they are typically at grade level.

124. **a.** A terrace is a raised patio.

125. **b.** A vulnerable spot on a metal railing is the base where it enters concrete. Railings often rust at this point.

126. **d.** A cavity wall is not a type of retaining wall.

127. **b.** The biggest enemy of retaining walls is water.

128. **a.** The use of shoring is not a retaining wall problem.

129. **d.** Ratchet effect is a mode of failure for retaining walls.

130. **a.** Gabion is a gravity retaining wall.

131. **d.** Preserved wood foundation pressure treating is quite effective and would form the most rot-resistant wood retaining wall. If given a choice, wood is a poor one for retaining walls, but they are popular because they fit into landscaping and are relatively inexpensive.

132. **c.** Weep holes in retaining walls should typically be about 4 inches in diameter.

133. **c.** Weep holes in retaining walls should typically be no more than 10 feet apart.

134. **c.** Deadmen are connected to tiebacks in retaining walls.

135. **c.** Cantilevered construction does not necessarily result in leaning retaining walls. That is a standard type of construction.

2. STRUCTURAL SYSTEMS

Practice Questions

1. Brick veneer walls are not watertight.
   a. True
   b. False

2. The masonry veneer is a load-bearing part of the structure.
   a. True
   b. False

3. With wood frame walls, the lintel size is independent of the number of stories above.
   a. True
   b. False

4. It is acceptable to notch a bird's mouth into the bottom plate of an I-joist.
   a. True
   b. False

5. As long as the footing is below the frost line, it is not a problem to let the temperature in the basement drop below freezing.
   a. True
   b. False

6. Cracks due to horizontal forces rarely result in a structural problem.
   a. True
   b. False

7. Steel beams should not be shimmed with wood.
   a. True
   b. False

8. Joists may sit on top of beams or be attached to the sides of beams.
   a. True
   b. False

9. Joists see vertical loads only.
   a. True
   b. False

10. Joists are often used to provide lateral support for solid masonry walls.
    a. True
    b. False

11. Fire-cutting joists is a serious structural error.
    a. True
    b. False

12. Joists notched at their end are weaker than normal joists.
    a. True
    b. False

13. Joists resting on foundation walls at or near grade level are prone to rot.
    a. True
    b. False

14. Holes in joists should be near the bottom rather than the middle of the joists.
    a. True
    b. False

15. Partition walls exert no load on floor joists because they are not load-bearing walls.
    a. True
    b. False

16. All concrete floors in houses are suspended slabs.
    a. True
    b. False

17. Hollow concrete blocks are weaker if laid on their side.
    a. True
    b. False

18. Bricks laid on their sides forming windowsills are a structural problem.
    a. True
    b. False

19. Patched cracks on brick are a sure sign of serious structural movement.
    a. True
    b. False

20. Bearing walls and partition walls are built in substantially the same way.
    a. True
    b. False

21. Walls see vertical loads only.
    a. True
    b. False

22. Openings in partition walls *DO NOT* normally need lintels.
    a. True
    b. False

23. Wall-framing problems are often tough to identify because wall-framing details usually are concealed.
    a. True
    b. False

24. With masonry walls, the lintel size is independent of the number of stories above.
    a. True
    b. False

25. Masonry resting on wood is a less than ideal arrangement.
    a. True
    b. False

26. The top of the exposed edge of a steel lintel should be caulked.
    a. True
    b. False

27. It is acceptable for wood I-joists to lean against each other at the peak, the way rafters can.
    a. True
    b. False

28. Missing firestopping is more common on platform construction.
    a. True
    b. False

29. The function of a footing is to
    a. provide lateral support for foundation walls.
    b. transmit the weight of the house to the soil.
    c. provide support for the basement floor slab.
    d. resist hydrostatic pressure.

30. Footing failures can most positively be diagnosed by
    a. sagging floors.
    b. vertical cracking in foundation walls.
    c. horizontal cracking above windows.
    d. bowing foundation walls.

31. When installing a basement walkout an important consideration, often overlooked, is
    a. undermining footings.
    b. potential for termite infestation.
    c. frost penetration below the footings.
    d. damage to foundation walls on the original building.

32. When lowering a basement floor, if the soil is excavated only to the bottom of the footing (i.e., not below the footing), which problem may have been created?
    a. Inadequate end bearing for floor joists
    b. Excessive grade height
    c. Disturbed soil below footing
    d. Lost lateral support for the footing

33. All of the following are dead loads *EXCEPT*
    a. the weight of the structure above the foundation.
    b. snow loads.
    c. the weight of the soil surrounding the foundation.
    d. the weight of the shingles on the roof.

34. Footings that are continuous around the perimeter of the house are called
    a. pad footings.
    b. grade beams.
    c. spread footings.
    d. piers.

35. Which of the following is the best soil type for building homes?
    a. Fine sand
    b. Organic
    c. Gravel
    d. Coarse sand

36. Differential settlement is
    a. settlement that occurs at a control joint.
    b. when one part of the house settles and the rest does not.
    c. the cause of all horizontal foundation cracks.
    d. associated with shrinkage cracks.

37. The maximum slope for a lot depends on soil type and other conditions, but in general the maximum slope is
    a. 1 in 2.
    b. 1 in 3.
    c. 1 in 4.
    d. 1 in 5.

38. The best way to determine whether a crack is active is
    a. to determine how many planes of movement there are.
    b. if the crack is greater than a ¼ inch, it's active.
    c. to monitor the crack over time.
    d. to determine whether the cracks go through the masonry units or the mortar joints.

39. Step footings are
    a. used for underpinning.
    b. required when lowering the basement floor below the original footing depth.
    c. often used on houses built on sloped lots.
    d. the same as bench footings.

40. All of the following statements are true of frost heave *EXCEPT*
    a. frost heave can be caused by raising the exterior grade height.
    b. frost heave can be caused by insulating the basement.
    c. frost heave can be caused by lowering the grade level on the outside of the foundation.
    d. movement due to frost heave is often a combination of upwards and inwards movement.

41. Where lateral forces have caused cracking, bowing, bulging, or leaning of foundation walls, corrective action is often required. All of the following are typical corrective actions *EXCEPT*
    a. adding buttresses on the inside of the foundation wall.
    b. building a separate foundation wall on the interior of the foundation.
    c. building a separate exterior wall against the foundation.
    d. adding steel beams or channels horizontally along the crack.

42. Cinder block is
    a. a concrete block with steel reinforcement.
    b. much stronger than concrete block.
    c. very resistant to moisture.
    d. made from slag and has a rougher, darker texture than concrete block.

43. A cold joint is
    a. a deliberate crack built into the foundation to allow for concrete shrinkage.
    b. a result of pouring the concrete foundation at two separate times.
    c. a result of pouring the concrete when the temperature is below the freezing point.
    d. a joint between concrete blocks where insufficient mortar thickness was used. This joint will be substantially reduced in strength.

44. Pilasters typically
    a. prevent heaving.
    b. support beams.
    c. are wood.
    d. see primarily tension forces.

45. Laterally unsupported foundation walls
    a. must be poured concrete.
    b. have no reinforcing bar.
    c. are not supported by floor framing.
    d. cannot have exterior basement stairwells.

46. A buttress
    a. primarily resists vertical forces.
    b. resists lateral thrust.
    c. is used with step footings.
    d. is not effective in freezing climates.

47. Horizontal cracks in foundation walls are usually caused by all of the following *EXCEPT*
    a. soil pressure.
    b. improper backfilling.
    c. sinking footings.
    d. hydrostatic pressure.

48. Which of the following terms do *NOT* fit together?
    a. Monolithic slab, supported slab, floating slab
    b. Compression, tension, shear
    c. Underpinning, bench footing, lowered basements
    d. Expansive soils, slip joint, pilaster

49. Which provides the best base on which to build a foundation?
    a. Organic soils with a six-inch bed of gravel
    b. Undisturbed soil
    c. Eight-inch-wide footings
    d. Concrete block footings

50. Piles are
    a. used where soil quality is poor.
    b. driven into the ground as far as the frost line.
    c. always driven into the ground until they hit bedrock.
    d. never driven to bedrock.

51. All of the following materials have been used for foundations *EXCEPT*
    a. wood.
    b. brick.
    c. gypsum.
    d. concrete block.

52. Interior footings (under columns, for example) are usually subject to what kinds of loads?
    a. Almost purely horizontal
    b. Horizontal and vertical
    c. Almost purely vertical
    d. Primarily tension

53. Which of the following statements is true of a settlement crack?
    a. Settlement cracks do not usually have corresponding cracks elsewhere in the building.
    b. Control joints are used to prevent settlement cracks from developing.
    c. Settlement cracks will occur at weak spots in the wall.
    d. Settlement cracks typically do not extend into footings.

54. In which situation are you most likely to see settlement cracks?
    a. Houses built on reclaimed land
    b. Houses built with slab-on-grade construction
    c. Houses with stone or brick foundations
    d. Houses built in an area with a very low water table

55. If two diagonal foundation wall cracks make a pyramid, most often
    a. the inside of the triangle is heaving.
    b. there is a shrinkage crack.
    c. the inside of the triangle is dropping.
    d. there is no significance to the pattern.

56. Which of the following would more likely indicate an active crack?
    a. The corners of the crack are rounded.
    b. The inside of the crack has paint in it.
    c. Recent cracking of patching material.
    d. The crack is horizontal.

57. Vertical joints every two-to-four-feet in the bottom section of the foundation wall could be evidence of
    a. mud-jacking.
    b. control joints.
    c. foundation irrigation.
    d. underpinning.

58. In most frost areas
    a. the bottom of the footing rests on top of the basement slab.
    b. the top of the footing is even with the top of the basement slab.
    c. the bottom of the basement slab rests on top of the footing.
    d. the bottom of the footing is even with the bottom of the basement slab.

59. Why might a deck or a driveway cause the frost depth to be greater than normal?
    a. Shoveled driveways or a deck prevent the insulating snow from limiting the frost depth.
    b. Driveways and areas under decks do not usually drain well.
    c. Snow tends to drift on driveways and decks.
    d. The snow layer causes deeper frost penetration.

60. Adfreezing
    a. is the result of insufficient footing depth.
    b. is more common in free-draining soils.
    c. helps reduce heat loss.
    d. won't occur in dry soils.

61. Which of the following can cause additional horizontal loads on the foundation?
    a. Driveway slopes toward the house
    b. Removal of a tree near the home
    c. Undersized footings
    d. Lack of lateral support

62. Moisture penetration through the foundation wall can cause the foundation to flake off on the interior. This condition is called
    a. honeycombing.
    b. cold joints.
    c. efflorescence.
    d. spalling.

63. A bench footing is used
    a. on sloping lots.
    b. where the water table is high.
    c. with pier footings only.
    d. when lowering basements.

64. All of these are good inspection techniques *EXCEPT*
    a. looking for what is missing.
    b. backtracking.
    c. focusing exclusively on details.
    d. checking connections carefully.

65. When must you go into crawl spaces?
    a. Wherever you can physically fit
    b. When headroom is greater than 30 inches
    c. When it is not dangerous and you will not damage anything
    d. When you suspect there may be a problem within

66. Floor structures may experience what kinds of loads? (3 answers)
    a. Live and dead loads
    b. Vertical loads
    c. Horizontal loads
    d. Compression loads

67. Wood framing members
    a. should not contact concrete that is below grade.
    b. should not contact concrete directly.
    c. should not contact masonry directly.
    d. should not contact steel directly.

68. Sills see forces that are primarily
    a. tension parallel to the grain.
    b. tension perpendicular to the grain.
    c. compression parallel to the grain.
    d. compression perpendicular to the grain.

69. Sills below grade level
    a. are more likely to fail in bending than sills above grade.
    b. are more susceptible to crushing than sills above grade.
    c. are more susceptible to rot than sills above grade.
    d. are more susceptible to warping than sills above grade.

70. Anchor bolts holding sills to foundations
    a. need nuts and washers.
    b. should extend 14 inches down into the foundation.
    c. should never be used within one foot of building corners.
    d. should be spaced every 10 feet.

71. Common sill problems include all of the following *EXCEPT*
    a. crushing.
    b. poor anchoring.
    c. gaps under sills.
    d. sagging.

72. The implications of failed sills include all of these *EXCEPT*
    a. sloped or sagging floors.
    b. heaved floors.
    c. differential settlement.
    d. structural collapse.

73. Steel columns resting on wood sills
    a. should be nailed to the sills tightly.
    b. should be bolted to the sills tightly
    c. should be separated from the sill by a sill gasket.
    d. may crush the sill.

74. Sills may do all of the following *EXCEPT*
    a. anchor the superstructure to the foundation.
    b. provide a level surface for wall and floor construction.
    c. provide a nailing surface for floor joists.
    d. act as the structural support for framing over basement windows.

75. Columns built into exterior walls are called
    a. studs.
    b. piers.
    c. pilasters.
    d. concealed posts.

76. Common column materials include all of these *EXCEPT*
    a. steel.
    b. Concrete.
    c. plywood.
    d. masonry.

77. The function of columns is most like
    a. beams.
    b. studs.
    c. rafters.
    d. piers.

78. Rust on steel columns is
    a. usually found at the top.
    b. usually found at the bottom.
    c. due to metal fatigue induced by expansion and contraction.
    d. only common on outdoor columns.

79. Rectangular or square solid wood columns should be at least
    a. 2 inches × 12 inches.
    b. 6 inches × 6 inches.
    c. 4 inches × 8 inches.
    d. 5 inches × 8 inches.

80. Steel columns may be secured to steel beams with
    a. bendable metal tabs.
    b. rivets.
    c. 4 nails, each 3½ inches long.
    d. wood transfer plates.

81. Spalling brick on columns usually results from
    a. insect activity.
    b. transverse loading.
    c. poor-quality mortar.
    d. moisture in the brick.

82. Beams are also called
    a. pilasters.
    b. purlins.
    c. girders.
    d. I-joists.

83. Ends of beams should rest on
    a. columns only.
    b. foundations only.
    c. 3½ inches of solid material.
    d. wood shims.

84. Are beams allowed to rest on concrete block walls?
    a. Only if there are wood shims between the beam and the block.
    b. Only if at least the top seven inches of block is filled with concrete.
    c. Only if there is at least six inches of end bearing.
    d. This is not allowed.

85. Notches in beams should
    a. not be present.
    b. not be in the middle ⅓ of the beam span.
    c. be in the middle ⅓ of the beam span.
    d. be in the bottom ¼ of the beam.

86. The weakest joist-to-beam connection is
    a. a joist on top of a wood beam running across the full width of the beam.
    b. a joist and beam fastened with a mortise and tendon joint.
    c. a ledger board.
    d. a joist resting on a wood beam by one-half of an inch.

87. One function of floor joists may be to
    a. vertically support beams.
    b. laterally support columns.
    c. vertically support foundations.
    d. laterally support masonry walls.

88. All of these are common joist problems *EXCEPT*
    a. overspanning.
    b. sagging.
    c. joists running parallel to walls below.
    d. rot.

89. Floor openings around stairs
    a. are called cantilevers.
    b. are supported by the staircase.
    c. are usually supported by columns.
    d. often require doubling of joists.

90. Sagging floors
    a. indicate undersized subflooring.
    b. indicate foundation failure.
    c. can be reinforced by sistering.
    d. may result from truss uplift.

91. If a 2×8 joist has a 3 inch $\times$ 3 inch notch at the bottom where it rests on a beam
    a. the beam should also be notched.
    b. the head room is reduced below.
    c. the beam should be steel.
    d. the joist may have a crack that extends horizontally from the notch.

92. Joist hangers
    a. are all suitable for every size of joist.
    b. can only be used on the first floor.
    c. should be secured with roofing nails, because the large heads provide good support.
    d. should fit tightly against the bottoms of joists.

93. Bridging, blocking, and strapping do all of these *EXCEPT*
    a. damp vibration.
    b. spread loads among joists.
    c. prevent joist twisting.
    d. allow thinner sheathing.

94. Holes are
    a. best near the top of joists.
    b. best near the bottom of joists.
    c. best near the middle of joists.
    d. not allowed in joists.

95. Partition walls (nonload-bearing walls)
    a. add very little load to the floor joists below.
    b. are best if they are parallel to and directly above a floor joist below.
    c. are best if they are perpendicular to floor joists below.
    d. should not be offset from the beam or wall below.

96. Wood floor trusses
    a. are often referred to as scissor trusses.
    b. cannot be supported by beams.
    c. should always be fire-cut.
    d. typically have longer spans than dimensional lumber.

97. The subflooring material most likely to fail by swelling is
    a. waferboard.
    b. plywood.
    c. plank.
    d. LVL.

98. Subflooring can be thought of as
    a. little studs.
    b. little columns.
    c. little joists.
    d. little collar ties.

99. Unsupported subflooring ends are a problem common with
    a. tongue-and-groove plywood laid perpendicular to joists.
    b. waferboard.
    c. plank laid diagonally to joists.
    d. plank laid perpendicular to joists.

100. Walls may perform all of these functions *EXCEPT*
    a. resistance to racking.
    b. support of exterior and interior finishes.
    c. acting as supply ductwork for heating systems.
    d. providing chases for wires and pipes.

101. Masonry walls may be any of these *EXCEPT*
    a. single wythe.
    b. triple wythe.
    c. cavity walls.
    d. sandwich walls.

102. Solid masonry walls typically need
    a. vented rain screens.
    b. wide soffits.
    c. foundations and footings.
    d. pilasters.

103. Solid masonry walls typically need all of these *EXCEPT*
    a. a way to hold the wythes together.
    b. arches or lintels over openings.
    c. mortar.
    d. corbelling.

104. Masonry walls are strongest in
    a. compression.
    b. vertical tension.
    c. vertical bending.
    d. horizontal bending.

105. Which single wall is most likely to contain both an arch and a lintel?
    a. solid brick.
    b. wood frame.
    c. wood frame brick veneer.
    d. a cavity wall.

106. Cracks in brick walls
    a. are common.
    b. always require repair.
    c. should always be caulked.
    d. always need a structural engineer's analysis.

107. More serious cracks tend to be
    a. diagonal.
    b. vertical.
    c. random.
    d. in more than one plane.

108. Cracks may result from building movement that
    a. has stopped.
    b. is moving at a steady rate.
    c. is slowing down.
    d. all of the above.

109. Which wall will show cracks first if the foundation moves?
    a. Brick
    b. Clapboard
    c. Aluminum siding
    d. Board and batten siding

110. Rusting lintels typically cause
    a. diagonal cracks, forming a triangle above windows.
    b. vertical cracks, above window corners.
    c. horizontal cracks, radiating out from the top corners of windows.
    d. vertical cracks, below window corners.

111. In a solid masonry wall, which of these is usually visible?
    a. brick ties
    b. header courses
    c. diagonal headers
    d. weep holes

112. Which wall gets taller over time?
    a. Concrete block
    b. Poured concrete
    c. Brick
    d. Wood frame

113. All of these wood frame walls commonly carry floor loads *EXCEPT*
    a. 2-by-6s, 16 inches on center.
    b. 2-by-6s, 24 inches on center.
    c. 2-by-4s, 12 inches on center.
    d. 2-by-4s, 24 inches on center.

114. Double-top plates on wood frame walls
    a. can be omitted if joists are directly above studs.
    b. can be omitted if the top plate is oak.
    c. are needed on partition walls.
    d. must be locked at their joints with metal ties.

115. When it comes to resisting wind loads, wood frame walls can be thought of as
    a. beams on their sides.
    b. columns laying flat.
    c. floors installed on their sides.
    d. collar ties on their ends.

116. Bottom plates on platform framed bearing walls
    a. must rest completely on a subfloor.
    b. must rest at least 1 inch of its width on a subfloor.
    c. must rest at least ⅔ of its width on a subfloor.
    d. must rest at least ⅓ of its width on a subfloor.

117. Girts in a bearing wall are necessary if
    a. there is no masonry veneer.
    b. there is no finish on either side of the wall.
    c. there is only drywall on one side of the wall and nothing on the other.
    d. there is only plywood siding on one side of the wall and nothing on the other.

118. Sheathing functions include all of these *EXCEPT*
    a. supporting siding.
    b. stiffening walls to prevent racking, for example.
    c. helping to keep wind out of the building.
    d. supporting metal ties for brick veneer.

119. Partition or nonload-bearing walls
    a. can be identified by tapping on them.
    b. always have structural supports below.
    c. do not provide end support for joists.
    d. must have sheathing.

120. Condensation in northern climates forms in walls
    a. on their warmest surfaces only.
    b. as a result of indoor air leaking into the walls.
    c. as a result of outdoor air leaking into the walls.
    d. which prevents rot by keeping all of the wood at the same moisture content.

121. Racking of wood frame walls can be prevented by all of these *EXCEPT*
    a. diagonal bracing.
    b. collar ties.
    c. plaster and lath.
    d. plywood sheathing.

122. In wood frame walls, all of these may cause top plates to sag *EXCEPT*
    a. a single top plate.
    b. a splice in the midspan of the top plate.
    c. two-by-four top plates on a two-by-six wall.
    d. concentrated loads.

123. Offset walls supporting floor loads above
    a. can cause a floor to sag near the wall.
    b. are not permitted.
    c. cannot be offset by more than three feet from their support below.
    d. are unlimited in location as long as they are perpendicular to the joists below.

124. A lack of firestopping in a platform framed house is most common
    a. on exterior walls.
    b. around chimneys and pipes.
    c. at electrical chases.
    d. on interior walls.

125. Masonry veneer has a function similar to
    a. studs.
    b. sheathing.
    c. buttresses.
    d. aluminum siding.

126. Brick ties are
    a. usually aluminum.
    b. visible.
    c. fastened to studs.
    d. fastened to sheathing.

127. Vented rain screen walls
    a. are only needed on north facing walls.
    b. vent indoor moisture.
    c. reduce water driving through brick walls.
    d. has the brick installed tight against the sheathing behind to prevent moisture penetration.

128. All of these are components of vented rain screens *EXCEPT*
    a. weep holes.
    b. flashings.
    c. sheathing paper.
    d. headers.

129. Cored bricks or hollow concrete blocks on their sides are prone to
    a. spalling.
    b. efflorescence.
    c. crushing.
    d. mortar deterioration.

130. Most modern brick is
    a. glazed on the exterior side.
    b. made from reconstituted stone.
    c. waterproof with low permeability and porosity.
    d. not designed to be in the soil.

131. If an arch over a four foot window in the middle of a three story masonry wall failed completely
    a. the wall would collapse.
    b. a triangular hole over the window would develop.
    c. the window was probably leaking.
    d. it was probably the result of lateral thrust.

132. Steel lintels
    a. should not be used in masonry walls.
    b. are usually stainless steel.
    c. need six inches of endbearing in most areas.
    d. have a minimum span of six feet, six inches.

133. Rusting steel lintels
    a. should be caulked.
    b. tend to expand.
    c. tend to shrink.
    d. only occur in masonry veneer walls.

134. Which statement is true?
    a. Increasing the insulation makes the attic warmer.
    b. If the attic is cold, then warm, moist air leaking into the attic from the house will condense more quickly.
    c. If you increase the insulation level in a roof, you should decrease the ventilation.
    d. The insulation and ventilation cannot affect the structure of a roof.

135. Ceiling joists are
    a. similar to rafters but found on low-slope roofs.
    b. horizontal members used with rafters and sometimes with roof joists.
    c. 2-by-4s, 2-by-6s, 2-by-8s, or 2-by-10s and are used to support the sheathing.
    d. structural members that support the dead load of the roof sheathing, the roofing material, and the live loads above.

136. Joints in ceiling joists should be securely spliced
    a. to prevent rafter spread.
    b. because if they are firmly attached, collar ties are not required.
    c. to prevent rafter sag.
    d. to provide a supporting surface for the purlins.

137. The span of a rafter is defined as the
    a. horizontal projection of the rafters, from one side of the house to the other.
    b. length of the rafter, from the collar tie to the ridge board.
    c. horizontal projection, from one support to another.
    d. distance from the center of one rafter to the center of the next; most commonly 16 inches.

138. All of the following statements are true of ridge boards *EXCEPT*
    a. ridge boards are only used on roofs with a slope of 2-in-12 or less.
    b. ridge boards are typically a nominal one inch board.
    c. ridge boards are usually one size larger than the rafters.
    d. if there is a ridge board, some authorities may allow opposing rafters to be offset by their width.

139. All of these are components of asphalt shingles *EXCEPT*
    a. sealing strips.
    b. organic felt.
    c. synthetic rubber.
    d. granule surfacing.

140. Sagging rafters may be a result of
    a. undersized rafters.
    b. overspanned rafters.
    c. excessive roof weight.
    d. all of the above.

141. Purlins are
    a. horizontal members supporting the midspan of rafters.
    b. part of the framing of a truss roof system.
    c. part of the framing of a raised foundation.
    d. none of the above.

142. What are some of the properties of trusses?
    a. Middle web boards can be altered as needed.
    b. They typically need no midlength support.
    c. They are engineered structural members.
    d. Both b and c describe properties of trusses.

143. What is another term for beam?
    a. Span
    b. Girder
    c. Joist
    d. Header

144. What is the likely cause of sag in roof sheathing where the trusses are 24 inches on center with a clear span of 36 feet?
    a. Undersized trusses
    b. Sheathing is too thin
    c. Undersized purlins
    d. Inadequate fastening of sheathing to trusses

145. Collar ties are installed in roof framing to
    a. prevent purlin sag.
    b. provide lateral support for the top of the walls.
    c. support the end walls of gable roofs.
    d. prevent rafters from sagging.

146. A roof truss that has been cut in order to accommodate a skylight can be resupported by
    a. a skilled carpenter.
    b. special engineering design.
    c. doubling trusses on either side of the skylight opening.
    d. no special consideration necessary.

147. All of the following are styles of roofs *EXCEPT*
    a. shed roof.
    b. hip roof.
    c. garage roof.
    d. butterfly roof.

148. Which of the following is the least common spacing for rafters, roof joists and ceiling joists?
    a. 12 inches
    b. 20 inches
    c. 24 inches
    d. 36 inches

149. All of the following terms can be used when discussing roof structures *EXCEPT*
    a. shoes.
    b. toes.
    c. hips.
    d. birds' mouths.

150. While inspecting the exterior of the house, you notice that there is a gap between the soffit and the exterior wall. The gap is wider near the midpoint of the wall and closes to nothing at the corners. Which of the following conditions would you suspect?
    a. The rafters are not adequately attached at the ridge boards.
    b. The purlins are not continuous and are inadequately spliced at the joints.
    c. The rafters are resting on toes, rather than heels.
    d. The ceiling joists are not tying opposing rafter bottoms together properly.

151. All of the following perform essentially the same function as a knee wall *EXCEPT*
    a. purlins.
    b. struts.
    c. strongbacks.
    d. birds' mouths.

152. What is a gusset plate used for in a roof structure?
    a. It connects members of a truss together.
    b. A gusset plate is used only in earthquake-prone and hurricane-prone areas.
    c. It connects edges of roof sheathing together when they do not bear directly on top of a rafter or truss.
    d. It connects the purlins to the rafters.

153. All of the following statements are true of truss uplift *EXCEPT*
    a. truss uplift is a cyclical problem.
    b. truss uplift occurs in the winter.
    c. truss uplift is a serious structural problem and is very difficult to deal with.
    d. the best solution to truss uplift is to conceal the movement.

154. All of the following statements are true of wood I-joists *EXCEPT*
    a. a bird's mouth cut is acceptable in a wood I-joist.
    b. wood I-joists cannot be hung from the top chord only.
    c. wood I-joists must rest on a wall or a ridge beam.
    d. wood I-joists can perform the same functions as rafters, roof joists, or ceiling joists.

155. Plywood, waferboard, and OSB require edge support at all edges. All of the following are considered adequate edge support *EXCEPT*
    a. H-clips.
    b. top and bottom edges, butted and glued together.
    c. 2 × 2 blocking.
    d. an edge resting directly on a rafter or truss.

156. While inspecting the attic of a row house built in the mid-1970s, you notice that the plywood next to the party wall is delaminating and has a white powder underneath. Which of the following might explain this?
    a. The attic is much colder near the party walls, and there is almost always more condensation on the underside of the sheathing in this area.
    b. This condition is an example of pyrolysis, where the sheathing in contact with the masonry party wall deteriorates prematurely.
    c. The plywood next to the party wall is probably FRT plywood. FRT plywood has been found to deteriorate prematurely.
    d. This type of plywood has oriented strands and can only be installed in one direction. Often the last piece is installed in the wrong direction to make it fit between the party walls.

157. The webs of a truss
    a. are compression members.
    b. are tension members.
    c. may be in compression or tension.
    d. have no load on them.

158. Which of the following is a truss style?
    a. Lambert
    b. Panel scissor
    c. Briggs & Stratten
    d. Inverted Belgian

159. All of the following could indicate spreading rafters *EXCEPT*
    a. sag in roof or ridge.
    b. top of exterior wall bowed out.
    c. gap between the soffit and the exterior wall
    d. cracks in interior ceilings, running perpendicular to the outside walls.

160. Collar ties are
    a. always loaded in compression.
    b. always loaded in tension.
    c. potentially in compression or tension but are most often in tension.
    d. potentially in compression or tension but are most often in compression.

161. For a house with wood frame walls, the roof structure can be nailed directly to the wall structure. If the exterior walls are solid masonry, how is the roof framing attached to the walls?
    a. A wood sill is bolted to the top of the wall, and the roof framing is nailed to this sill.
    b. Each rafter is bolted to the masonry wall with bolts that are about ½-inch-in-diameter and about 3½ inches long.
    c. If the exterior walls are solid masonry, the roof structure can simply rest on top of the wall. There is no need to secure them as long as the bottoms of opposing rafters are tied together to prevent rafter spreading.
    d. It is attached by joist hangers and concrete nails.

162. Which of the following statements is true of knee walls and struts?
    a. Knee walls and struts should not bear directly on a supporting wall.
    b. Knee walls and struts supporting purlins sometimes bear close to, but not directly on, bearing walls.
    c. Where knee walls and struts supporting purlins bear directly on supporting walls, the joists should be the next size larger than they otherwise would be.
    d. None of the above statements is true.

163. Which of the following truss types will have two top chords and two bottom chords?
    a. Fink
    b. Howe
    c. Scissor
    d. Belgian

164. All of the following are functions of roof sheathing *EXCEPT*
    a. carrying live loads.
    b. providing lateral bracing for roof framing members.
    c. providing a nailing surface for roof coverings.
    d. providing vertical support for roof framing members.

165. Jack rafters are
    a. rafters at hips and valleys.
    b. rafters that tie into a header at an opening in the roof (such as a skylight).
    c. rafters that have been doubled.
    d. the same as I-joists.

166. Which of the following are truss conditions that should be reported? (3 answers)
    a. Hole at the ¼ point of web (less than ⅓ thickness)
    b. Weak gusset connection
    c. Truss uplift
    d. Insulation completely covering the bottom chord of the truss

167. In which of the following situations is roof sheathing NOT required?
    a. Where lateral bracing is achieved with struts
    b. Where a wood batten system has been used with concrete tile
    c. Where two layers of ice and water protection have been used
    d. None of the above

168. H-clips are used for
    a. attaching rafters to ceiling joists.
    b. attaching members of trusses together.
    c. edge support for roof sheathing.
    d. splicing rafters.

ANSWERS AND EXPLANATIONS

1. **a.** Brick veneer walls are not watertight.

2. **b.** Masonry veneer does not carry the live or dead loads of the structure.

3. **b.** With wood frame walls, the lintel size depends on the number of stories above, due to the fact that the lintel is subjected to all of the vertical loads above that opening.

4. **b.** Wood I-joists cannot have bird's mouth cuts.

5. **b.** If the building is not heated, the frost line will be lowered. If the depth of frost is two feet, for example, it may be expected to be two feet below the basement floor if the home is not heated.

6. **b.** Cracks dues to horizontal forces often represent serious structural problems.

7. **a.** Steel beams should be supported only with steel shims.

8. **a.** Joists may sit on top of beams or be attached to the sides of beams.

9. **b.** Joists see both vertical and lateral loads.

10. **a.** Joists are often used to provide lateral support for solid masonry walls.

11. **b.** Fire-cutting joists is a useful technique to prevent masonry walls from tipping over in case of a serious fire.

12. **a.** Joists notched at their end are weaker than normal joists.

13. **a.** Joists resting on foundation walls at or near grade level are prone to rot.

14. **b.** Holes in joists should be near the middle rather than the top or bottom.

15. **b.** Although they don't bear a load from above, partition walls themselves are loads on the floor joists below.

16. **b.** Very few concrete floors in houses are suspended slabs.

17. **a.** The strength of hollow concrete blocks is greatly reduced if they are installed on their side.

18. **b.** Bricks laid on their sides forming window-sills are not a structural problem.

19. **b.** Patched cracks on brick may indicate either a minor, one-time issue or serious structural movement.

20. **a.** Bearing walls and partition walls are built in substantially the same way.

21. **b.** Walls see lateral as well as vertical loads.

22. **a.** Door openings in partition walls normally do not require lintels.

23. **a.** You normally can't see much of the wall framing directly, so problems are difficult to identify and often based on deduction.

24. **a.** With masonry walls, the lintel carries the weight of the masonry immediately above the opening, not all the stories above.

25. **a.** We generally don't want masonry bearing on wood.

26. **b.** The top of the exposed edge of a steel lintel should not be caulked; doing so will trap water inside the wall.

27. **b.** When used in a rafter orientation, wood I-joists must rest on or against a ridge beam. Metal hangers are appropriate supports.

28. **b.** Lack of firestopping is more prevalent on balloon frame construction than platform framing.

29. **b.** The function of a footing is to transmit the weight of the house to the soil.

30. **b.** Vertical cracking in foundation walls indicates footing failures.

31. **c.** Frost penetration into the soil below the footings is an issue when you excavate to create a basement walkout.

32. **d.** Excavating to the bottom of a footing exposes the side of the footing. This removes the lateral support of the soil from the footing.

33. **b.** Snow loads are live loads.

34. **c.** Spread footings are continuous around the perimeter of the house.

35. **c.** Gravel is the strongest soil type for building homes on this list.

36. **b.**   Differential settlement occurs when one part of the house settles and the rest does not, or when two parts settle at different rates.

37. **a.**   The maximum slope is 1 in 2.

38. **c.**   You have to monitor a crack over time to determine whether it is active.

39. **c.**   Step footings are typically used for houses built on sloped lots.

40. **a.**   Frost heave cannot be caused by raising the grade height. This is more likely to protect the foundation from frost than make it worse.

41. **d.**   Steel beams or channels added horizontally along the crack are not likely to be successful. Beams or channels added vertically are better.

42. **d.**   Cinder block is made from slag and has a darker, rougher texture than concrete block. It is more susceptible to deterioration upon exposure to moisture.

43. **b.**   A cold joint is the result of pouring the concrete foundation at two different times.

44. **b.**   Pilasters typically support beams.

45. **c.**   Floor framing gives foundation walls the lateral support.

46. **b.**   A buttress resists lateral thrust.

47. **c.**   Horizontal cracks in foundation walls can be caused by soil pressure, hydrostatic pressure, or improper backfilling.

48. **d.**   Expansive soils, slip joints and pilaster do not fit together.

49. **b.**   Undisturbed soil is the best base for building a foundation.

50. **a.**   Piles are typically used where soil quality is poor. They are driven into the ground until they hit bedrock or the friction is enough to resist downward movement. Piles aren't usually related to a frost issue.

51. **c.**   Gypsum is not a foundation material.

52. **c.**   Interior footings see almost a purely vertical load.

53. **c.**   Settlement cracks typically occur at weak spots in walls. This includes door and window openings.

54. **a.**   Houses built on reclaimed land are prone to settlement cracks because the soil is disturbed.

55. **c.**   When two diagonal cracks form a pyramid, the inside of the pyramid is usually dropping.

56. **c.**   Active cracks are indicated by sharp corners on the crack and/or recent cracking of patch material.

57. **d.**   Vertical joints every two-to-four-feet around the foundation may suggest an underpinning job.

58. **c.**   In most frost areas, the basement slab bottom rests on the top of the footing.

59. **a.**   Snow is an insulator. Shoveling off the driveway or deck allows the frost to go deeper.

60. **d.**   Adfreezing won't occur in dry soils.

61. **a.**   Driveways may slope towards the house, increasing the load from water and ice. Large vehicles parked adjacent to the house can impose a large horizontal load.

62. **d.**   Flaking off of concrete or masonry material is called spalling.

63. **d.**   You use bench footings when lowering basements.

64. **c.**   You should not focus exclusively on details.

65. **c.**   Go into crawl spaces when it is safe, and when no damage to anything will occur.

66. **a, b,** and **c.**   Floors see live and dead loads that might be vertical and/or horizontal.

67. **a.**   Wood framing members should not contact concrete that is below grade.

68. **d.**   Sills see compression forces perpendicular to the grain.

69. **c.**   Sills below grade are much more susceptible to rot than sills above grade.

70. **a.**   Anchor bolts holding sills to foundations need nuts and washers.

71. **d.**   Sills don't typically sag because they are continuously supported by the foundation.

72. **b.**   Heaved floors do not indicate failed sills.

73. **d.**   Steel columns sitting on wood sills can crush the sill due to the concentrated load.

74. **d.**   Sills should not be asked to carry the framing loads over basement windows.

75. **c.**   Columns built into walls are called pilasters.

76. **c.**   Columns are not typically made of plywood.

77. **d.**   Columns are most like piers.

78. **b.**   Rust on columns is usually at or near the bottom, often as a result of chronically-wet basement problems, or flooding from plumbing or heating water, or sewer backup.

79. **b.**   Wood columns should be at least 6 inches × 6 inches.

80. **a.**   Steel columns can be secured to beams with bendable metal tabs.

81. **d.**   Spalling brick is usually the result of moisture in the brick.

82. **c.**   Beams are also called girders.

83. **c.**   Beams should rest on at least 3½ inches of solid material.

84. **b.**   Beams can sit on hollow concrete block walls if at least the top seven inches of the block is filled with concrete.

85. **a.**   Beams should not be notched.

86. **d.**   A joist resting on a beam by only one-half of an inch is scary. It won't take much movement for that joist to fall off.

87. **d.**   Joists may be called upon to laterally support masonry walls.

88. **c.**   It is okay if joists run parallel to the walls below.

89. **d.**   Floors around stairs often require doubling of the joists around the opening.

90. **c.**   Sagging floors can be reinforced by sistering. Undersized subflooring is usually not the issue.

91. **d.**   A notched joist may have a crack that extends out horizontally from the notch.

92. **d.**   Joist hangers should fit tightly against the bottom of joists.

93. **d.**   Bridging, blocking, and strapping do not allow thinner sheathing.

94. **c.**   Holes are best near the middle of joists, rather than the top or bottom.

95. **c.**   Partition walls are best perpendicular to the floor joists below. This way their load is spread out over several joists.

96. **d.**   Wood floor trusses typically have longer spans than would be allowed with ordinary lumber.

97. **a.**   Waferboard subflooring is likely to swell when it gets wet.

98. **c.**   Subflooring can be thought of as little joists.

99. **c.**   Planks laid diagonally to joists are often unsupported at their ends.

100. **c.**   Walls cannot act as supply ducts for heating systems because the warm air is too hot.

101. **d.**   Masonry walls can be single, double, triple wythe, or cavity walls. A sandwich wall is not a designation for a masonry wall.

102. **c.**   Solid masonry walls typically need foundations and footings.

103. **d.**   Solid masonry walls do not need corbelling.

104. **a.**   Masonry walls are strongest in compression. It is hard to squash a masonry wall.

105. **c.**   A wood frame brick veneer wall may have a lintel on the wood frame section and an arch in the brick section.

106. **a.**   Cracks in brick walls are common.

107. **d.**   The most serious cracks tend to be in more than one plane.

108. **d.**   Cracks may result from building movement that has stopped, is moving at a steady rate, or is speeding up/slowing down.

109. **a.**   Brick is the most brittle of these systems and will crack first if the foundation moves.

110. **c.**   Rusting lintels usually result in horizontal cracks radiating out from the top corners of windows.

111. **b.**   Header courses are usually visible.

112. **c.**   Brick walls get taller over time.

113. **d.**   Two-by-fours, 24 inches on center are not common. This doesn't provide great support for sheathing or drywall. Two-by-fours on 12-inch centers are commonly used where the floor framing is on 12-inch centers.

114. **a.** Double-top plates on wood frame walls can be omitted if the joists are directly above the studs.

115. **c.** Wood frame walls can be thought of floors on their sides with respect to wind loads. The wind load feels the same to a wall as people standing on a floor.

116. **c.** Two-thirds of the width of a bottom plate must rest on the sub floor.

117. **b.** Bearing walls need girts if there is no sheathing or drywall, for example, on either side.

118. **d.** Sheathing should not be asked to support the metal ties for brick veneer. The ties should be supported by the studs.

119. **c.** Partition walls do not provide end support for joists.

120. **b.** Condensation usually results from indoor air leaking into the walls.

121. **b.** Collar ties are not found in wall construction.

122. **c.** Two-by-four top plates on a two-by-six wall are not a problem, although they are not common.

123. **a.** Offset load-bearing walls may result in a floor sagging near the wall because the load is not transferred directly to the bearing wall or beam below.

124. **b.** A lack of firestopping is most common around chimneys and pipes.

125. **d.** Masonry veneer's function is similar to aluminum siding. It is not a structural member.

126. **c.** Brick ties should be fastened to studs.

127. **c.** Vented rain screen walls help to reduce the water driving through the brick walls.

128. **d.** Headers are not part of a vented rain screen. They are part of a solid masonry wall.

129. **c.** Hollow bricks installed on their sides may be easily crushed.

130. **d.** Modern brick is not designed to be in the soil.

131. **b.** If you made a hole in a masonry wall, a triangular hole over the window would develop. The wall would not fall down.

132. **c.** Steel lintels need six inches of end bearing in most areas.

133. **b.** Rusting steel lintels tend to expand.

134. **b.** Warm moist air leaking into the attic from the house will condense more quickly if the attic is cold.

135. **b.** Ceiling joists are horizontal members used with rafters and (sometimes) roof joists.

136. **a.** Ceiling joists help to prevent rafter spread if they are adequately tied to the bottom of the rafters.

137. **c.** The span of a rafter is the horizontal projection from one support to another.

138. **a.** Ridge boards should not be used below a slope of 4-in-12.

139. **c.** Synthetic rubber is not a component of asphalt shingles.

140. **d.** Sagging rafters may result from undersized or overspanned rafters. Excessive roof weight may also cause sagging.

141. **a.** Purlins are horizontal members supporting the midspan of rafters.

142. **d.** Trusses need no midlength support typically and are engineered systems.

143. **b.** Girder is another term for beam.

144. **b.** Where sheathing between trusses 24 inches on center sags, it is usually because the sheathing is too thin.

145. **d.** Collar ties prevent rafter sagging.

146. **b.** Special engineering design is necessary to resupport cut trusses.

147. **c.** A garage roof is not a style of roof.

148. **d.** Thirty-six inches is not a common rafter or joist spacing.

149. **a.** A "shoe" is not a common structural term.

150. **d.** A gap between the soffit and the wall suggests rafter spreading, usually because the ceiling joists don't tie the opposing rafter bottoms together.

151. **d.** Birds' mouths are notches not structural members.

152. **a.** A gusset plate connects truss members together.

153. **b.**   Truss uplift is not a serious structural problem and is reasonably easy to deal with.

154. **a.**   A bird's mouth notch is not acceptable in an I-joist.

155. **b.**   You can't glue the butt edges of plywood together.

156. **c.**   This is probably FRT (Fire Resistant Treated) plywood that is deteriorating.

157. **b.**   A panel scissor is a style of truss.

158. **c.**   Webs may be in tension or compression.

159. **d.**   Cracks in ceilings running perpendicular to outside walls do not suggest rafter spreading.

160. **d.**   Collar ties can be loaded in compression and tension but are most often in compression.

161. **a.**   A wood sill is bolted to the top of a wall and the framing is nailed to this sill.

162. **b.**   Knee walls in struts supporting purlins sometimes bear close to, but not directly on, bearing walls.

163. **c.**   Scissor trusses have two top chords and two bottom chords.

164. **d.**   Roof sheathing does not provide vertical support for roof framing members.

165. **a.**   Jack rafters are rafters at hips and valleys.

166. **a, b,** and **c.** Truss problems include holes in webs, weak gusset connections, and truss uplift.

167. **b.**   You don't need roof sheathing if wood battens are used to support roof tiles.

168. **c.**   H-clips are used to provide edge support for roof sheathing.

3. ROOFING SYSTEMS
Practice Questions

1. You should always walk on clay tile roofs.
   a. True
   b. False

2. Concrete tiles are often laid over a waterproof membrane on the roof.
   a. True
   b. False

3. Inspectors should walk on concrete tile roofs.
   a. True
   b. False

4. Fiber cement shingles can be bent without breaking.
   a. True
   b. False

5. Rust on metal roofs occurs only on the surface.
   a. True
   b. False

6. Caulking is an acceptable substitute to letting the flashing into the mortar joints.
   a. True
   b. False

7. Ice damming can be an issue on skylights.
   a. True
   b. False

8. During an inspection of a skylight, you should never lift on the edge of the skylight.
   a. True
   b. False

9. The roof covering is typically part of the structure of the home.
   a. True
   b. False

10. You will never find three layers of asphalt shingles on a roof.
    a. True
    b. False

11. Slate roofs are among the most expensive to install and maintain.
    a. True
    b. False

12. Inspectors should walk on slate roofs.
    a. True
    b. False

13. A flashing is not required on the bottom edge of the chimney.
    a. True
    b. False

14. Your chimney inspection is finished when you get down off of the roof.
    a. True
    b. False

15. Leaking skylights can lead to structural problems.
    a. True
    b. False

16. Drip edge flashings are always required.
    a. True
    b. False

17. A flat roof surfaced with roll roofing is considered to be a high quality roof surface, and is usually seen on more expensive houses.
    a. True
    b. False

18. It is good practice to apply new built-up roof membranes over old ones.
    a. True
    b. False

19. A metal surface is a common and inexpensive way to cover large flat roofs.
    a. True
    b. False

20. Roll roofing is considered a temporary surface.
    a. True
    b. False

21. The base flashing on a flat roof is a "shedding system."
    a. True
    b. False

22. Low-slope is a possible problem with all these materials *EXCEPT*
    a. asphalt shingles.
    b. wood shakes.
    c. roll roofing.
    d. fiber cement shingles.

23. The following materials are all brittle *EXCEPT*
    a. wood.
    b. slate.
    c. roll roofing.
    d. clay.

24. Which material has the shortest life expectancy?
    a. Concrete
    b. Fiber cement
    c. Slate
    d. Roll roofing

25. Which material commonly imitates clay?
    a. Asphalt shingle
    b. Roll roofing
    c. Slate
    d. Concrete

26. Ice dams are most likely on roofs
    a. with asphalt shingles.
    b. with low slopes and wide overhangs.
    c. with low slopes and small overhangs.
    d. with steep slopes and small overhangs.

27. Patches on roofs almost always indicate
    a. good maintenance.
    b. prior leakage.
    c. poor installation.
    d. multiple layers of roofs.

28. Multiple layers of roofing are most common with
    a. clay.
    b. slate.
    c. wood.
    d. asphalt shingles.

29. A low-slope asphalt shingle application can go down to a slope of
    a. 6-in-12.
    b. 5-in-12.
    c. 4-in-12.
    d. 2-in-12.

30. Common failure modes for asphalt shingles include all of these *EXCEPT*
    a. spalling.
    b. blisters.
    c. loss of granules.
    d. cupping or clawing.

31. As asphalt shingles get close to the end of their life, the slots (keyways) between shingle tabs
    a. lengthen.
    b. narrow.
    c. widen.
    d. disappear.

32. New shingles applied in cold weather may be prone to
    a. breaking, because they are brittle.
    b. blistering when they warm, because of thermal shock.
    c. tabs tearing off, because sealing strips don't hold.
    d. surface cracking, because of organic felt shrinkage.

33. Roofing problems are most common
    a. at the eaves.
    b. at the ridges.
    c. above bathrooms and kitchens.
    d. at flashings and roof penetrations.

34. Two layers of asphalt shingle roofing material
    a. are good, because they provide double protection against leaks.
    b. may result in a shorter life for the second layer of shingles.
    c. improve attic insulation.
    d. are not permitted due to the extra load on the roof structure.

35. These are all common wood roof problems *EXCEPT*
    a. slots that are too wide.
    b. splitting.
    c. rot.
    d. burn-through.

36. On which roof is interlay (or interlayment) most likely be found?
    a. asphalt shingle
    b. wood shingle
    c. wood shake
    d. clay

37. No. 1 Blue-grade wood shingles are
    a. 100 percent edge-grain.
    b. 100 percent heartwood.
    c. free from knots (100 percent clear).
    d. All of the above

38. The problem with butting adjacent wood shingles too closely together is that
    a. attic ventilation is reduced.
    b. shingle drying is slowed.
    c. leakage is more likely.
    d. the shingles may buckle when wet.

39. Flat-grain wood shingles
    a. are superior quality.
    b. are found only on No. 3 Black grade shingles.
    c. can be identified by a flame pattern.
    d. are more resistant to cupping and curling than edge-grain shingles.

40. Moss on a wood roof
    a. should never be removed.
    b. provides additional protection from ultraviolet light.
    c. helps to insulate the wood from thermal shock.
    d. holds water against the wood, promoting rot.

41. If you drilled a hole through a properly laid wood shingle roof, how many shingles would you go through?
    a. 1
    b. 2
    c. 3
    d. 4

42. If you drilled a hole through a properly laid slate roof, how many slates would you go through?
    a. 1
    b. 2
    c. 3
    d. 4

43. If you drilled a hole through a properly laid Spanish-style clay roof, how many tiles would you go through?
    a. 1
    b. 2
    c. 3
    d. 4

44. If you drilled a hole through a properly laid, shingle-style flat clay roof, how many tiles would you go through?
    a. 1
    b. 2
    c. 3
    d. 4

45. If you drilled a hole through a properly laid, flat interlocking tile roof (concrete or clay), how many tiles would you go through?
    a. 1
    b. 2
    c. 3
    d. 4

46. If you drilled a hole through a properly laid, fiber cement roof, how many shingles would you go through?
    a. 1
    b. 2
    c. 3
    d. 4

47. If you drilled a hole through a properly laid, wood shake roof, how many shakes would you go through?
    a. 1
    b. 2
    c. 3
    d. 4

48. If you drilled a hole through a properly laid, metal shingle roof, how many shingles would you go through?
    a. 1
    b. 2
    c. 3
    d. 4

49. If you drilled a hole through a properly laid, roll roofing installation, how many layers would you go through?
    a. 1
    b. 2
    c. 3
    d. 4

50. All of these are common slate failure modes *EXCEPT*
    a. curling.
    b. breakage.
    c. delaminating.
    d. getting soft or crumbly.

51. Slate roofing is all of these *EXCEPT*
    a. very expensive.
    b. nailed in place.
    c. laid over 30-pound felt underlay.
    d. properly repaired with tar.

52. Dormer flashings may include all of the following *EXCEPT*
    a. stack flashings.
    b. ridge flashings.
    c. valley flashings.
    d. roof/sidewall flashings.

53. Clay tile roofs are effective shedding-style roofs by themselves under what circumstances?
    a. Never—a watertight membrane below is always needed
    b. On low-slope roofs only (less than 4-in-12)
    c. On steep-slope roofs only (more than 4-in-12)
    d. Only if glazed tile is used

54. Concrete tiles may be secured to the roof with any of these *EXCEPT*
    a. nails.
    b. staples.
    c. clips.
    d. battens.

55. A standing seam is found on
    a. a wood roof.
    b. a metal roof.
    c. a slate roof.
    d. a fiber cement roof.

56. Ice dam evidence includes everything listed here *EXCEPT*
    a. electric heating cables.
    b. siding discoloration starting at the soffit.
    c. water damage at interior wall/ceiling intersections.
    d. water running down along rafters from peak.

57. Cutting the points applies to
    a. clay.
    b. concrete.
    c. metal.
    d. asphalt shingles.

58. Mission clay tiles
    a. are lower quality than concrete tiles.
    b. have top pieces and bottom pieces.
    c. are always installed over a waterproof membrane.
    d. are prone to splitting.

59. Roll roofing fails
    a. after 20 years of life, typically.
    b. if it's not cemented directly to the sheathing.
    c. by cracking, buckling, or blistering.
    d. if installed on slopes of less than 1 in 12.

60. Metal roofing
    a. cannot be installed with an overlap.
    b. can never have exposed fasteners.
    c. must have a slope greater than 5-in-12.
    d. can be installed as shingles or sheets and panels.

61. Which cedar shingle is most rot-resistant?
    a. One on a north exposure of a 5-in-12 roof
    b. One on a low-sloped roof
    c. One in the path of a downspout discharging from a higher roof
    d. One on a 12-in-12 roof

62. The pitch of a valley in a sloped roof with a 4-in-12 pitch is approximately
    a. 2-in-12.
    b. 3-in-12.
    c. 4-in-12.
    d. 5-in-12.

63. The valley flashings should widen at the bottom to
    a. improve the aesthetics of the roof.
    b. make it easier to install the shingles.
    c. minimize the risk of ice damming.
    d. allow for the greater accumulation of water that collects here.

64. Open valley flashings made of roll roofing typically consist of
    a. 2 layers, 18 inches wide and 36 inches wide.
    b. 2 layers, each 18 inches wide.
    c. 2 layers, 12 inches wide and 18 inches wide.
    d. 3 layers, each 18 inches wide.

65. Metal valley flashings should *NOT* be longer than 10 feet because
    a. expansion and contraction may cause buckling.
    b. it would not be aesthetically pleasing.
    c. longer lengths of metal are too expansive.
    d. longer pieces are more difficult to handle.

66. Considerable wrinkling and tautness of EPMD and PVC roof membranes at wall intersections would typically be caused by
    a. improper base flashing detail.
    b. shrinkage of the membrane.
    c. poor securement of fascia to roof deck.
    d. lack of a proper counterflashing.

67. The bottom cap flashing for a masonry chimney has a single piece of metal let into the mortar joint and nailed to the shingle surface so that it won't lift up. The flashing extends over the shingle surface approximately 4 inches. No leakage is evident inside the home. You tell your client that,
    a. "The chimney base flashing has been properly installed."
    b. "The bottom cap flashing should extend down the shingle surface by at least six inches. The flashing has to be replaced."
    c. "This is not an ideal installation as the nail holes may leak and movement of the roof deck relative to the chimney may pull the flashing out, but it is typical and acceptable." Because the flashing hasn't been pulled yet, you recommend monitoring, rather than replacement.
    d. "This is not a proper cap flashing, as a hem was not created. The flashing should be replaced."

68. When walking around the outside of a house, you notice efflorescence on the chimney brickwork, just below the roofline. The most likely problem is
    a. a blocked chimney flue.
    b. the lack of a proper liner for the chimney.
    c. a leaking roof flashing.
    d. leaking soffits.

69. If the flange for a plumbing stack flashing appears to have pulled away from the roof, this would typically be caused by
    a. structural settlement of the house.
    b. settlement of the stack.
    c. incompatible flashing materials.
    d. none of the above.

70. If a recessed area is noted in the stack flashing around the pipe, this is commonly caused by
    a. structural settlement of the house.
    b. settlement of the stack.
    c. too many nails in the stack flashing.
    d. incompatible flashing materials.

71. Common installation problems with stack flashings include
    a. exposed or missing fasteners.
    b. the top half of flange exposed above roofing material.
    c. flashings being torn during installation.
    d. both a and b.

72. Apart from not providing a permanent seal, tarring over metal flashings is *NOT* desirable because
    a. tar and metal are not compatible.
    b. this may trap water and accelerate corrosion of the metal.
    c. it is difficult to determine the length of the flashing.
    d. it is difficult to determine if the flashing is let into masonry.

73. Concealed flashings for hips and ridges can include
    a. roofing felts.
    b. ice and water shield.
    c. mortar.
    d. All of the above

74. Ridge flashings can also act as
    a. venting systems.
    b. rain gutters.
    c. lightning protection systems.
    d. None of the above

75. With concrete or clay tile roofs, common problems with hip and ridge flashings include
    a. cracked or shrinking mortar.
    b. rusted metal.
    c. gaps in curved tile hip and ridges.
    d. both a and c.

76. The most vulnerable areas on roofs are
    a. asphalt shingle "cut-outs" or slots.
    b. flashing details.
    c. gable ends.
    d. hips and ridges.

77. The preferred material for valley flashing is
    a. metal.
    b. heavy roofing felts.
    c. ice and water shield.
    d. the same material as the field of the roof.

78. The counterflashing where the top of a roof meets a wall is the
    a. metal skirt that covers the flashing or roofing material below.
    b. flashing that extends up from below the roofing material.
    c. caulking details at the intersection of the wall surface and roofing material.
    d. triangular blocking that allows the roof membrane to 45° bends rather than one 90° bend.

79. A part of a chimney flashing most prone to leakage is the part
    a. protruding through the ridge of the roof.
    b. adjacent to the gutters.
    c. facing the high side of the roof.
    d. facing the eaves.

80. Solarium enclosures tend to leak
    a. at the seals of the double-glazed glass.
    b. where the glass roof meets the glass wall at the eave of the solarium.
    c. where the glass roof meets the top of the gable wall of the solarium.
    d. at the intersection of the house wall and glass roof.

81. Common valley flashing materials include all of the following *EXCEPT*
    a. galvanized steel.
    b. roll roofing.
    c. lead.
    d. brass.

82. If you can't get onto the roof, you should
    a. advise your client of this limitation.
    b. make an educated guess of the condition of the roof, based on the age, type, and location of the home.
    c. inspect the roof with binoculars, but report the roof as worse than it looks, because you may miss something.
    d. inspect the roof only from inside the attic and the interior of the home.

83. All flashings are
    a. exposed.
    b. concealed.
    c. metal.
    d. prone to leakage.

84. Flashings are typically located at
    a. valleys.
    b. roof penetrations.
    c. intersections with other materials.
    d. All of the above

85. Which of these is the most typical skylight problem?
    a. Rust
    b. Mechanical damage
    c. Leakage
    d. Cracked glazing

86. Mechanical damage to skylights is commonly caused by all of the following *EXCEPT*
    a. reroofing activities.
    b. building shifting.
    c. snow and ice removal.
    d. overhanging trees.

87. Double-glazed skylights
    a. are hermetically sealed.
    b. are vented.
    c. will never show condensation between the panes.
    d. are either a or b.

88. Which skylight is the best at resisting leakage?
    a. skylights with integral curbs
    b. curb-less skylights
    c. flush-mounted skylights
    d. skylights set on site-built curbs

89. Skylight leakage is most commonly caused by
    a. building shifting.
    b. poor installation.
    c. too steep a roof slope.
    d. poor quality skylights.

90. The most common solarium problem is
    a. excess heat gain in the summer.
    b. cracked glass due to normal building settlement.
    c. leakage.
    d. drafts.

91. Solarium inspections *DO NOT* include
    a. determining whether the roof glazing is tempered.
    b. checking the glass/frame joints.
    c. looking for excess caulking.
    d. looking for streaking inside.

92. Drip edge flashings are usually
    a. metal.
    b. ice and water shield.
    c. installed at valleys.
    d. roll roofing.

93. The functions of drip edge flashings include all of these *EXCEPT* to
    a. protect the gutters.
    b. protect the fascia.
    c. direct roof runoff into gutters.
    d. direct roof runoff away from the roof.

94. Drip edge flashing
    a. is installed over the eave protection or underlayment.
    b. cannot be aluminum.
    c. has its bottom edge between the gutter and the fascia.
    d. has a 45° bend in the bottom ½-inch.

95. Drip edge flashing
    a. may extend roughly three inches up the roof surface.
    b. may extend roughly one inch up the roof surface.
    c. is always required along rakes.
    d. cannot be used with eave protection.

96. Drip edge flashing problems include all of the following *EXCEPT*
    a. rust.
    b. copper used as a drip edge.
    c. looseness.
    d. flashings that are too short

97. A drip edge flashing that sits proud above the roof sheathing
    a. helps to prevent ice dams.
    b. is found only on wood roofs.
    c. may trap water on the roof, like a dam.
    d. helps to better protect the roof sheathing.

98. Dormer flashings
    a. has a valley if it's a gable dormer.
    b. cannot use siding as a valley flashing.
    c. are complex.
    d. should not have step (base) flashings.

99. Shed dormers NEVER have
    a. base (step) flashings.
    b. counterflashings.
    c. valley flashings.
    d. siding acting as counterflashing.

100. Valley flashings on dormers
    a. should always be metal.
    b. discharge onto the field of the roof below.
    c. must have a slope greater than 6-in-12.
    d. are used instead of roof/sidewall flashings.

101. The dormer siding can act as
    a. counterflashing.
    b. step (base) flashing.
    c. valley flashing.
    d. hip flashing.

102. A standing seam roof is
    a. a wood roof.
    b. an asphalt shingle roof.
    c. a gravel roof.
    d. a metal roof.

103. A scupper is
    a. a roof-to-wall flashing.
    b. movement of the flood coat.
    c. a roof drain opening through a wall.
    d. a drip edge made with a decorative trim detail.

104. If a built-up roof has seams every 12 inches, how many plies are there (not including the dry-laid base)?
    a. 2
    b. 3
    c. 4
    d. 5

105. An inspector should not walk on a roof
    a. if it could cause damage or is unsafe.
    b. ever.
    c. when the owner is home.
    d. when it is a flat roof.

106. What are common problems with EPDM roofs?
    a. Open seams and flashings
    b. Discoloration due to oil
    c. Tenting
    d. All of the above

107. The typical life of roll roofing on a flat roof is
    a. 5 years.
    b. 10 years.
    c. 15 years.
    d. 25 years.

108. Flat roofing systems are
    a. shedding systems.
    b. watertight systems.
    c. evaporation systems.
    d. ballasted systems.

109. Blisters in a built-up roof may be caused by
    a. asphalt that is too cold when applied.
    b. air or water trapped between the roof sheathing and the membrane.
    c. air or water trapped between the plies of the membrane.
    d. both b and c.

110. Which conditions can contribute to slippage of a built-up roof membrane?
    a. Wrong type of asphalt used
    b. Too many plies
    c. Asphalt too thick
    d. Both a and c

111. A ponding roof is any roof that still has water on it
    a. 12 hours after a rain.
    b. 24 hours after a rain.
    c. 36 hours after a rain.
    d. 48 hours after a rain.

112. Which of the following statements is/are true of a modified bitumen roof?
    a. The seams are spaced every 12 inches and the surface has a rubbery feel
    b. There is evidence of bleed-out of asphalt at the seams and the seams are spaced every 3 feet.
    c. There are no exposed nails.
    d. Both b and c are true.

113. Which of the following statements is/are *TRUE?*
    a. With roll roofing, the flashings are often also made of roll roofing.
    b. Modified bitumen is more flexible than roll roofing.
    c. Roll roofing is another name for modified bitumen.
    d. Both a and c are true.

114. One of the following roof membranes feels like rubber. When you stretch it, it rebounds.
    a. ABS
    b. EPDM
    c. PVC
    d. Built-up

115. Which of the roof membranes may be damaged by oils left from a Freon leak at a roof-mounted air conditioner?
    a. PVC
    b. Mod bit
    c. EPDM
    d. roll roofing

116. Which of the following roof membranes DO NOT require a layer of field-installed gravel to protect it from the sun?
    a. Built-up
    b. PVC
    c. Roll roofing
    d. Both b and c

117. Which roof membrane has had shattering problems when it is cold outside?
    a. PVC
    b. Mod bit
    c. Unprotected roll roofing
    d. Built-up

118. The purpose of a cant strip is
    a. to seal the top of a parapet counterflashing.
    b. to replace a reglet as the counterflashing.
    c. to make the roof membrane less likely to crack at a change in direction.
    d. both a and b.

119. The base flashing on flat roof should
    a. extend up the vertical wall above the highest expected depth of water on the roof.
    b. extend about 8 to 14 inches above the roof deck.
    c. be embedded in a reglet.
    d. be both a and b.

120. A water stain on a ceiling below a flat roof does not necessarily indicate a leak immediately above, because
    a. water can travel between the plies of the roof before emerging on the interior.
    b. a flood coat of asphalt is often applied to the roof sheathing below the membrane, which will redirect the water.
    c. vapor retarders may carry water some distance horizontally before it leaks through.
    d. of reasons a and c.

121. A parapet wall is
    a. the curb wall around the perimeter of a skylight.
    b. a perimeter wall which extends above the roofline.
    c. an interior wall which meets a flat roof at its top.
    d. a wall around a balcony.

122. All of the following are common built-up roof problems *EXCEPT*
    a. oil-canning.
    b. blisters.
    c. alligatoring.
    d. ridging.

123. Drip edge flashings are found at
    a. plumbing stacks.
    b. skylights.
    c. perimeters.
    d. pitch pockets.

124. Ponding water on flat roofs
     a. attracts birds that may damage the roof.
     b. increases the weight on the roof.
     c. increases the severity of a leakage problem.
     d. causes both b and c.

125. Wood decks on roofs may do all of the following *EXCEPT*
     a. protect the roof from ultraviolet light.
     b. protect the roof from mechanical damage.
     c. make the roof more difficult to inspect and repair.
     d. protect the roof from condensation damage.

126. Exposed felts
     a. may wick water into the roof.
     b. can cause gravel erosion.
     c. replace the flood coat.
     d. allow the inspector to determine the number of plies in the roof.

127. Which of the following is *NOT* a common problem on modified bitumen?
     a. Shattering
     b. Loss of granules
     c. Open seams
     d. Surface cracking

128. Good flat roof flashings do all the following *EXCEPT*
     a. make watertight joints between roofing and other materials.
     b. last 50 percent as long as the membrane.
     c. protect joints from ultraviolet light.
     d. protect joints from mechanical damage.

129. A pitch pocket would most likely be used on
     a. a skylight.
     b. a plumbing stack.
     c. an antenna base.
     d. a parapet wall taller than 16 inches.

130. Termination bars are sometimes used instead of
     a. counterflashings.
     b. cant strips.
     c. drip edge flashings.
     d. copings.

131. The top of parapet wall cap flashings
     a. should slope down away from the roof.
     b. should slope down toward the roof.
     c. should be level.
     d. shouldn't matter.

132. Fasteners for metal counterflashings should
     a. never be exposed.
     b. always be screwed.
     c. never be exposed on horizontal surfaces.
     d. always be caulked.

133. A reglet is used to
     a. attach a counterflashing to a wall.
     b. attach a drip edge flashing to a wall.
     c. seal around a plumbing stack.
     d. seal the heads of fasteners at a wall.

134. Skylights should rest on curbs not less than
     a. 4 inches in height.
     b. 6 inches in height.
     c. 8 inches in height.
     d. 10 inches in height.

135. Pitch pockets are *NOT* desirable because
     a. they indicate low quality workmanship.
     b. they require frequent maintenance.
     c. no one uses pitch any more.
     d. they tend to rot easily.

136. All of these are a likely cause of an asphalt base flashing sagging *EXCEPT*
     a. use of an inappropriate type of asphalt.
     b. dirty substrate.
     c. use of too little asphalt.
     d. use of improper fasteners.

137. Metal counterflashing that is close to the roof surface, but does not have a hem
     a. can cut the roof membrane, due to thermal expansion and contraction.
     b. is more likely to rust.
     c. will require greater maintenance.
     d. requires a reglet.

138. Using mastic for a minor repair on a modified bitumen roof
     a. can cause damage to the surface (incompatible material).
     b. is considered a temporary repair.
     c. requires ultraviolet protection in the form of aggregate.
     d. will cause the granular surface to erode.

139. For a built-up roof with a wood deck on top, which of these statements are true?
    a. Aggregate is required on the surface of the roof.
    b. The deck support should be designed such that proper drainage of the roof is not impeded.
    c. No gravel is needed because the deck protects the surface from ultraviolet light.
    d. Both b and c are true.

140. Which of the following flat roofs have been most susceptible to lifting off in a wind?
    a. Modified bitumen
    b. Built-up
    c. Copper
    d. Roll roofing

141. A "flood coat" refers to
    a. "spray on" EPDM. This is used in areas where very large volumes of water are expected.
    b. a method of sealing modified bitumen roof layers.
    c. the layer of asphalt that is applied to the bare wood deck prior to installing the first layer of felts.
    d. the layer of asphalt applied over the felts, into which gravel is embedded.

142. Blisters on a built-up roof
    a. will become vulnerable to UV damage.
    b. can be repaired by cutting them open, drying, sealing, and covering them with gravel.
    c. Both a and b are true.
    d. Neither a nor b is true.

ANSWERS AND EXPLANATIONS

1. **b.** You should not walk on clay tile roofs.

2. **a.** Concrete tiles often are laid over a waterproof membrane of roofing felts mopped into hot asphalt or ice and water shield.

3. **b.** You should not walk on concrete tile roofs.

4. **b.** Fiber cement shingles are very brittle and subject to impact damage.

5. **b.** Metal roofs may rust around fasteners as well as on the surface.

6. **b.** A caulked joint will be an ongoing maintenance item.

7. **a.** In areas where snow accumulates on roofs, heat loss through skylights creates the potential for ice damming around and below the skylight.

8. **b.** You should lift the edge of the skylight to get a sense of how well it is secured.

9. **b.** The roof covering has no structural role.

10. **b.** You may find three layers of asphalt shingles on a roof. However, this is not recommended.

11. **a.** Slate roofs are among the most expensive to install and maintain.

12. **b.** You should not walk on slate roofs.

13. **b.** Flashing is required on the bottom, sides, and top of a chimney.

14. **b.** You must inspect the area below the chimney flashing for evidence of leakage.

15. **a.** Leaking skylights can lead to rot damage to framing members, weakening the structure in the area of the skylight.

16. **b.** Detail edge flashings are not required; however, they are a helpful detail.

17. **b.** Roll roofing is a low quality surface.

18. **b.** It is not recommended practice to apply new built-up roof membranes over old ones.

19. **b.** Flat metal roofing is not a common way to cover an entire house roof. Most metal roofs are very expensive.

20. **a.** Roll roofing is a low quality system and often considered temporary.

21. **b.** The base flashing on a flat roof is a watertight system.

22. **c.** Roll roofing can be installed on a flat roof. All of the other materials listed need to be on a sloped roof.

23. **c.** Roll roofing is not brittle. All of the other materials on this list are brittle.

24. **d.** Roll roofing has the shortest life expectancy of the common roofing materials.

25. **d.** Concrete tiles commonly imitate slate tiles.

26. **b.** Ice dams are common on roofs with low slopes and wide overhangs.

27. **b.** Patches on roofs almost always indicate prior leakage.

28. **d.** Multiple layers of roofing are most common with asphalt shingles.

29. **d.** A low-sloped shingle application can go down to a slope as low as 2-in-12.

30. **a.** Spalling is not a failure mode for asphalt shingles.

31. **c.** The slots between asphalt shingles get wider as the shingles get closer to the end of their life.

32. **c.** Asphalt shingles applied in cold weather may be prone to tabs tearing off because the sealing strips don't hold.

33. **d.** Roofing problems are most common at fastenings and roof penetrations.

34. **b.** Two layers of shingles may result in a shorter life for the second layer.

35. **a.** Slots being too wide is not a common problem on wood roofs.

36. **c.** Interlayment is typically found on wood shakes.

37. **d.** Number 1 blue-grade shingles are 100 percent edge-grain, 100 percent heartwood, and 100 percent clear.

38. **d.** If wood shingles are butted too tightly together, they may buckle when wet.

39. **c.** Flat-grain wood shingles can be identified by a flame pattern.

40. **d.** Moss on a wood roof holds water against the roof, promoting rot.

41. **c.** In a wood shingle roof, you would typically go through 3 layers of shingles.

42. **b.** On a slate roof you would typically go through 2 layers of slate.

43. **a.** On a Spanish-style clay roof you would typically go through 1 layer of tile.

44. **b.** On a shingle-style flat clay roof you would typically go through 2 layers of tile.

45. **a.** On a flat interlocking tile roof you would typically go through 1 layer.

46. **b.** On a fiber cement roof you would typically go through 2 layers of roofing.

47. **b.** On a wood shake roof you would typically go through 2 layers of wood.

48. **a.** On a metal roof you would typically go through 1 layer of metal.

49. **a.** On roll roofing, you would typically go through 1 layer of roofing material.

50. **a.** Curling is not a failure mode for slate.

51. **d.** Slate roofing should not be repaired with tar.

52. **a.** Dormer flashings are very different from stack flashings. Stack flashings surround pipes.

53. **c.** Clay tile roofs are effective shedding systems only if the slope is more than 4-in-12.

54. **b.** Staples cannot be used to fasten concrete tiles.

55. **b.** A standing seam can be found on a metal roof.

56. **d.** Ice dam evidence typically does not include water running down along the rafters, because ice dams form at the bottom of the rafters to begin with.

57. **d.** Cutting the points applies to the corners of asphalt shingles at valleys.

58. **b.** Mission clay tiles have top pieces and bottom pieces.

59. **c.** Roll roofing typically fails by cracking, buckling, or blistering.

60. **d.** Metal roofing can be installed as shingles or sheets and panels.

61. **d.** A cedar shingle roof on a 12-in-12 slope is most rot-resistant. It will tend to get rid of its water quickly.

62. **b.** The pitch of a valley in a 4-in-12 roof is roughly 3-in-12.

63. **d.** Valley flashings should widen to allow for the greater accumulation of water near the bottom of the valley.

64. **a.** Roll roofing valley flashings are typically 2 layers, with the bottom layer being 18 inches wide and the top layer being 36 inches wide.

65. **a.** Metal valley flashing sections should be no longer than 10 feet because the expansion and contraction may cause buckling.

66. **b.** Wrinkling or tautness (sometimes called tenting) is typically caused by membrane shrinkage.

67. **c.** This is not an ideal installation because you shouldn't be securing the flashing to both the chimney and the roof. However, it is very common, and if nothing has moved yet it would be recommended to monitor this situation rather than replace it.

68. **c.** The deposit on the chimney brickwork just below the roofline probably means a leaking roof flashing.

69. **a.** Settlement of the house may cause the flange for the plumbing stack flashing to look like it has pulled away from the roof. Actually, the roof is dropping relative to the stack.

70. **b.** A low area in the stack flashing around the pipe is commonly a result of the settlement of the stack.

71. **d.** Common installation problems with stack flashings include exposed or missing fasteners and exposure of the top half of the flange above the roofing material.

72. **b.** Putting tar on metal flashings may trap water and accelerate the rusting of the metal.

73. **d.** Concealed flashings for hip and ridge systems can include roofing felts, ice and water shield, and mortar.

74. **a.** Ridge flashings can also act as venting systems.

75. **d.** Common hip problems with tile roofs include cracked or shrinking mortar and gaps in curved tile pieces.

76. **b.** The most vulnerable areas on roofs are flashing details.

77. **a.** The preferred material for valley flashing is metal.

78. **a.** Counterflashing at a roof to wall intersection is the metal skirt that covers the flashing or roofing material below.

79. **c.** A chimney flashing is most prone to leakage at the high side.

80. **d.** Solarium enclosures tend to leak at the intersection of the house wall and the glass roof.

81. **d.** Brass is not a common valley flashing material.

82. **a.** If you can't get onto the roof, you should advise your client of this limitation.

83. **d.** All valley flashings are prone to leakage.

84. **d.** Flashings are typically located at valleys, roof penetrations, and intersections with other materials.

85. **c.** Leakage is the most typical skylight problem.

86. **b.** Building shifting usually has no effect on skylights.

87. **d.** Double glazed skylights may be hermetically sealed or vented.

88. **d.** Skylights set on site-built curbs are best at resisting leakage.

89. **b.** Skylight leakage is most commonly caused by poor installation.

90. **c.** Leakage is the most common solarium problem.

91. **a.** It is unnecessary to determine whether glazing is tempered in a solarium.

92. **a.** Drip edge flashings are usually metal.

93. **a.** Drip edge flashings do not protect gutters.

94. **d.** Drip edge flashing typically has a 45° bend in the bottom half-inch.

95. **a.** Drip edge flashing may extend three or four inches up the roof surface.

96. **b.** It's just fine to use copper as a drip edge.

97. **c.** A drip edge flashing that sits proud may trap water on the roof, like a dam.

98. **a.** However, dormer flashings don't necessarily include valley flashings. Shed dormers, for example, do not have valleys.

99. **c.** Shed dormers never have valley flashings.

100. **b.** Valley flashings on dormers discharge their water onto the field of the roof below.

101. **a.** Dormer siding can act as counterflashing.

102. **d.** A standing seam roof is a metal roof.

103. **c.** A scupper is a roof drain opening through a wall.

104. **b.** There are three plies in a built-up roof with seams every 12 inches.

105. **a.** An inspector should not walk on a roof if it could cause damage to the roof or is unsafe.

106. **d.** Common EPDM roof problems include open seams and flashings, discoloration due to oil, and tenting.

107. **a.** Roll roofing on a flat roof typically lasts 5 years.

108. **b.** Most flat roofing systems are water tight systems.

109. **d.** Blisters in a built-up roof may be caused by air or water trapped between the sheathing and the membrane, or trapped between plies in the membrane.

110. **d.** The wrong type of asphalt or asphalt that is too thick may result in slippage of a built-up membrane.

111. **d.** A ponding roof is any roof that still has water on it 48 hours after a rain.

112. **d.** Evidence of bleed out at the seams and seams spaced every three feet are common in a modified bitumen roof. The absence of exposed nails is also typical of a modified bitumen roof.

113. **b.** Mod bit is more flexible than roll roofing.

114. **b.** EPDM stretches and rebounds like rubber.

115. **c.**   EPDM can be damaged by oils.

116. **d.**   PVC roofs and roll roofing do not require additional protection from the sun. This is a bit misleading; roll roofing does require protection, but it is already built into the roofing material.

117. **a.**   PVC has suffered from shattering problems in cold weather.

118. **c.**   A cant strip makes the membrane less likely to crack at a change in direction because it takes two 45° turns instead of one 90° turn.

119. **d.**   Base flashing on a flat roof should extend up the wall above the height of water. This is typically 8 to 14 inches above the roof deck.

120. **d.**   The stain may not indicate a leak immediately above because the water can travel horizontally between the plies of the roof before emerging on the interior, and vapor barriers may carry water horizontally some distance before it leaks through.

121. **b.**   The parapet wall is a perimeter wall protruding above the roofline.

122. **a.**   Oil canning is not a problem on a built-up roof.

123. **c.**   Drip edge flashings are found at roof perimeters.

124. **d.**   Ponding water on flat roofs increases the weight on the roof and the severity of a leak when it occurs.

125. **d.**   Wood decks do not protect the roof from condensation damage.

126. **a.**   Exposed felts may wick water into the roof.

127. **a.**   Shattering is not a common problem on mod bit roofs.

128. **b.**   Roof flashings should last equally as long as the membrane.

129. **c.**   A pitch pocket is most likely to be used on an antenna base.

130. **a.**   Termination bars are sometimes used instead of counterflashings.

131. **b.**   The top surface of a parapet wall should slope slightly toward the roof. You don't want water accumulating on the cap, as this may cause rust. You don't want water dripping off the cap down the side of the building or onto people below, either.

132. **c.**   Fasteners for metal counterflashings should never be exposed on horizontal surfaces.

133. **a.**   Reglets are used to attach counterflashings to walls.

134. **c.**   Skylight curbs should be eight inches in height.

135. **b.**   Pitch pockets require frequent maintenance to keep them watertight.

136. **d.**   Improper fasteners are not a likely cause of sagging for asphalt base flashing.

137. **a.**   A metal flashing without a hem may cut the roof membrane.

138. **b.**   Mastic is a temporary repair.

139. **d.**   Deck support should be arranged so that roof drainage is not interfered with. The deck protects the roof surface from ultraviolet light.

140. **c.**   Copper has been traditionally susceptible to wind liftoff on flat roofs.

141. **d.**   A flood coat is a layer of asphalt applied over the felts, into which the gravel is embedded.

142. **c.**   Blisters on roofs will become sensitive to UV damage because the gravel is typically eroded away from the blister. Blisters can be repaired by cutting them open, drying them, sealing them, and covering them with gravel again.

4. ELECTRICAL SYSTEMS
Practice Questions

1. The service size is determined by the amperage and voltage ratings of the service.
   a. True
   b. False

2. The drip loop should be as close to the roof surface as possible.
   a. True
   b. False

3. A 200-amp service will have two 100-amp fuses in the service panel.
   a. True
   b. False

4. There can be up to 10 throws to disconnect all of the electricity in a house.
   a. True
   b. False

5. Service entrance conductors run from the service drop to the service box or service panel.
   a. True
   b. False

6. Electrical wiring in a house is direct current.
   a. True
   b. False

7. A 120-volt circuit uses a black and red wire.
   a. True
   b. False

8. Larger appliances usually have 240 volts.
   a. True
   b. False

9. The drip loop is typically part of the service drop.
   a. True
   b. False

10. All service entrance conductors must be in a conduit.
    a. True
    b. False

11. Load calculations are a required part of a home inspection.
    a. True
    b. False

12. Aluminum is an acceptable service entrance conductor material.
    a. True
    b. False

13. If you can't read the size of the fuses in the service box, you should remove them to try to get a better look.
    a. True
    b. False

14. The service box can be inside, outside, or in a garage.
    a. True
    b. False

15. The service box may stand alone or may be combined with the distribution panel.
    a. True
    b. False

16. You are allowed to ground to the gas piping.
    a. True
    b. False

17. Wires run directly from the service box to the branch circuits.
    a. True
    b. False

18. Subpanels must be immediately adjacent to the main panel.
    a. True
    b. False

19. Typical distribution panels have 60 circuits.
    a. True
    b. False

20. The red and black wires of multiwire circuits should be on separate bus bars.
    a. True
    b. False

21. Outlets should be as far away from bathtubs and showers as possible.
    a. True
    b. False

22. Outlets should be as close to basins as possible.
    a. True
    b. False

23. All junction boxes should be concealed.
    a. True
    b. False

24. Knob-and-tube writing was commonly installed without junction boxes.
    a. True
    b. False

25. One smoke detector is needed in each home near the kitchen, because that's where most house fires start.
    a. True
    b. False

26. An ungrounded conductor is
    a. uninsulated.
    b. called the neutral.
    c. usually white in color.
    d. often called the hot conductor.

27. The standard house voltage is
    a. 100 A.
    b. 120 V.
    c. 120/208 V.
    d. 120/240 V.

28. The unit for the measure of electrical power is
    a. amps.
    b. watts.
    c. joules.
    d. kWh.

29. How much current does a 120-V, 1200-W hair dryer draw?
    a. 10 A
    b. 144 A
    c. 10 W
    d. 0.10 A

30. Ohm's Law, the relationship between voltage, current, and resistance in a simple circuit, states that
    a. $V = IR$.
    b. $I = VR$.
    c. $R = I/V$.
    d. $V = I/R$.

31. If electricity costs $0.10 per kWh, how much does it cost to run a 120-V whirlpool bath that draws 5 A for ½ hour?
    a. $0.06
    b. $0.03
    c. $3.00
    d. $0.30

32. Following the grounded conductor from the service box toward the street, you would find that it connects to
    a. the ground rod for the house.
    b. the utility's transformer.
    c. the main water pipe.
    d. the meter.

33. If two 60-W light bulb branch circuits are wired in parallel, and another parallel 60-W light bulb branch circuit is added
    a. the bulb closest to the voltage source will be brightest.
    b. each bulb will have the same brightness.
    c. the total current in the circuit stays the same.
    d. the current in each branch will decrease.

34. The service drop wires
    a. are a reliable indicator of service size.
    b. are usually the homeowner's responsibility.
    c. connect to the house at the drip loop.
    d. must always be in conduit.

35. Overhead service wires must
    a. be 3 feet away from windows, in most areas.
    b. clear a flat roof by 3 feet or more, in most areas.
    c. not be run over decks under any circumstances.
    d. be at least 10 feet above a driveway.

36. Water stains on the soffit around the hole where service mast passes through is most likely the result of
    a. improper flashing where the mast penetrates the roof.
    b. a lack of a drip loop.
    c. a lack of caulking between the soffit and the mast.
    d. a cracked masthead.

37. You notice rust in the service panel. Which of the following may be the cause?
    a. No drip loop
    b. Undersized conduit
    c. Damaged masthead
    d. Both a and c.

38. Which one of the following is *NOT* a possible cause of the service mast, conduit, or cable letting water in?
    a. Movement of the components
    b. Deterioration of materials over time
    c. Conduit undersized
    d. Building settlement

39. Four service entrance conductors indicate
    a. a 240-V service.
    b. a three-phase service.
    c. a 120-V service.
    d. a 400-A service.

40. A 60-A service
    a. is not allowed in new construction in North America.
    b. requires a minimum #3 AWG copper wire.
    c. is not suitable for a 240-V service.
    d. can be adequate in some cases.

41. Assuming copper, standard wire type, and normal temperature rating, what is the typical conductor size (in AWG) for a 60-A service?
    a. #10
    b. #6
    c. #4
    d. #3

42. Assuming copper, standard wire type, and normal temperature rating, what is the typical conductor size (in AWG) for a 200-A service in the United States?
    a. #2
    b. 1/0
    c. 2/0
    d. 3/0

43. A 100-A service for a 1,000-square-foot house with 3 bedrooms, an electric stove, an electric dryer, a 2-ton central A/C unit (FLA = 12 amps), and two 1,500-W, 240-volt electric baseboard heaters would be considered
    a. clearly inadequate.
    b. adequate for no more than two adults.
    c. most likely adequate.
    d. clearly oversized.

44. A service box with a black wire, a red wire, a white wire, and two 200-A fuses indicates a
    a. 120/240-V, 400-A service.
    b. 120-V, 400-A service.
    c. 120-V, 200-A service.
    d. 120/240-V, 200-A service.

45. If the service entrance conduit is 2 inches, what conclusions can you draw as to the size of the electrical service?
    a. You would suspect a service greater than 100 A, but would have to confirm elsewhere.
    b. The service is 200 A.
    c. The service is 100 A.
    d. The service conduit is oversized.

46. What valuable information can be obtained by looking at the electrical meter of the house?
    a. The service amperage
    b. The maximum service that the house can support
    c. None
    d. The age of the house

47. What would two wires entering the service weatherhead indicate to you?
    a. A three-phase system
    b. An older 120-V system
    c. A 100-A service
    d. A 240-V system

48. The grounded service conductor
    a. is called the neutral.
    b. connects to the water pipe and/or the ground rod.
    c. cannot be aluminum.
    d. must be bonded to the gas piping.

49. Electrical resistance
    a. increases with increasing wire diameter.
    b. decreases with increasing wire diameter.
    c. decreases with increasing wire length.
    d. is higher for copper than for aluminum.

50. The power available in a typical 15-A, 120-V household circuit is
    a. 1,500 W.
    b. 1,000 W.
    c. 1,800 W.
    d. 3,600 W.

51. What is the frequency (cycles/second) of household electricity?
    a. 60 Hz
    b. 50 Hz
    c. 30 Hz
    d. 66 MHz

52. Why are some main switches sealed by the utility?
    a. For safety
    b. To prevent air leakage
    c. To prevent tapping of power prior to the meter
    d. Both a and c.

53. You observe #6-gauge copper wires entering a service box with two 60 A fuses inside. From the service box, #3 copper conductors lead to a newer combination panel that has a 100 A main breaker. You should report the service size as
    a. 100 A.
    b. 160 A.
    c. 60 A.
    d. 120 A.

54. At the drip loop you notice that the service drop conductors are smaller in diameter than the service entrance conductors. You should conclude that
    a. it was a faulty installation and should be corrected.
    b. the service entrance conductors must be aluminum, and report them as such.
    c. the house service must be 200 A.
    d. this is a normal situation and is acceptable.

55. With respect to electricity, rain water is
    a. an insulator.
    b. a conductor.
    c. no different from distilled water.
    d. similar to air.

56. If P = 120 watts, and the circuit powers only the outlet that a gas dryer is plugged into, what is I?
    a. 0.5 A
    b. 120 ohms
    c. 1.0 A
    d. 1.0 W

57. An overcurrent protection device
    a. can be a fuse or breaker.
    b. regulates voltage in a circuit.
    c. usually indicates an obsolete panel.
    d. refers to the plastic washers installed in fuse sockets.

58. Service entrance (SE) cable must be securely clamped to the house
    a. using brass clamps and screws.
    b. every 12 inches, using rustproof fasteners.
    c. every 6 feet.
    d. every 30 inches, generally.

59. If an auxiliary panel has been added, the wires connecting it to the service panel are protected by
    a. overcurrent protection provided in the service panel.
    b. overcurrent protection provided in the auxiliary panel that is sometimes allowed, so long as the feeder wire is in rigid conduit.
    c. a drip loop.
    d. both a and b.

60. The top end of an SE cable service
    a. should be bent into a U-shaped drip loop before removing the cable sheathing.
    b. should not be clamped within 36 inches of the top.
    c. should have a gooseneck before the splice.
    d. must be spliced to the service drop at least 3 feet from the side of the house.

61. Can gas piping be used to ground the electrical system?
    a. Yes
    b. Yes, if there is no other grounding electrode available
    c. Only if the main plumbing pipe is plastic
    d. No

62. Is it permissible to use an aluminum grounding wire?
    a. Yes
    b. Only if it is at least #3 AWG
    c. Only in dry environments within the United States
    d. Only in some provinces and states

63. In most areas, for what distance can service entrance wires run inside the building before going into the service box, without special permission?
    a. 5 feet
    b. 10 feet, if in conduit
    c. 0 feet, or as short as possible
    d. Maximum of 3 feet

64. The function of bonding is to
    a. ensure that two electrical conductors are at the same potential.
    b. ensure an electrical conductor is at zero potential.
    c. provide a primary path for ground faults from the electrical system.
    d. ensure that the black and red conductors are at the same potential.

65. What is linking?
    a. Linking ensures that light switches only operate the fixtures installed in the same room.
    b. Linking is the same as bonding.
    c. Linking ensures that two fuses or circuit breakers are disconnected at the same time.
    d. Linking refers to connections made in a junction box.

66. A damaged or nicked wire is a safety hazard because
    a. the damaged wire may corrode.
    b. the effective diameter of the wire has been decreased, thereby decreasing the resistance of the wire.
    c. the effective resistance of the wire is increased so the fuse can no longer adequately protect the wire from overheating.
    d. the wire is more likely to break.

67. A kitchen split receptacle is a
    a. switched circuit operating a wall receptacle.
    b. receptacle with a test button required near kitchen sinks.
    c. circuit servicing a separate cooktop and oven.
    d. receptacle with the top and bottom halves on different circuits.

68. The wire size used in household circuits fused at 15 amps is
    a. #14-gauge copper.
    b. #12-gauge aluminum.
    c. #10-gauge tinned copper.
    d. both a and b.

69. You see two circuit breakers linked together in a panel. One has a black wire attached to it and the other has a red wire attached to it. The cable has no white (neutral) wire. Assuming a proper installation, you are most likely seeing
    a. an electric dryer circuit.
    b. a 120-V dedicated microwave circuit.
    c. a furnace circuit.
    d. a 240-V balanced load, such as a baseboard heater.

70. A type-P fuse is a
    a. time-delay fuse.
    b. heat sensitive fuse.
    c. GFCI fuse.
    d. "power" fuse, for 30-A, or greater, loads.

71. Which of the following is not an approved grounding method?
    a. Metallic underground water piping
    b. Metal frame of a building
    c. Ground rods
    d. Gas piping

72. Subpanels are
    a. prohibited in bathrooms.
    b. prohibited in clothes closets.
    c. prohibited on building exteriors.
    d. both a and b.

73. These are all problems with fuses *EXCEPT*
    a. a difference between the fuse manufacturer and the panel manufacturer.
    b. looseness.
    c. a broken fuse holder.
    d. not having links on multiwire circuit fuses.

74. The wire that connects the system neutral to the water supply, well casing, or ground rods is called the
    a. grounding electrode conductor.
    b. grounded conductor.
    c. electrode.
    d. ground fault interrupter.

75. As a general rule, how much clear space should be in front of the service box?
    a. One foot
    b. Three feet
    c. Five feet
    d. Six feet

76. With respect to amperage ratings, the main fuses or breaker
    a. must be greater than the service box rating.
    b. should be sized to adequately protect the service entrance wires.
    c. should be no larger than the rating of the service box.
    d. must be both b and c.

77. After entering the service box, the neutral service entrance conductor should
    a. connect to the terminal with the grounding electrode conductor and the service neutral.
    b. connect to the main breaker.
    c. go directly to the distribution panel.
    d. connect to the main fuses on the line side.

78. Overfusing is
    a. the clipping of breaker handles so that they operate together.
    b. installing too many fuse receptors into a panel, causing a potential overload.
    c. installing fuses in a holder that requires two to be removed at once.
    d. installing a fuse or breaker that is rated too big for the conductor.

79. In a distribution panel, a black wire and a red wire are connected to separate breakers that are four breakers apart, on the same bus bar. Both wires are part of the same cable. The neutral from the cable connects to the neutral bus. The potential problem with this arrangement is that
    a. the 240-V appliance may not operate properly.
    b. the breakers may not be linked.
    c. the neutral wire may overheat.
    d. all of the above are true.

80. When replacing the panel cover, it's hard to get it back on without pinching or compressing the wires inside the box. You should conclude that
    a. the panel is overcrowded.
    b. the panel cover is too small for the panel.
    c. the wires are probably larger than is necessary.
    d. both a and c are true.

81. Which of the following is not an appropriate place to terminate a grounding system?
    a. Buried grounding plates or rings
    b. Under ground
    c. Metal water supply pipes
    d. Metal siding of buildings

82. In general, modern 120-V circuits can accommodate how many outlets and/or light fixtures?
    a. 8
    b. 10
    c. 12
    d. 16

83. A 14-gauge copper wire is protected by a 20-amp fuse. You should report that
    a. this is a defect, and recommend improvement.
    b. this is always allowable.
    c. this indicates poor wiring.
    d. this may be acceptable, depending on what the circuit load is.

84. Putting a penny in a fuse holder is dangerous because
    a. the penny will melt, causing a short circuit.
    b. the penny will corrode, leading to overheating.
    c. the circuit has no overcurrent protection.
    d. the fuse receptor will react with the copper in the penny, causing it to degrade.

85. A multiwire circuit has
    a. protection from circuit breakers, but not fuses.
    b. two neutral wires.
    c. two ground wires.
    d. a red and a black wire.

86. Common copper wire sizes for an electric water heater are
    a. #12 and #10.
    b. #16 and #8.
    c. #16 and #18.
    d. #10 and #8.

87. A fuse and its holder in the panel are hot. The possible cause is that
    a. the fuse is the wrong size for the circuit.
    b. the fuse was over-tightened.
    c. the fuse beside the affected fuse was over-tightened, causing the bus bar to bend.
    d. both a and c are true.

88. All of the breakers in a service panel are white, except one, which is black. You should be checking
    a. that the black breaker is correctly sized for the wire.
    b. that the black breaker is suitable for use in the panel, if this is determinable.
    c. that the black breaker isn't loose.
    d. All of the above

89. Which one of the following is NOT a cause of a loose or damaged breaker?
    a. Manufacturing defect
    b. Undersized wire
    c. Rough handling
    d. Wear and tear

90. All of the following are panel wire problems EXCEPT
    a. overheating.
    b. wires crossing bus bars.
    c. sheathing removed.
    d. abandoned wires.

91. Openings in panels and boxes should be sealed so that people don't inadvertently touch live electrical systems. There is another reason to keep these openings sealed. What is it?
    a. To prevent insects and other pests from nesting in the panel
    b. To help contain a fire inside the panel
    c. To keep the panel rigid so it won't rack—too many openings in the panel will cause it to lose rigidity.
    d. Condensation is more likely to form in the panel.

92. What happens if the neutral wire bypasses the service box?
    a. The house electrical system won't work properly.
    b. The grounding electrode conductor can't get to the water piping and/or ground rods.
    c. The neutral and grounding system will not be properly connected.
    d. The ground wire will carry electricity under normal conditions.

93. Putting the fuses upstream of the disconnect switch in the service box
    a. makes it dangerous to change the fuses even when the house power is shut off.
    b. may cause a short circuit through the fuses.
    c. is a result of connecting the service conductors to the line side, rather than the load side.
    d. is a result of installing the box upside-down.

94. All of these are functions of grounding systems *EXCEPT*
    a. protection of homeowners.
    b. providing an emergency path for electricity to escape.
    c. dissipation of static charges.
    d. prevention of short circuits.

95. Which one does *NOT* defeat the ground wire connected to a water supply/plumbing system?
    a. Connecting to an abandoned pipe
    b. A dielectric connector
    c. A jumper across the meter
    d. Plastic piping

96. Common branch circuit wire materials include all of these *EXCEPT*
    a. copper.
    b. aluminum.
    c. solder-dipped copper.
    d. silver-dipped copper.

97. Of the GFIs that you find in a house, which ones must be tested?
    a. All of them
    b. Those at the panel
    c. Exterior GFIs
    d. Kitchen GFIs and exterior GFIs

98. Which of these wires is a home inspector required to inspect?
    a. Telephone wiring
    b. Security wiring
    c. Cable television wiring
    d. Wiring for a clock receptacle

99. NMD cable is
    a. rigid.
    b. armored.
    c. suitable for dry indoor use.
    d. suitable for outdoor use but not underground.

100. Plastic sheathing on branch wiring became popular in the
    a. 1950s.
    b. 1960s.
    c. 1970s.
    d. 1980s.

101. Extension cords are typically
    a. stranded wire.
    b. solid wire.
    c. designed to be held in place with staples.
    d. best protected if run under carpets.

102. Number 10-gauge wires are typically used for all of these *EXCEPT*
    a. air conditioners.
    b. clothes dryers.
    c. dishwashers.
    d. saunas.

103. Twist-on connectors (wire nuts)
    a. replace junction boxes.
    b. are not permitted on knob-and-tube wiring.
    c. are also called solderless connectors.
    d. should be used only on soldered connections.

104. Supports for branch circuit wires are needed
    a. every 3 feet.
    b. only where wires may be exposed to mechanical damage.
    c. within 12 inches of leaving a box.
    d. only where the wires are run horizontally.

105. Which of the following is a suitable location for a branch circuit wire?
     a. Attached to a baseboard with suitable staples every four feet
     b. Under carpets
     c. Within one inch of the face of a stud
     d. Stapled to two-by-four studs

106. Loose connections
     a. may start fires.
     b. are never located in junction boxes.
     c. are never found in panels.
     d. are common only with aluminum wiring.

107. Wires should be kept
     a. tight against heating ducts or pipes.
     b. at least one inch away from heating ducts or pipes.
     c. at least two inches away from heating ducts or pipes.
     d. at least nine inches away from heating ducts or pipes.

108. How far should wires be kept from the metal vent connector on a gas appliance?
     a. One inch
     b. Six inches
     c. Nine inches
     d. Eighteen inches

109. Wires should not be run across the tops of ceiling joists in attics unless
     a. the ceiling is not insulated.
     b. the attic height is less than 40 inches.
     c. knob-and-tube wiring is used.
     d. the wiring is NMW.

110. White wires can sometimes act as black wires
     a. in 240-volt circuits.
     b. in multiwire branch circuits.
     c. by design on a reverse polarity circuit.
     d. on a dedicated circuit for a clothes dryer.

111. All of these are common branch circuit problems *EXCEPT*
     a. NMD wires run through floor joists without tubes or grommets.
     b. damaged wires.
     c. open splices.
     d. undersized wire.

112. Original knob-and-tube connections
     a. were always in metal junction boxes.
     b. employed solder.
     c. should all be replaced.
     d. were always concealed.

113. Knob-and-tube wiring issues include all of the following *EXCEPT*
     a. connections to modern wire not in boxes.
     b. wires buried in insulation.
     c. brittle wire, insulation, or sheathing.
     d. overheated neutrals on multiwire branch circuits.

114. Knob-and-tube wire buried in insulation
     a. is not permitted in some jurisdictions if the insulation is combustible.
     b. ensures the wires won't come in contact with each other.
     c. is never permitted.
     d. may be more prone to attack by pests than wires above insulation.

115. Fused neutrals
     a. provide enhanced protection for the neutral wire.
     b. will never trip because the voltage drop across a neutral wire is negligible.
     c. are required on multiwire branch circuits.
     d. are dangerous.

116. Panels used with aluminum wire should
     a. be circuit breaker rather than fuse-type.
     b. contain at least 20 branch circuits.
     c. be rated CUAL.
     d. be rated CO/ALR

117. The disadvantage of pigtailing aluminum to copper wire is that
     a. the two metals are not compatible.
     b. it adds more connections and leads to overcrowding boxes.
     c. you can't pigtail different sized wire gauges together.
     d. the solder isn't likely to be effective.

118. Aluminum wiring is still used on
     a. 12-gauge circuits.
     b. 8-gauge circuits.
     c. 10-gauge circuits.
     d. commercial applications only.

119. Which of the following devices are most likely to be rated CO/ALR?
    a. Receptacles
    b. Wire nuts
    c. Panels
    d. Breakers

120. Problems with aluminum wiring include all of the following *EXCEPT* that
    a. it tends to creep.
    b. it lacked a ground wire.
    c. the aluminum oxide is not a good conductor of electricity.
    d. aluminum is softer than copper and easier to damage.

121. Special grease on aluminum wires is
    a. found on number 12-gauge and 10-gauge wires.
    b. found on stranded wires.
    c. found on service entrance wires only.
    d. used to control creep.

122. All of the following are common outdoor wiring problems *EXCEPT*
    a. NMW wiring used outdoors.
    b. garage door openers powered with an extension cord.
    c. unprotected wires within 4 feet of the garage floor.
    d. wires running through downspouts.

123. All of these are common lighting problems *EXCEPT*
    a. light fixtures that are damaged.
    b. lights above closet shelves.
    c. lights that are missing.
    d. lights above stairwells.

124. Overheating is commonly caused by any one of these *EXCEPT*
    a. a defective fixture.
    b. oversized bulbs.
    c. bulbs installed with the base down.
    d. a damaged wire.

125. How hot is the surface of a 100-watt incandescent bulb, typically?
    a. 280°
    b. 380°
    c. 480°
    d. 580°

126. Light fixtures are required in all the following locations *EXCEPT*
    a. stairwells with more than six treads.
    b. each room.
    c. on the outside of the home near every exterior door.
    d. in clothes closets.

127. When looking at a spotlight you see the letters IC. This means it is
    a. for incandescent bulbs only.
    b. to be used on interior ceilings only.
    c. for use in insulated ceilings.
    d. not designed to be left on continuously, and is designed for intermittent control.

128. All of these are common receptacle problems *EXCEPT*
    a. damaged receptacles.
    b. loose receptacles.
    c. overheated receptacles.
    d. GFI receptacles used outdoors.

129. All of the following are common receptacle problems *EXCEPT*
    a. worn receptacles.
    b. a pin that has broken in the receptacle.
    c. the receptacle being too close to the basin.
    d. bathroom outlets that are too far from basins.

130. Three-slot receptacles on ungrounded circuits are safety hazards because
    a. people will use grounded appliances, thinking the receptacle is grounded.
    b. people may try to put three appliances, rather than two, into the duplex receptacles.
    c. computers may not be able to dissipate static charges.
    d. radio devices won't be able to use the ground wire as an antenna.

131. When you find three-slot receptacles on ungrounded circuits, you might recommend any of the following *EXCEPT* to
    a. replace the circuit with a grounded circuit.
    b. fill the ground hole with epoxy, if permitted by the relevant authority.
    c. replace the receptacle with a GFI.
    d. label the circuit at the panel "ungrounded."

132. The term *service drop* defines
  a. the underground wires from the utility, to the point of connection, to the house.
  b. the wires that connect the meter to the service box.
  c. the wires that run down the outside of the house into the meter.
  d. the overhead wires coming from the utility pole, to the point of connection, to the house.

133. A properly polarized circuit
  a. has the black wire connected to the silver screw on the receptacle.
  b. has the neutral and ground connections bonded-together at the receptacle.
  c. will always be grounded.
  d. will result in the threaded collar of a lamp being neutral.

134. GFI receptacles
  a. protect all of the receptacles upstream in the same circuit.
  b. are best tested with a circuit analyzer with a GFI test button.
  c. only work on grounded circuits.
  d. are accepted as an alternative for grounding under some circumstances.

135. Overloading the neutral wire on a multiwire branch circuit
  a. is likely if the black and red wires are powered from the same bus.
  b. means that the neutral wire was undersized.
  c. indicates a short in the circuit.
  d. is the result of failing to fuse the neutral.

136. The best location for an outlet is
  a. on a floor.
  b. immediately beside a basin in a bathroom.
  c. immediately beside a bathtub in a bathroom.
  d. 6 inches to 12 inches above a garage floor.

137. Three-way switches control
  a. lights from three different locations.
  b. lights from two different locations.
  c. three or more light fixtures.
  d. two or more light fixtures.

138. Common junction box problems include all of the following *EXCEPT*
  a. wire nuts inside boxes.
  b. missing boxes.
  c. boxes missing cover plates.
  d. overcrowded boxes.

ANSWERS AND EXPLANATIONS

1. **a.** The size of the electrical service is a function of both the voltage and amperage.

2. **b.** The bottom of the drip loop should be well above the roof 12 to 24 inches, depending on jurisdiction.

3. **b.** Two 100-amp fuses indicate 100-amp service. You cannot add the two fuses together to determine the service size.

4. **b.** There can be up to six throws to disconnect all of the electricity in the house.

5. **a.** Service entrance conductors pick up where the service drop wires end and extend down to the service panel.

6. **b.** Electric wiring in a house is alternating current.

7. **b.** Some 120-volt circuits use a black wire and a white wire; others use a red wire and a white wire.

8. **a.** A 240-volt circuit is used for large appliances such as stoves, electric water heaters, electric clothes dryers, air conditioners, and saunas.

9. **b.** The drip loop is part of the service entrance wires, not the service drop.

10. **b.** The service entrance wires may be in a conduit on the outside of the building or there may be a special Service Entrance (SE) cable that does not require a conduit.

11. **b.** Home inspectors are not required to perform load calculations.

12. **a.** Service entrance conductors may be aluminum or copper.

13. **b.** DO NOT touch anything in the service box. The fuses may be live and could kill you.

14. **a.** These are all acceptable locations for a service box.

15. **a.** The service box may be a stand-alone box or a combination panel (also called a service panel).

16. **b.** You are not allowed to use gas piping as a way to ground the electrical system, because much of the gas underground piping is plastic. Plastic is not a good electrical conductor.

17. **b.** Wires for house services should come off the distribution panel, not the service box.

18. **b.** Subpanels can be located anywhere in the house and can be difficult to find.

19. **b.** Typical distribution panels have 10 to 20 circuits.

20. **a.** The red and black wires of multiwire circuits should be on separate bus bars.

21. **a.** Most electrical authorities like to have outlets as far away from bathtubs or showers as practical. Any outlet closer than three feet is potentially dangerous.

22. **a.** Electrical authorities like receptacles in bathrooms to be close to the basin but not directly over it, because an appliance's cord may droop in the water.

23. **b.** Conjunction boxes must be accessible.

24. **a.** Original knob-and-tube spliced connections were not in junction boxes.

25. **b.** Smoke detectors should be near all sleeping areas, with at least one-per-floor in a home.

26. **d.** An ungrounded conductor is often called the hot conductor.

27. **d.** The standard house voltage is 120/240 V.

28. **b.** The unit for the measure of electrical power is watts.

29. **a.** The hair dryer will draw 10 amps ($P = V \times I$, $I = P/V$, $I = 1,200/120$).

30. **a.** $V = IR$.

31. **b.** The cost is 3 cents. ($P = V \times I$), ($P = 120 \times 5 = 600$ watts). (600 watts = 0.6 kilowatts). (0.6 kilowatts operating for 1 hour would consume 0.6 kilowatt hours). (0.6 kilowatts working for 1/2 hour will consume 0.3 kilowatt hours). At 10 cents per kilowatt hour, 0.3 kilowatt hours costs 3 cents.

32. **b.** The grounded or white conductor goes to the utility's transformer. From there it goes down, typically through a grounding wire at the base of the pole, and into a ground rod located there.

33. **b.** In a parallel circuit, any bulbs that you add will have the same brightness, so long as the circuit is not overloaded.

34. **c.** Service drop wires join the house at the drip loop.

35. **a.** Overhead service wires must be 3 feet away from windows.

36. **a.** Water stains on the soffit, where the mast goes through the roof, usually indicate a flashing problem.

37. **d.** Rust in the service panel may be a result of no drip loop or a damaged masthead.

38. **c.** Undersized conduit can't be the cause of water getting into the electrical system.

39. **b.** Four service entrance conductors indicate a three-phase service which is beyond our scope.

40. **d.** A 60-amp service can be adequate in some cases.

41. **b.** #6-gauge wire is adequate for 60-amp service.

42. **c.** A 200-amp service must have 2/0-gauge wire in the United States.

43. **c.** A 100-amp service in a single family, three-bedroom home with an electric stove and clothes dryer, a two-ton air-conditioning unit, and two 1,500-watt electric baseboard heaters is probably adequate. Keep in mind that the air-conditioning unit and the electric baseboard heaters would not likely be used at the same time.

44. **d.** A black, red, and white wire and 200-amp fuses indicates a 120/240-volt, 200-amp service.

45. **a.** The size of the conduit is not a reliable indicator of the service size. This would be common for a 200-amp service, but they could run smaller wires in the conduit.

46. **c.** No valuable information can be obtained by looking at the meter.

47. **b.** Two wires entering the service head indicates a 120-volt system.

48. **a.** The grounded service conductor is the neutral.

49. **b.** Electrical resistance gets smaller as the wire gets bigger because there is more room for the electrons to move through the wire.

50. **c.** P = VI, P = 120 × 15 = 1,800 watts.

51. **a.** Household electricity is 60 Hertz.

52. **d.** Switches are sealed by the utility company to ensure safety, to prevent tampering, and to stop people stealing electricity upstream of the meter.

53. **c.** This is a 60-amp service, limited by the service entrance conductors and the main fuses. It doesn't matter what is downstream of that.

54. **d.** The service drop conductors can be smaller than the service entrance conductors because the service drop conductors are in free air, whereas the service entrance conductors are in cable or conduit.

55. **b.** Rainwater is a conductor.

56. **c.** (P = VI), (I = P/V), (I = 120/120 = 1). The first part of the question is a bit of a red herring. All you have to know is that the wattage is 120. You know that the voltage is 120 because it is a gas clothes dryer that plugs in.

57. **a.** An over-current protection device can be a fuse or breaker.

58. **d.** Service entrance cable should be clamped to the house every 30 inches, generally.

59. **d.** The protection for wires servicing an auxiliary panel is ideally in the service panel. Fuses or breakers can be in the auxiliary panel as long as the wire powering the auxiliary panel is in rigid conduit and is reasonably short (five feet in some jurisdictions).

60. **c.** The top end of a service entrance cable should have a gooseneck before the splice.

61. **d.** Gas piping cannot be used to ground the electrical system.

62. **c.** Aluminum grounding conductors can only be used in dry environments in the United States.

63. **c.** Service entrance wires should not run inside the building. Some rules say no distance is permitted. Other rules indicate that they should be as-short-as-possible.

64. **a.** The function of bonding is to ensure that two electrical conductors are at the same potential (not necessarily zero).

65. **c.** Linking ensures that two fuses or circuit breakers are disconnected at the same time. This is important on 240-volt circuits or multiwire branch circuits.

66. **c.** A damaged or nicked wire is a problem because the resistance of the wire is effectively increased where it is nicked. The fuse will not adequately protect that part of the wire from overheating.

67. **d.** A kitchen split receptacle is a duplex receptacle with the top and bottom halves on different circuits.

68. **d.** Typical household circuits are 14-gauge copper or 12-gauge aluminum.

69. **d.** This is a 240-volt balanced load, often an electric baseboard heater.

70. **b.** A type P fuse is a heat sensitive fuse.

71. **d.** Gas piping is not an approved grounding method.

72. **d.** Subpanels are prohibited in bathrooms and clothes closets.

73. **a.** A difference between fuse manufacturer and panel manufacturer is not a problem.

74. **a.** The grounding electrode conductor is the wire that connects the system neutral to the water supply, well casing, or ground rods.

75. **b.** There should be three feet of clear space in front of a service box.

76. **d.** The main fuses or breakers should be sized to adequately protect the service entrance wires and should be no bigger than the rating of the service box.

77. **a.** The neutral service entrance conductor should connect to the terminal with the grounding conductor and the service neutral.

78. **d.** Overfusing is installing a fuse or breaker that is too big for the conductor.

79. **d.** The problem is that the 240-volt appliance may not operate properly, because both wires are on the black bus. The breakers may not be linked. The neutral may overheat if the black and red wires are on the same bus.

80. **a.** The panel is overcrowded if you can't get the cover back on without pinching wires.

81. **d.** Metal siding on buildings cannot be used to ground an electrical system. Some jurisdictions require that the siding be bonded to the electrical system, but that is different.

82. **c.** Roughly 12 outlets and/or light fixtures are permitted.

83. **a.** A 14-gauge copper wire is usually not permitted on a 25-amp fuse.

84. **c.** Putting a penny in a fuse holder means that the circuit has no overcurrent protection.

85. **d.** A multiwire circuit has a red and black wire.

86. **a.** Common wire sizes for water heaters are 12-gauge and 10-gauge.

87. **c.** If the fuse is hot, it may be because of a poor connection to the bus bar. This is often because the adjacent fuse was over tightened.

88. **d.** You should check that the breaker is properly sized and is compatible with this panel. You should make sure that it was professionally installed (and not forced into place) and that the breaker isn't loose.

89. **b.** An undersized wire won't cause a loose or damaged breaker.

90. **c.** Sheathing that has been removed on the panel wires is not a problem.

91. **b.** Openings in panels should be kept sealed to help keep fire inside the panel.

92. **c.** If the neutral wire bypasses the service box, the neutral and grounding system will not be properly connected to each other.

93. **a.** Putting fuses upstream of the disconnected switch in the service box makes it more dangerous to change the fuses. Even when the house power is shut off, there will be power to the fuse terminals.

94. **d.** Grounding does not prevent short circuits.

95. **c.** A jumper across the meter does not defeat the grounding system. It ensures that it is continuous.

96. **d.** Silver-dipped copper wires are not made, as far as anyone knows.

97. **a.** All GFIs must be tested.

98. **d.** We are required to inspect the wiring for a clock receptacle.

99. **c.** NMD cable is suitable for dry indoor use.

100. **c.** Plastic sheathing on branch wiring became popular in the 1970s.

101. **a.** Extension cords are typically stranded wire. This is so they will be more flexible than solid wire.

102. **c.** Number 10-gauge wires are not used for dishwashers. Dishwashers typically have #12-gauge or #14-gauge wire.

103. **c.** Wire nuts are also called solderless connectors.

104. **c.** Branch circuit wires should be supported within 12 inches of leaving a box.

105. **d.** Branch circuit wires can be stapled to 2 × 4 studs.

106. **a.** Loose connections may start fires.

107. **b.** Wires should be kept at least one inch away from heating ducts or pipes.

108. **b.** Wires should be kept six inches away from metal vent connectors on a gas appliance.

109. **b.** Wires should not be run across the top of ceiling joists unless the attic height is less than 40 inches.

110. **a.** White wires can sometimes act as black wires in 240-volt circuits.

111. **a.** NMD wires run through floor joists without tubes or grommets are not a problem.

112. **b.** Original knob and tube connections employed solder.

113. **d.** Overheated neutrals on multiwire branch circuits are not specific to knob and tube wiring. Multiwire branch circuits are, in fact, very rare on knob and tube wiring.

114. **a.** Knob and tube wiring buried in insulation is not permitted in some jurisdictions if the insulation is combustible.

115. **d.** Fused neutrals are dangerously poor practice.

116. **c.** Panels used with aluminum wires should be rated CUAL.

117. **b.** Pigtailed connections with aluminum wire add more connections to the box and may lead to overcrowding.

118. **b.** Aluminum wiring is still used on #8-gauge circuits. Stranded aluminum wire is still common. That includes wires that are #8-gauge and larger.

119. **a.** Receptacles are most likely to be rated CO/ALR.

120. **b.** Lacking a ground wire is not a common problem with aluminum wire.

121. **b.** The special grease on aluminum wires is typically used on stranded wires.

122. **a.** NMW wire used outdoors is not a problem.

123. **d.** Lights above stairwells are not problems.

124. **c.** Overheating is not likely to be caused by bulbs installed with the base down. This is the optimum arrangement for incandescent bulbs. The fixture and bulb are more likely to overheat if installed with the base at the top.

125. **b.** The surface temperature of a 100-watt bulb might be 380°.

126. **d.** Light fixtures are not required in clothes closets.

127. **c.** A pot light rated IC is intended for use in insulated ceilings.

128. **d.** GFI receptacles used outdoors are not problems. In fact, that is the most desirable outdoor receptacle.

129. **c.** The receptacle that is too close to the basin is not a problem.

130. **a.** Ungrounded three-slot receptacles are a problem because people might use grounded appliances and expect the receptacle to be grounded.

131. **d.** It is not much help to label the circuit back at the panel.

132. **d.** The service drop refers to the overhead wires coming from the utility pole to the house.

133. **d.** A properly polarized circuit has the lamp collar connected to the neutral.

134. **d.** GFI receptacles are accepted as an alternative for grounding under most retrofit circumstances.

135. **a.** Overloading the neutral wire on a multiwire branch circuit is likely if the black and red wires are powered from the same bus.

136. **b.** Outlets should be immediately beside a basin in a bathroom.

137. **b.** Three-way switches control lights from two different locations.

138. **a.** Wire nuts should be found inside boxes.

5. HEATING AND COOLING SYSTEMS

Practice Questions

1. A return grille allows us to modulate the volume of airflow.
   a. True
   b. False

2. The vent in a high-efficiency furnace should slope up away from the furnace gently to allow combustion gases to rise more easily.
   a. True
   b. False

3. Monoport burners are popular because they work equally well in any orientation.
   a. True
   b. False

4. Backdraft refers to an abnormal flame pattern.
   a. True
   b. False

5. Vent connectors other than B-vents require a six-inch clearance from combustibles.
   a. True
   b. False

6. The fan control switch is a safety device.
   a. True
   b. False

7. Poor or no heating is the most significant implication of heat exchanger problems.
   a. True
   b. False

8. The fan control switch is a required operating control on gravity furnaces.
   a. True
   b. False

9. Every oil furnace must have a barometric damper.
   a. True
   b. False

10. Power venters are never allowed on conventional oil furnace vent connectors.
    a. True
    b. False

11. The vent connector from an oil furnace must connect to the chimney above a vent connector from a water heater.
    a. True
    b. False

12. The oil filter is similar to the size and shape of the oil filter on a car.
    a. True
    b. False

13. Oil burners in conventional oil furnaces are natural draft.
    a. True
    b. False

14. The typical required combustible clearance between an oil burner and combustibles is 24 inches.
    a. True
    b. False

15. Aluminum is a commonly used material for exhaust flues on oil furnaces.
    a. True
    b. False

16. Oil burners are typically inside the furnace cabinet.
    a. True
    b. False

17. Closed systems must have circulators.
    a. True
    b. False

18. If you find a radiator with the balancing valve completely shut off, then there will be no water in the radiator.
    a. True
    b. False

19. It is possible to have a pressure-relief valve that is too small for the boiler.
    a. True
    b. False

20. The pressure-reducing valve on a boiler is a safety control that prevents the pressure in a boiler system from building beyond 30 psi.
    a. True
    b. False

21. Outdoor air thermostats are commonly used with residential hot water boilers.
    a. True
    b. False

22. Bleed valves on radiators are used to let water out to help balance the heating in individual rooms.
    a. True
    b. False

23. Boilers do not require venting systems.
    a. True
    b. False

24. A missing automatic air vent is a common problem with hot water boilers.
    a. True
    b. False

25. You can see the elements on an electric furnace.
    a. True
    b. False

26. When you compress gas, you cool it.
    a. True
    b. False

27. The evaporator coil is outdoors in a split system.
    a. True
    b. False

28. Oversized distribution ductwork is a common problem with central air-conditioning.
    a. True
    b. False

29. An undersized air conditioner is better than an oversized one.
    a. True
    b. False

30. The typical temperature drop from outdoors to indoors with a properly operating air-conditioning system would be about 15°F.
    a. True
    b. False

31. Evaporator coils should be upstream of furnace heat exchangers.
    a. True
    b. False

32. A compressor can be thought of as a pump.
    a. True
    b. False

33. Compressors typically are located indoors on an air-to-air, split-system air-conditioning system.
    a. True
    b. False

34. The larger refrigerant line contains a liquid.
    a. True
    b. False

35. The smaller refrigerant line is called the suction line.
    a. True
    b. False

36. The larger refrigerant line is called the return line.
    a. True
    b. False

37. Flex ducts have less friction loss than rigid ductwork.
    a. True
    b. False

38. One Btu is the amount of heat required to raise
    a. one gallon of water one degree Fahrenheit.
    b. one liter of water one degree Centigrade.
    c. one pound of water one degree Fahrenheit.
    d. one pound of water one degree Centigrade.

39. Which of the following is *NOT* a method of heat transfer?
    a. Conduction
    b. Induction
    c. Radiation
    d. Convective loops

40. For complete combustion, and ignoring dilution air requirements, natural gas requires approximately
    a. $\frac{1}{15}$ volume ratio of gas/air.
    b. $\frac{1}{100}$ volume ratio of gas/air.
    c. one pound of air for one pound of fuel.
    d. $\frac{10}{1}$ volume ratio of gas/air.

41. A conventional gas-fired, forced-air furnace rated at 100,000 Btu input is in a four-foot by four-foot by eight-foot-high furnace room with a door.
    a. A single 50-square-inch opening should be provided at roughly the elevation of the draft hood.
    b. Two openings should be provided, one near the bottom and one near the top of the room, each 50 square inches.
    c. Two openings should be provided, one near the bottom and one near the top of the room, each sized at 100 square inches.
    d. One opening should be provided, sized at 500 square inches.

42. Natural gas
    a. is lighter than air.
    b. is piped as a compressed liquid.
    c. has a strong natural odor.
    d. contains about 2,500 Btu-per-cubic-foot.

43. Which of the following is *NOT* a problem with a natural gas burner?
    a. Flame lifting
    b. Flame rollout
    c. Inactive flame
    d. Delayed ignition

44. Flame rollout would *NEVER* be caused by
    a. overfiring of the burner.
    b. cracked heat exchanger.
    c. lack of combustion air.
    d. underfiring of the burner.

45. Heat exchangers
    a. separate the combustion air from the house air.
    b. can be easily repaired or replaced.
    c. are typically made of aluminum.
    d. should be completely inspected during a standard home inspection.

46. The right burner in a two-burner, conventional efficiency furnace ignites from the pilot readily, but the left burner ignition is delayed. When it does ignite, it does so with a flash and pop. What is likely wrong?
    a. The pilot is dirty.
    b. The flame sensor is malfunctioning.
    c. The left burner is damaged.
    d. The crossover igniter needs adjustment.

47. The flame of the left burner in a two-burner, conventional efficiency furnace touches the heat exchanger when the blower is not running. What is likely to be the problem?
    a. The heat exchanger is cracked on the left side.
    b. The right burner is dirty.
    c. The left burner is dirty.
    d. The left burner is misaligned.

48. The fan/limit switch will typically turn the blower on at
    a. 80°F–110°F.
    b. 120°F–150°F.
    c. 170°F–200°F.
    d. 220°F–250°F.

49. The high-limit setting for a forced-air, gas furnace is typically
    a. 150°F.
    b. 200°F.
    c. 250°F.
    d. 300°F.

50. The anticipator on a thermostat is used to
    a. start the furnace, in anticipation of a temperature drop.
    b. stop the furnace early to reduce overheating of the house.
    c. control current flow to the furnace gas valve.
    d. prevent the air conditioner from cycling if it is too cold outside.

51. Of the following, which is the best location for the thermostat?
    a. In the front vestibule, on an interior wall
    b. In the living room across from the fireplace
    c. In the second-floor master bedroom, away from all windows
    d. On an interior dining room wall by the light switch

52. In the operating sequence of a conventional gas-fired, forced-air furnace, which step is out of sequence?
    a. The thermocouple verifies that the pilot is on.
    b. The house air fan comes on.
    c. The gas valve opens.
    d. The burners are ignited.

53. A conventional gas-fired, forced-air furnace has an input rating of 100,000 Btu. Its output rating is 80,000 Btu. The seasonal efficiency is
    a. greater than the steady state efficiency.
    b. less than the steady state efficiency.
    c. independent of off-cycle losses.
    d. minimized by the presence of an induced-draft fan.

54. Corrosion in the draft hood and on the inside of the access cover indicates
    a. excess flue gas temperature.
    b. inadequate flue gas temperature.
    c. backdrafting.
    d. excess draft air.

55. Heat exchanger failure in a conventional efficiency furnace may lead to all these *EXCEPT*
    a. carbon monoxide in the house.
    b. soot buildup on the burner-side of the heat exchanger.
    c. high house humidity levels.
    d. flame pattern disruption when the house air fan comes on.

56. Which of the following statements, with respect to vent connectors, is *FALSE*?
    a. The temperature of diluted exhaust products from conventional gas-fired furnaces is 500°F to 700°F.
    b. The vent connector joins the furnace to the chimney or vent.
    c. The vent connector should slope up from the furnace to the chimney at roughly ¼-inch-per-foot.
    d. The implications of vent connector problems are exhaust spillage and condensation.

57. All of the following affect the amount of air delivered to each room *EXCEPT*
    a. duct shape.
    b. duct location.
    c. duct length.
    d. blower size.

58. All of the following are problems you'll commonly find on house air fans *EXCEPT*
    a. dirt.
    b. fans poorly secured.
    c. a loose fan belt.
    d. fans installed backwards.

59. All of the following are common furnace filter problems *EXCEPT*
    a. missing filters.
    b. filters installed upstream of blower
    c. filters installed backwards.
    d. loose or collapsed filters.

60. The single cold-air return in a small bungalow is located beside the main supply register to the living room. What is the concern with this?
    a. The supply and return can be easily blocked with furniture.
    b. The living room will get the worst airflow.
    c. The return will pull the supply air in.
    d. The furnace could overheat with this setup.

61. The homeowner has tucked the supply and return plenums up tight along a wood beam. Are there concerns with this?
    a. Yes, the ducts are too close to the combustible wood.
    b. No, the ceiling is now easier to finish.
    c. Yes, the airflow is lowered due to the tight bends.
    d. No, duct vibration is less likely to occur.

62. Supply air registers in a forced-air heating system are best located
    a. high on interior walls.
    b. low on interior walls.
    c. low on exterior walls.
    d. centrally located on ceilings.

63. Poor airflow may be the result of all of the following *EXCEPT*
    a. dirty ducts.
    b. obstructed or collapsed ducts.
    c. leaking ducts.
    d. uninsulated ducts.

64. An early generation, midefficiency gas furnace has a vent damper. Which of the following list of conditions is *NOT* a safety concern?
    a. The vent damper is stuck open.
    b. The vent damper is stuck closed.
    c. The vent damper motor runs continuously.
    d. The vent damper is not interlocked with the burner.

65. Off-cycle losses on a conventional gas-fired forced air furnace waste
    a. 5 percent of the heat generated.
    b. 10 percent of the heat generated.
    c. 20 percent of the heat generated.
    d. 30 percent of the heat generated.

66. Which of the following is *NOT TRUE?*
    a. Annual Fuel Utilization Efficiency is the same as seasonal efficiency.
    b. Off-cycle losses include chimney losses and standing pilot losses.
    c. Induced-draft fans always have standing pilots.
    d. Induced-draft fans are used for purging the furnace.

67. Ignition devices commonly found on mid-efficiency gas furnaces include all these *EXCEPT*
    a. electronic ignition.
    b. spark igniters.
    c. hot-surface igniters.
    d. thermocouples.

68. Natural gas burners can have several different draft mechanisms. All of the following are possible examples *EXCEPT*
    a. natural draft.
    b. induced draft.
    c. reverse draft.
    d. forced draft.

69. A midefficiency, induced-draft gas furnace is manifolded with a natural-draft water heater. Is this a concern?
    a. No, this is always allowed.
    b. No, not if the vent is large enough to handle both.
    c. Yes, if the furnace vent pressure is positive.
    d. Yes, this situation is never allowed.

70. Midefficiency, gas-fired furnaces
    a. may be vented through the sidewall.
    b. never had plastic venting.
    c. always have an induced-draft fan.
    d. have seasonal efficiencies in the 85 percent to 90 percent range.

71. Induced-draft fans improve efficiency by doing all of the following *EXCEPT*
    a. using less house air than a natural-draft burner.
    b. eliminating off-cycle losses up the chimney.
    c. condensing the exhaust gases.
    d. eliminating the need for dilution air.

72. Midefficiency furnaces with induced-draft fans may have all of the following components *EXCEPT*
    a. an air-proving switch.
    b. a draft hood.
    c. electronic ignition.
    d. a spillage switch.

73. High-efficiency gas furnaces improve efficiency by
    a. reducing airflow across the heat exchanger.
    b. increasing airflow and increasing flue gas exhaust temperature.
    c. reducing temperature rise and condensing flue gases.
    d. increasing blower speed and evaporating flue gases.

74. A common temperature rise across a modern high-efficiency gas furnace is
    a. 10°F to 50°F.
    b. 35°F to 65°F.
    c. 50°F to 85°F.
    d. 70°F to 100°F.

75. Corrosion noted inside a high-efficiency, gas-furnace blower compartment may be
    a. indicative of humidifier leakage.
    b. indicative of condensate line blockage.
    c. indicative of induced-draft fan failure.
    d. All of the above

76. Direct-vent heating systems
    a. take combustion air from outside the dwelling.
    b. require 1 square inch of vent space per 1,000 Btu/hour input.
    c. usually have standing pilots and forced-draft fans.
    d. have their combustion occur outside the building.

77. High-efficiency gas furnaces are designed to condense because
    a. of the desire to capture the latent heat of vaporization.
    b. the heat exchangers have been made more corrosion-resistant anyway, so condensation doesn't matter.
    c. new technology allows us to collect and dispose of the condensation.
    d. the condensation is used to help cool the induced-draft fan.

78. Which of the following is *NOT* a normal installation on a pulse high-efficiency furnace?
    a. Vibration damping in the duct connections
    b. Flexible gas connector
    c. Exterior duct insulation
    d. A tailpipe

79. The seasonal efficiency of a high-efficiency gas furnace can be
    a. 75 percent to 85 percent.
    b. 80 percent to 90 percent.
    c. 85 percent to 95 percent.
    d. 95 percent to 100 percent.

80. The exhaust gas temperature from a high-efficiency furnace is typically
    a. 50°F to 100°F.
    b. 100°F to 150°F.
    c. 150°F to 200°F.
    d. 200°F to 250°F.

81. The exhaust from a high-efficiency gas furnace terminates underneath an enclosed deck. Is this a concern?
    a. No, the exhaust gases are low-temperature, so there is no combustibility problem.
    b. Yes, the wood is combustible.
    c. Yes, the exhaust gases will spill into the house.
    d. Yes, the exhaust gases will rot the deck.

82. A pulse furnace has all of the following *EXCEPT*
    a. a purge blower.
    b. an air intake vacuum switch.
    c. direct spark ignition.
    d. an induced-draft fan.

83. Common problems with high-efficiency furnaces include all of the following *EXCEPT*
    a. induced-draft fan problems.
    b. vent damper problems.
    c. heat exchanger problems.
    d. clogged condensate systems.

84. Common heat exchanger problems on mid-efficiency and high-efficiency furnaces include all of the following *EXCEPT*
    a. rust.
    b. cracking.
    c. vibration.
    d. overheating.

85. Common condensate problems on high-efficiency furnaces include all of the following *EXCEPT*
    a. leaking condensate lines.
    b. lack of an automatic air vent in condensate lines.
    c. poor discharge location.
    d. a missing or clogged neutralizer.

86. Sidewall vents from midefficiency or high-efficiency furnaces should be at least
    a. 6 feet away from windows and other building openings.
    b. 1 foot off the ground.
    c. 10 feet from soffits.
    d. 10 feet away from gas regulators.

87. The implication of improper slope on the exhaust flue from a high-efficiency gas furnace is
    a. water damage outside.
    b. frost closure at the discharge.
    c. moisture being drawn-in through the combustion air intake.
    d. corrosion of the vent material.

88. The exhaust flue on a midefficiency furnace should have a six-inch combustible clearance. On a high-efficiency furnace exhaust flue, the required clearance is
    a. six inches.
    b. three inches.
    c. two inches.
    d. zero inches.

89. Combustion in a direct-spark ignition, condensing gas furnace is sensed by
    a. the primary control.
    b. the flame sensor.
    c. the thermocouple.
    d. the ignition module.

90. Combination furnaces
    a. use more than one vent.
    b. have more than one burner.
    c. use one burner to heat space and hot water.
    d. always have tempering valves.

91. The life expectancy of a conventional gas furnace is
    a. 20–25 years.
    b. 25–30 years.
    c. 30–35 years.
    d. 35–40 years.

92. The heat content of one gallon of No. 2 heating oil is approximately
    a. 2,500 Btu.
    b. 72,000 Btu.
    c. 140,000 Btu.
    d. 200,000 Btu.

93. Oil furnaces are like gas furnaces in all of the following respects *EXCEPT*
    a. ducts, registers, and grilles.
    b. heat exchangers.
    c. fan/limit switches.
    d. blast tubes.

94. You find an oil storage tank in the basement. The entire surface of the tank is rusting. What is the most likely cause?
    a. The basement leaks near the tank.
    b. The tank leaks.
    c. The clothes dryer vents into the tank area.
    d. The burner is backdrafting wet combustion gases.

95. When you turn up the thermostat, the oil burner does not operate. You know that the electrical power to the furnace is on. What is *NOT* a likely concern?
    a. A clogged nozzle
    b. The firepot having failed
    c. Clogging of the combustion air intake
    d. An empty fuel tank

96. Viewing the flame of an oil burner from the viewport shows a ragged, black-edged, yellow flame. This is
    a. normal for a flame-retention head burner.
    b. normal for a conventional oil burner.
    c. the result of a failed firepot.
    d. the result of a failed heat exchanger.

97. The viewport shows that the back wall of the ceramic felt combustion chamber is no longer white. It is browned and stained. What is the likely cause of this discoloration?
    a. The ceramic felt is saturated with oil.
    b. The felt is covered with soot from a dirty flame.
    c. The felt has turned this color with time and use.
    d. The heat exchanger has failed and is leaking creosote onto the firepot.

98. Combustion is verified in an oil furnace by
    a. the primary control.
    b. the thermocouple.
    c. the fan/limit switch.
    d. the electrodes.

99. The primary control on a modern flame-retention head oil burner is typically found
    a. on the heat exchanger.
    b. on the burner.
    c. on the exhaust flue.
    d. on the furnace cabinet.

100. The barometric damper for a conventional efficiency oil furnace is found on the
    a. furnace cabinet.
    b. burner.
    c. exhaust flue.
    d. heat exchanger.

101. When you turn up the thermostat on a conventional efficiency oil furnace, the burner fires but the barometric damper does not move. This may mean that
    a. the barometric damper has seized.
    b. the barometric damper is not needed for this furnace.
    c. the atmospheric pressure is greater than the flue pressure.
    d. the oil pressure to the burner is too high.

102. The required clearance from combustibles for an oil furnace vent connector is at least
    a. 0 inches.
    b. 3 inches.
    c. 6 inches.
    d. 9 inches.

103. All of the following are common vent connector issues on oil furnaces *EXCEPT*
    a. poor support.
    b. poor slope.
    c. loose fittings at plastic connections.
    d. poor connection to the chimney.

104. A high-static burner
    a. requires a barometric damper.
    b. uses higher air and oil pressure.
    c. is used at high altitudes.
    d. is an older-style oil burner.

105. The maximum steady-state efficiency for an oil burner is
    a. 72 percent.
    b. 77 percent.
    c. 82 percent.
    d. 87 percent.

106. Which of the following materials is *NOT* used for boiler heat exchangers?
    a. Plate steel
    b. Copper
    c. Nickel alloys
    d. Aluminum tubing

107. Heat is transferred from the fire-side of the heat exchanger to the water side by
    a. conduction.
    b. convection.
    c. radiation.
    d. All of the above

108. Heat is transferred from the radiator to the room by
    a. conduction.
    b. convection.
    c. Radiation.
    d. both b and c.

109. Piping in boiler systems is rarely made from
    a. black steel.
    b. polybutylene.
    c. galvanized steel.
    d. copper.

110. Boilers are connected to the domestic plumbing system to
    a. allow humidification to occur.
    b. to prevent backflow from occurring.
    c. to provide make-up water.
    d. to provide adequate water pressure in the plumbing system.

111. The pressure-relief valve
    a. prevents backflow from occurring.
    b. allows plumbing water to pressurize the boiler.
    c. prevents the formation of superheated water.
    d. allows the zone control valves to function.

112. Superheated water
    a. can be used for space heating and domestic water heating.
    b. can be prevented with a pressure-reducing valve.
    c. can cause steam explosions.
    d. develops if the tankless coil leaks.

113. Superheated water released suddenly into the atmosphere
    a. will not turn to liquid.
    b. will not turn to steam.
    c. will not explode.
    d. cannot cause death.

114. A boiler heat exchanger that has cracked will
    a. be very difficult to detect.
    b. be a life safety issue.
    c. leak water frequently.
    d. leak water, at least periodically.

115. Boiler water should *NOT* be drained in the summer because
    a. it is a nuisance to refill in the fall.
    b. fresh water will cause system corrosion.
    c. fresh water lowers the system response time.
    d. fresh water lowers the system efficiency.

116. Copper tube boilers should always
    a. have the pump running.
    b. have the pump running when the burner is firing.
    c. be installed with a bladder-style expansion tank.
    d. have radiators as the heat distributors.

117. The common high temperature-limit setting is
    a. 150°F.
    b. 170°F.
    c. 190°F.
    d. 210°F.

118. The outdoor-air thermostat may
    a. lower the water temperature as the outdoor temperature drops.
    b. fire the burner as the outdoor temperature drops.
    c. fire the burner as the outdoor temperature raises.
    d. remove operating control from the occupant of the building.

119. You come across a pressure-relief valve that is dripping. Which of the following is *NOT* a likely concern?
    a. The system pressure is too high.
    b. The pressure-relief valve seat is obstructed.
    c. The pressure-relief valve is the wrong capacity.
    d. The pipe extension is clogged.

120. The pressure-reducing valve needs to be adjustable because
    a. different boilers operate at different pressures.
    b. supply water pressures vary between locations.
    c. tall houses need higher pressure settings.
    d. each pump has a different pressure capability.

121. A circulator on a cast-iron boiler may start when the water temperature reaches
    a. 70–110°F.
    b. 110–140°F.
    c. 140–190°F.
    d. 190–210°F.

122. Circulators should NOT be mounted
    a. on the return piping.
    b. on the supply piping.
    c. at the lowest point in the piping.
    d. below any radiating surfaces.

123. Individual zoning control can be achieved by multiple
    a. circulators.
    b. pressure-reducing valves.
    c. expansion tanks.
    d. aquastats.

124. The expansion tank in an open system is typically located
    a. below the boiler.
    b. above the highest radiator.
    c. level with the circulator.
    d. below the pressure-reducing valve.

125. A closed, bladder expansion tank in a two-pipe system is typically located
    a. below the boiler.
    b. above the highest radiator.
    c. level with the boiler.
    d. at the lowest pipe level.

126. A reverse return system yields
    a. slightly more even heat distribution than a single-pipe system.
    b. slightly less even heat distribution than a single-pipe system.
    c. less head pressure on the circulator.
    d. smaller temperature rise across the boiler.

127. Heat distribution in hydronic systems can be balanced by adjusting the
    a. pressure-reducing valve setting.
    b. circulator capacity.
    c. valves at each radiator.
    d. boiler size.

128. A waterlogged expansion tank will cause
    a. the boiler heat exchanger to fail.
    b. the pressure-relief valve to drip.
    c. the pressure-reducing valve to drip.
    d. the circulator to stop.

129. Typical water pressure in a boiler at rest in a two-story house is
    a. 5–10 psi.
    b. 10–15 psi.
    c. 15–20 psi.
    d. 20–25 psi.

130. Typical water pressure at a boiler at rest in a three-story house is
    a. 1–5 psi.
    b. 5–10 psi.
    c. slightly higher than in a two-story home.
    d. lower than in a two-story home.

131. Circulators are NEVER controlled by
    a. the boiler electrical power.
    b. an aquastat.
    c. a pressure-relief valve.
    d. the burner coming on.

132. Which of these has the greatest heat delivery by length (e.g., a two-foot-long unit)?
    a. Radiators
    b. Convectors
    c. Baseboards
    d. Radiant piping

133. Of the following, the best location for a radiator in a living room, within a closed system having a circulator is
    a. on the interior wall.
    b. on the exterior wall, below the window.
    c. on the ceiling.
    d. anywhere, because the system has a circulator, and so it doesn't matter where the radiator is placed.

134. Where is the best location for a radiator in a basement room, in an open system (assuming the boiler is in the basement)?
    a. On the interior wall
    b. On the exterior wall
    c. On the ceiling
    d. Underneath the raised floor

135. Radiant piping systems are *NOT* made with
    a. iron.
    b. steel.
    c. plastic.
    d. nickel.

136. An inefficiency unique to tankless coil boilers is that the
    a. unit operates at higher pressures.
    b. unit must stay hot year-round.
    c. unit must deliver more heat.
    d. operating-efficiency of the boiler is less than that of most domestic water heaters.

137. The most difficult design problem on high-efficiency boilers is the
    a. return water temperature is too hot.
    b. return water temperature is too cold.
    c. circulator needs to be changed.
    d. new boiler operates at a higher pressure.

138. High-efficiency boilers prepurge the combustion chamber to
    a. remove any lingering exhaust gases.
    b. allow the hot surface igniter to warm.
    c. remove any lingering unburned fuel.
    d. prevent condensation in the boiler.

139. Older conventional efficiency, cast iron boilers have a life expectancy of
    a. 5–10 years.
    b. 10–15 years.
    c. 25–35 years.
    d. 35–50 years.

140. Backflow preventers
    a. keep the domestic water out of the boiler water.
    b. keep the boiler water out of the drinking water.
    c. prevent water from flowing out of the expansion tank.
    d. prevent reverse flow in the distribution system.

141. Pressure-reducing valve problems include all of the following *EXCEPT*
    a. pressure that is set too low.
    b. connection to the supply plumbing.
    c. inoperativity.
    d. backwards installation.

142. Air vents are
    a. safety controls.
    b. never used with diaphragm-type expansion tanks.
    c. also called air eliminators.
    d. never found on systems with pumps.

143. The device that keeps the boiler water hot on a standby basis is known by all these names *EXCEPT*
    a. stack relay.
    b. low-temperature limit.
    c. aquastat.
    d. primary control.

144. Flow control valves
    a. provide zone control.
    b. control the water-flow rate to the radiators.
    c. allow water to flow from the supply plumbing system into the boiler water.
    d. prevent water circulation when the system is at rest.

145. A common circulator pump problem is
    a. noisiness.
    b. use for zone control.
    c. use with copper tube boiler.
    d. running continuously.

146. A common radiator problem is
    a. lack of a balancing valve.
    b. location on the same system with convectors.
    c. location on an exterior wall.
    d. installation above the expansion tank.

147. Common tankless coil problems include all these *EXCEPT*
    a. leaks.
    b. rust.
    c. installation in direct contact with the boiler water.
    d. clogging.

148. How much heat is typically needed in an older, poorly insulated home in the northern United States?
    a. 5–10 Btu-per-square-foot
    b. 10–30 Btu-per-square-foot
    c. 30–60 Btu-per-square-foot
    d. 60–90 Btu-per-square-foot

149. Disadvantages of a steam system include all of the following *EXCEPT*
    a. there is no fan or pump to help move heat through the system.
    b. parts may be difficult to find.
    c. the environment inside the pipe is harsher than in a hot-water system.
    d. steam systems are complex because there are so many different kinds of systems and many of them have been modified.

150. All of the following are types of steam systems except one. Which one is *NOT*?
    a. Vapor system
    b. Vacuum system
    c. Two-pipe, reverse-flow system
    d. One-pipe, reverse-flow system

151. Boilers, piping, and radiators are commonly made of
    a. copper.
    b. cast iron.
    c. brass.
    d. aluminum.

152. Which of the following components would you find on a steam system?
    a. A high-temperature limit switch
    b. A pressure gauge
    c. A circulator pump
    d. Manual bleed valve on the rads

153. Which of the following would you typically find on a hot water boiler?
    a. Water temperature and pressure gauge
    b. Water level gauge
    c. Pressuretrol
    d. Hartford Loop

154. Typical steam pressure in a single family residential steam system would be
    a. 0.5–5 psi.
    b. 1–10 psi.
    c. 2–20 psi.
    d. 3–15 psi.

155. When the system is at rest, what will you find in the boiler?
    a. Steam
    b. Steam and water
    c. Air and water
    d. Air, water, and steam

156. When the heating system is at work, what would you expect to find in the radiators?
    a. Air
    b. Steam and water
    c. Steam
    d. Air and water

157. The purpose of an equalizer pipe in a steam boiler is to
    a. allow air to escape from the system so that steam can flow.
    b. equalize the steam pressure in the supply and return sides of the boiler.
    c. equalize water pressure in the supply and return mains.
    d. equalize pressure drop from the beginning to the end of the system.

158. All of these devices can cause the boiler to shut off, except for one. Which one will *NOT* shut the boiler off?
    a. Pressure-relief valve
    b. Low water cutout
    c. Pressuretrol
    d. Cutting off fuel supply

159. The purpose of a Hartford Loop is to
    a. equalize pressure throughout the system.
    b. prevent flooding of the boiler.
    c. prevent water from leaking out of the boiler if the wet return leaks.
    d. prevent flooding of main vents.

160. What is an appropriate slope for piping in a two-pipe steam system?
    a. ½–1-inch-per-foot
    b. 1-inch-in-2-feet
    c. 1-inch-in-5-feet
    d. 1-inch-in-20-feet

161. Where are the air vents in a one-pipe, parallel-flow system typically located?
    a. On the radiators
    b. At the steam header
    c. At the end of the return mains
    d. At the radiators and the end of return mains

162. Steam traps are typically located
    a. on the radiator in a one pipe system.
    b. on the return pipe from each radiator on a two-pipe system.
    c. at the end of the supply main on a two-pipe system.
    d. in places described by either b or c.

163. An F & T trap is
    a. a fast and tall trap.
    b. a float and thermostatic trap.
    c. a filling and timing trap.
    d. located half way up the side of a radiator.

164. Which of the following statements about condensate pumps is *FALSE?*
    a. Condensate pumps are only used on one-pipe systems.
    b. Condensate pumps have an air vent on the receiver.
    c. Condensate pumps have a check valve on the discharge line.
    d. Condensate pumps eliminate the need for Hartford Loops.

165. What is the normal setting of a pressure-relief valve on a steam system?
    a. 2 psi
    b. 5 psi
    c. 15 psi
    d. 30 psi

166. A blowdown valve
    a. is part of a Hartford Loop.
    b. is an automatic water make-up device.
    c. is used to test and flush the low water cutout.
    d. relieves pressures in excess of 30 psi.

167. All of the following are advantages of electric heat *EXCEPT*
    a. that electric furnaces have greater capacity than gas or oil heat furnaces.
    b. room by room control is possible.
    c. electric heating systems are less expensive to purchase and install than gas or oil systems.
    d. there are almost no off-cycle losses.

168. An electric heating system has
    a. a heat exchanger.
    b. a thermocouple.
    c. a draft hood.
    d. an overcurrent protection device.

169. A 20-kilowatt, 240-volt electric furnace would draw approximately how many amps for the heating elements?
    a. 43 amps
    b. 63 amps
    c. 83 amps
    d. 103 amps

170. A 20-kilowatt electric furnace has an output (in Btu-per-hour) capacity of roughly
    a. 48,000-Btu-per-hour.
    b. 68,000-Btu-per-hour.
    c. 88,000-Btu-per-hour.
    d. 108,000-Btu-per-hour.

171. All of the following are common electric space heaters *EXCEPT*
    a. baseboard heaters.
    b. wall-mounted heaters.
    c. duct heaters.
    d. toe-kick heaters.

172. Space heaters may be
    a. forced air.
    b. power vented.
    c. connected to ductwork.
    d. connected to piping and heating coils.

173. Which one of the following is *NOT* a common problem with space heaters?
    a. Inoperative heaters
    b. Obstructed heaters
    c. Electrical receptacles beside heaters
    d. 120-volt heaters installed on 240-volt circuits

174. How far above electric baseboard heaters should drapes be hung?
    a. Two inches
    b. Three inches
    c. Four inches
    d. Eight inches

175. Why don't you want electrical receptacles located above heaters?
    a. The fuse is likely to be undersized.
    b. An electrical cord resting on a heater poses a fire hazard.
    c. Whatever is plugged into the receptacle will obstruct the heater.
    d. The receptacle will be too hot to touch when plugging in an appliance.

176. Which one of the following is not a common electric fan problem?
    a. Noise
    b. Inoperativity
    c. Dirt
    d. Failure to stay on after thermostat is satisfied

177. Why is a 120-volt heater wired as 240-volts a problem?
    a. The room will overheat.
    b. The fuse will be undersized.
    c. The wire will be oversized.
    d. The heater may overheat.

178. A sequencer on an electric furnace is a
    a. device that shuts off the furnace when other large electrical appliances in the house are working.
    b. control to ensure that individual elements do not all come on at the same time.
    c. device to ensure that the furnace fan turns on and off at the correct times.
    d. device that limits the total-current draw of the furnace.

179. A staged electric furnace
    a. uses only the elements required to meet the heat loss.
    b. has all the elements come on at 10-second intervals.
    c. is always used in combination with an oil furnace.
    d. is always part of a heat pump system.

180. Ducts for electric furnaces
    a. cannot be located in subgrade areas.
    b. must be insulated.
    c. must be electrically grounded.
    d. are typically larger than ducts for gas or oil furnaces.

181. Electric boilers will NOT have a
    a. pressure-relief valve.
    b. Pressure-limit switch.
    c. draft hood.
    d. safe-fill switch.

182. Which types of electric heating systems should be removed from houses?
    a. Flex Heat radiant panels
    b. Radiant panels in drywall ceilings
    c. Electric furnaces on 240-volt circuits
    d. Baseboard heaters located on exterior walls, below windows

183. Which of the following was NOT a common radiant ceiling heating system?
    a. Panels laid on top of ceilings below insulation
    b. Wires embedded in lightweight concrete
    c. Wires embedded in lightweight plaster
    d. Prewired panels

184. Which of the following gas heating systems typically is designed to be connected to a duct system?
    a. Wall furnaces
    b. Floor furnaces
    c. Space heaters
    d. None of the above

185. Which of the following statements is true with respect to wall furnaces? They
    a. can always be unvented.
    b. require a two-inch clearance from combustibles on all sides.
    c. always use outside combustion air.
    d. use BW Vents.

186. Which of the following is NOT a problem with a wall furnace?
    a. The furnace top is 20 inches below the ceiling.
    b. The vent terminates 8 feet above the bottom of the furnace.
    c. The vent has a 30° offset.
    d. Ducts have been provided.

187. Which of the following is *NOT TRUE* with respect to a floor furnace?
    a. The grate should be 6 inches from any walls.
    b. The grate should have at least 24 inches clearance on at least two sides.
    c. The grate should be 2 inches from doors, drapes, or other combustibles.
    d. The grate should be at least 60 inches below any structure. including a bulkhead or stairway.

188. Which of the following is *NOT* a problem on a floor furnace?
    a. The heat exchanger cap is missing or damaged.
    b. There is restricted airflow.
    c. The unit is not listed, certified, or approved.
    d. The thermostat is mounted in the same room as the furnace.

189. Which of the following statements is true with respect to room heaters? They
    a. require 18 inches of clear space above the heater.
    b. may be installed on combustible floors.
    c. may be installed in masonry fireplaces.
    d. may be installed with four inches of clearance on all sides.

190. Which of the following statements, with respect to gas fireplaces, is *TRUE?*
    a. All gas fireplaces are decorative only.
    b. Gas fireplaces can be rated as space heaters.
    c. Gas fireplaces are very similar to wood-burning fireplaces.
    d. Gas fireplaces cannot have glass doors.

191. Gas logs
    a. do not need to be vented.
    b. may be vented through a chimney.
    c. should never be installed in an existing fireplace.
    d. must have electronic ignition.

192. Common problems with gas fireplace inserts or gas logs include
    a. missing four-inch firebrick.
    b. lack of an outdoor combustion air intake.
    c. lack of an ash pit.
    d. the damper in the existing fireplace not being fixed open.

193. Which of the following is an acceptable situation with gas-fired room heaters?
    a. It is unvented.
    b. It is not labeled for use in a fireplace.
    c. It has inadequate combustible clearance.
    d. There is no outdoor-combustion air supply.

194. For the purposes of inspection, fireplace inserts should be treated as
    a. gas logs.
    b. wood furnaces.
    c. wood stoves.
    d. wood fireplaces.

195. Heat pumps are designed to
    a. use circulating pumps to move liquid Freon.
    b. capture heat from the outdoors and bring it into the home.
    c. increase humidity levels in the home.
    d. convert electric energy to heat.

196. Which of the following statements is true?
    a. When a heat pump is in the cooling mode, the indoor coil is the condenser.
    b. When a heat pump is in the heating mode, the condensate line should be producing at least one quart of water every two hours.
    c. When a heat pump is in the cooling mode, the outdoor coil is the evaporator.
    d. When a heat pump is in the heating mode, the indoor coil is the condenser.

197. Which of the following statements is true with respect to heat pumps?
    a. The compressor must be outdoors.
    b. The compressor must be indoors.
    c. There may be two expansion devices.
    d. The expansion device must be indoors.

198. The reversing valve on a heat pump
    a. changes the direction of the piston in the compressor.
    b. changes the position of the expansion device.
    c. changes the liquid line to the suction line.
    d. changes the direction of the refrigerant flow.

199. The capacity of the heat pump
    a. is usually determined by the cooling load.
    b. is equal to the heating load.
    c. is fixed, regardless of the outdoor temperature.
    d. must be added to the backup gas furnace capacity to get the total heating capacity.

200. If a heat pump is sized for the heating load, it
     a. is probably undersized for the cooling load.
     b. may be oversized for the cooling load.
     c. may result in an extremely dry climate during the winter.
     d. will require a dual heat backup system.

201. With respect to heat pumps, the coefficient of performance (COP) is
     a. variable with outdoor temperature.
     b. the point at which the heat loss from the house exceeds the output capacity of the heat pump.
     c. the point at which heat loss from the house exceeds the input capacity of the heat pump.
     d. the ratio of the heating capacity to the cooling capacity.

202. If the backup heat is electric, when should the heat pump shut off?
     a. When the temperature falls below the balance point
     b. When the COP is below 1.0
     c. When the COP is below 3.0
     d. When the electric current draw of the compressor and the electric heat combined exceed 50 amps

203. If the backup heat for a heat pump is electric, when should the electric heat be shut off?
     a. When the relative humidity drops below 50 percent
     b. When the system drops below the balance point
     c. When the COP is greater than 3.0
     d. When the system is operating above the balance point

204. With respect to heat pumps, the balance point is the point
     a. at which the heating and cooling capacities are the same.
     b. at which the backup heat capacity and heat pump capacity are the same.
     c. at which the heat pump can just keep up with the heat loss.
     d. below which the backup heat must be abandoned.

205. Frost on the outdoor coil of a heat pump indicates a
     a. low refrigerant charge.
     b. high refrigerant charge.
     c. problem with the condensate system.
     d. normal operating condition.

206. A water source heat pump
     a. can be an open or closed system.
     b. typically uses water from the house plumbing system.
     c. has two piping systems buried directly in the earth.
     d. has a very limited capacity for heating and cooling.

207. Which of the following components would be found on a heat pump but NOT on a central air-conditioning system?
     a. Compressor
     b. Expansion device
     c. Reversing valve
     d. Indoor coil

208. Which of the following components would be found on a heat pump but *NOT* on a central air-conditioning system?
     a. Outdoor air fan
     b. Emergency heat switch
     c. Crankcase heater
     d. Insulated suction line

209. The purpose of the outdoor-air temperature sensor on a heat pump is to
     a. tell the heat pump when to come on.
     b. shut down the heat pump when the outdoor temperature is too low.
     c. tell the defroster when to come on.
     d. prevent freeze-up of the outdoor coil.

210. A two-stage thermostat is common on a heat pump. Its function is to
     a. allow a setback setting for the thermostat for nights.
     b. activate the backup heat when needed.
     c. engage both stages of a two-stage compressor.
     d. prevent a large surge in electrical demand when the heat pump and backup heat come on.

211. On a heat pump, an accumulator is
    a. a storage spot for excess liquid Freon.
    b. a storage spot for excess gas Freon.
    c. never found on a heat pump.
    d. located just downstream of the expansion device.

212. How much air should move past a three-ton heat pump indoor coil every minute?
    a. 450 cubic feet
    b. 900 cubic feet
    c. 1,350 cubic feet
    d. 1,800 cubic feet

213. Above which outdoor temperature should you avoid testing a heat pump in the heating mode?
    a. 50°F
    b. 60°F
    c. 65°F
    d. 75°F

214. Below which outdoor temperature should you avoid testing a heat pump in the cooling mode?
    a. 85°F
    b. 75°F
    c. 70°F
    d. 65°F

215. Which is the best location for an outdoor coil on a heat pump?
    a. Under the drip line of the roof
    b. On the east side of the house
    c. Under a deck
    d. With its base one inch below grade level to avoid snow blowing under the unit

216. All of these are causes for inoperative heat pumps in heating mode *EXCEPT* if the
    a. outdoor temperature is 47°F.
    b. system is set for Emergency Heat.
    c. outdoor temperature is (−10)°F.
    d. outdoor temperature is below the balance point temperature and the backup heat is a gas furnace.

217. With respect to heat pumps, weak airflow on forced-air systems at the registers is caused by all of these *EXCEPT*
    a. a dirty filter.
    b. a clogged indoor coil.
    c. dirt on the fan blades.
    d. a low refrigerant charge.

218. Backup heat problems on heat pumps include all of the following *EXCEPT* the backup heat
    a. doesn't operate, although the thermostat is calling for it to operate.
    b. operates constantly.
    c. operates every time the heat pump operates and the outdoor temperature is 45°F.
    d. is controlled by the second stage of a two-stage thermostat.

219. If a heat pump compressor has been running and is shut off, it should not be turned back on for five minutes because
    a. the refrigerant pressure on the discharge side is too high.
    b. the refrigerant pressure on the discharge side is too low.
    c. the refrigerant is too cold.
    d. the oil needs to return to the sump before the system can start up.

220. The single most expensive and important component of a heat pump is the
    a. expansion device.
    b. compressor.
    c. condenser coil.
    d. evaporator coil.

221. Types of heat pumps include all of the following *EXCEPT*
    a. a water-to-water system.
    b. a water-to-air system.
    c. an earth-to-air system.
    d. a bivalent system.

222. If operating a heat pump in the heating mode when the outdoor temperature is above 65°F, it may
    a. overheat the home.
    b. damage the defrost system.
    c. damage the compressor.
    d. damage the expansion device.

223. If operating a heat pump in the cooling mode when the temperature is below 60°F to 65°F, it
    a. maximizes the efficiency.
    b. minimizes the efficiency.
    c. risks damaging the compressor.
    d. overloads the crankcase heater.

224. The purpose of the Emergency Heat switch on a heat pump is
    a. to lock out the backup heat.
    b. to bypass the heat pump.
    c. to bypass the thermostat.
    d. to have both the backup heat and the heat pump operating simultaneously.

225. A heat pump should go into the defrost mode if an ice build-up is
    a. visible.
    b. more than ⅛-inch-thick.
    c. more than ¼-inch-thick.
    d. more than ½-inch-thick.

226. Why does ice build up on the outdoor section of the heat pump?
    a. The heat pump is faulty.
    b. The cold outdoor air has high relative humidity.
    c. The outside temperature is too cold for the heat pump to be operating.
    d. The system is locked in the cooling mode, rather than in the heating mode.

227. The electric backup heating system on a heat pump should be
    a. upstream of the indoor coil.
    b. downstream of the indoor coil.
    c. interlocked, so that the electric heat will not be on when the heat pump is on.
    d. interlocked, so that the electric heat must be on when the heat pump is on.

228. A bivalent heat pump has
    a. two outdoor coils.
    b. a gas burner.
    c. a defrost cycle.
    d. electric backup heat.

229. When a heat pump is operating in 35°F weather, the temperature of the liquid refrigerant line upstream of the expansion device may be
    a. 30°–50°F.
    b. 78°–90°F.
    c. 105°–115°F.
    d. over 120°F.

230. When a heat pump is operating in 35°F weather, the temperature of the liquid refrigerant line downstream of the expansion device may be
    a. below 30°F.
    b. 30°–50°F.
    c. 70°–90°F.
    d. 100°–120°F.

231. When a heat pump is operating in 35°F weather, the temperature of the refrigerant line immediately downstream of the compressor may be
    a. 70°–90°F.
    b. 100°–120°F.
    c. 120°–140°F.
    d. over 140°F.

232. Conventional air-cooled central air-conditioning systems help to cool the home. They are also capable of
    a. heating the home.
    b. dehumidifying the home.
    c. humidifying the home.
    d. deionizing the house air.

233. Which of the following statements about the refrigerant Freon is *FALSE?*
    a. It is noncorrosive.
    b. It is nonflammable.
    c. It is nontoxic.
    d. It is a liquid at atmospheric temperature and pressure.

234. In the evaporator coil of an air-cooled air conditioner, Freon
    a. heats up as it changes from a liquid to a gas.
    b. cools as it changes from a gas to a liquid.
    c. cools as it changes from a liquid to a gas.
    d. changes from a warm liquid to a cool liquid.

235. In the condenser coil of an air-cooled air conditioner, the refrigerant
    a. heats up as it changes from a liquid to a gas.
    b. cools as it changes from a gas to a liquid.
    c. cools as it changes from a liquid to a gas.
    d. changes from a warm liquid to a cool liquid.

236. In the compressor of an air-cooled air conditioner, the refrigerant
    a. heats up as it expands.
    b. cools as it expands.
    c. changes from a liquid to a gas.
    d. heats up as it is squeezed.

237. In the metering device of an air-cooled air conditioner
    a. the warm gas changes to a cool gas.
    b. the warm liquid changes to a cool liquid.
    c. the pressure on the gas is increased.
    d. the gas condenses to a liquid.

238. The latent heat of vaporization is
    a. the energy consumed when converting water at 212°F to steam at 212°F.
    b. the amount of heat consumed in converting steam to one pound of water.
    c. the equivalent of 180 Btu.
    d. the amount of heat required to raise the temperature of steam from 212°F to 970°F.

239. Lower humidity levels in the home during the summer are more comfortable for people because
    a. their skin doesn't dry out as much.
    b. the air can absorb more cooking moisture and odors.
    c. it is easier for moisture on the skin to evaporate.
    d. mold and mildew cannot form.

240. The function of a compressor in an air-conditioning system is to
    a. convert the gas to a liquid.
    b. warm up the cool liquid.
    c. warm up the cool gas.
    d. convert the liquid to a gas.

241. The purpose of the crankcase heater on an air-conditioning compressor is to
    a. help the system defrost.
    b. warm the Freon so that it can be condensed.
    c. boil the refrigerant out of the lubricating oil.
    d. heat the lubricating oil to reduce its viscosity.

242. An air conditioner compressor often does not start up for five-minutes-or-so if it has been shut off for just a few seconds because this allows
    a. the pressures on the suction and discharge side of the compressor to equalize.
    b. the Freon on the suction side of the compressor to heat up.
    c. the Freon on the discharge side of the compressor to cool down.
    d. avoiding damage to the evaporator coil.

243. Which of the following is not a common problem with an air conditioner compressor?
    a. Excess noise or vibration
    b. Inoperativity
    c. Short cycling or running continuously
    d. Overcooling the Freon in the condenser

244. Where is the condenser on a split-system, air-cooled central air-conditioning system located?
    a. In the attic
    b. In the furnace cabinet
    c. In the outdoor cabinet anywhere inside the house
    d. Adjacent to the metering device

245. Which of the following is NOT a common problem with condenser coils?
    a. Exposure to direct sunlight
    b. Mechanical damage
    c. Rust
    d. Having less than six feet of clearance from the discharge side

246. Which of the following statements about conventional water-cooled air-conditioning systems is FALSE?
    a. The condenser is often located indoors.
    b. There is no fan associated with this condenser coil.
    c. The heat is typically dissipated into water drawn from the swimming pool.
    d. The water passing through the coil is typically a single-pass system.

247. Which of the following is NOT a common location for an evaporator coil in a split-system air conditioner?
    a. The attic
    b. The furnace supply plenum
    c. A cabinet outside at grade level
    d. A basement

248. The implications of a dirty evaporator coil in a split-system air conditioner could be any of the following except for one. Which one does NOT apply?
    a. The airflow is restricted.
    b. The cooling is inadequate.
    c. The compressor may be damaged trying to pump a liquid rather than a gas.
    d. The condenser coil may ice up and be damaged.

249. Frost on the evaporator coil of a split-system air conditioner may mean that
    a. there is excess air flow over the coil.
    b. there is a dirty air filter.
    c. there is an oversized fan.
    d. the ducts are oversized.

250. Which is the most precise expansion device for an air conditioner on this list?
    a. Filter/dryer
    b. Capillary tube
    c. Thermostatic expansion valve
    d. Capacitor

251. Which of the following is *NOT* a common problem with a condensate collection system on a split-system air conditioner?
    a. The condensate goes into a ¾-inch drain line.
    b. The pan is leaking.
    c. The drain is blocked.
    d. The discharge point is improper.

252. A trap in the condensate line of a split-system air conditioner
    a. is more important on pans upstream of the house air fan.
    b. is not required if the condensate drains into a waste plumbing stack.
    c. prevents heated air in the winter from being blown outside through the condensate drain line.
    d. will not work if the condensate drain line is under negative pressure.

253. The liquid refrigerant line in a split-system air-conditioning system
    a. is the larger of the two copper lines.
    b. runs from the condenser to the expansion device.
    c. is the low-pressure side of the system.
    d. is cooler than the suction line when the system is operating.

254. Central air conditioners are most like which household appliance?
    a. Stove
    b. Refrigerator
    c. Microwave oven
    d. Garbage disposal

255. Condenser fans in split-system air conditioners are typically located
    a. in the attic.
    b. in the furnace plenum.
    c. outside.
    d. just upstream of the duct heater.

256. The function of the condenser fan in split-system air conditioners is to
    a. cool the refrigerant by boiling it.
    b. heat the refrigerant by boiling it.
    c. cool the refrigerant by turning it into a liquid.
    d. heat the refrigerant by turning it into a liquid.

257. Which of the following statements about evaporator fans in a split-system air conditioner is *FALSE?*
    a. The evaporator fan should move roughly 100 cfm of air for each ton of air conditioning.
    b. The fan can be belt driven.
    c. The fan can be direct driven.
    d. The fan can be part of a fan coil unit.

258. Which of the following statements about air-conditioning ducts is *FALSE?*
    a. They can use the same ducts as the heating system.
    b. They cannot be flexible ducts.
    c. They should be larger than heating ducts in cold climates.
    d. They can use returns made of combustible materials.

259. The ideal location for a supply register on an air-conditioning system is
    a. at or near floor level on an outside wall.
    b. at or near floor level on an interior wall.
    c. at or near ceiling level on an exterior wall.
    d. at or near ceiling level on an interior wall.

260. The ideal location for a return grille on an air-conditioning system is
    a. at or near floor level on an outside wall.
    b. at or near floor level on an interior wall.
    c. at or near ceiling level on an exterior wall.
    d. at or near ceiling level on an interior wall.

261. Common problems with duct systems for air conditioners include all of the following *EXCEPT*
    a. too few supply or return registers.
    b. poor location for supply and return registers.
    c. obstructed registers.
    d. oversized ducts.

262. Which of the following statements about air-conditioning thermostats is *FALSE?*
    a. The thermostat can control both the heating and cooling systems.
    b. The thermostat typically turns on the house fan, condenser fan, and compressor all at the same time.
    c. The thermostat should be located in the warmest room of the house in order to provide the best cooling.
    d. A mechanical thermostat must be installed approximately level.

263. Which of the following statements about evaporative coolers is *FALSE?*
    a. They are also known as swamp coolers.
    b. They use a recirculating duct system.
    c. They include an air handler, a water reservoir, and a pump.
    d. They may be rotary, spray, or drip type.

264. Which of the following statements about an evaporative cooler is true?
    a. These units dehumidify and cool the home.
    b. These units are suitable in the southeastern United States.
    c. An air gap should be provided for the water reservoir.
    d. The system should be interconnected with the house heating duct system.

265. Several things may cause an evaporative cooler to leak. They include all of the following *EXCEPT*
    a. the water tray may rust.
    b. drains may become obstructed.
    c. the condensate trap may split.
    d. spider tubes may split.

266. Which of the following statements about whole-house fans is *FALSE?*
    a. House air is typically drawn from the top story of the home and discharged into the attic.
    b. The whole-house fan is not really an air-conditioning system.
    c. When the fan is not running, louvers below the fan fall closed.
    d. The fan operation is interlocked with the house heating thermostat.

ANSWERS AND EXPLANATIONS

1. **b.** Grilles allow us to modulate the direction the air is flowing, but not the volume of airflow.

2. **b.** The reason a vent should slope up away from a high-efficiency furnace is to allow any condensate in the vent to run back to the furnace so it can be collected and carried away.

3. **a.** Upflow, downflow, and horizontal furnaces can use the same monoport burners.

4. **b.** Backdraft, sometimes referred to as spillage, occurs when combustion products flow out of the furnace into the room through the burner or draft hood, rather than up the chimney. This is a life-threatening situation.

5. **a.** Single-wall vents require a six-inch combustible clearance. B-vents, which are double-walled, with an air space between the walls, require only a one-inch clearance.

6. **b.** The fan control switch is an operating control, not a safety control.

7. **b.** The most significant implication of heat exchanger problems is the possibility of exhaust products leaking in the house air. This is a life-threatening situation.

8. **b.** Because gravity furnaces do not have fans, they do not need a fan control switch.

9. **b.** Some new, energy-efficient oil burners do not use a draft damper.

10. **b.** Power venters can be used with oil equipment in some areas to reduce the risk of backdrafting on an excessively long flue.

11. **b.** When multiple vent connectors go into the same chimney, the vent from the smaller input appliance (the water heater) should go above the vent from the bigger appliance (the furnace).

12. **a.** The oil filter on an oil furnace is similar in size and shape to the one on a car.

13. **b.** Oil burners in conventional oil furnaces are forced draft.

14. **a.** Make sure that combustibles (including drywall) are at least 24 inches from the oil burner.

15. **b.** Because of the high temperature of oil combustion products (around 500°F) aluminum generally is not allowed. Some areas may permit it if it is very thick.

16. **b.** Oil burners typically are outside the furnace cabinet.

17. **b.** A few closed systems do not have pumps (circulators).

18. **b.** Even if the balancing valve is completely shut off, there will still be water in the radiator.

19. **a.** Pressure-relief valves come in various sizes, and it is possible to have one that is too small for the boiler. The relief valve setting should always be equal-to-or-greater-than the burner rating.

20. **b.** The pressure-reducing valve maintains an adequate amount of water in the boiler at the desired pressure (12 psi to 15 psi). It is an operating control. The pressure-relief valve is the safety control that prevents high pressure within the boiler.

21. **b.** Outdoor air thermostats are used more in commercial than residential construction, although you may find them in large homes.

22. **b.** Bleed valves are used to let trapped air out, so the water can circulate properly.

23. **b.** Boilers, like furnaces, require venting systems to exhaust combustion products out of the house.

24. **b.** An air vent is not mandatory, although some boilers come with an integral vent.

25. **b.** The elements in an electric furnace are not visible after removing the cover designed for homeowner access.

26. **b.** When you compress gas, you heat it.

27. **b.** The evaporator coil is indoors in a split system.

28. **b.** Undersized ducts are a common problem; oversized ducts are not common.

29. **a.** Many air-conditioning manufacturers and installers recommend slightly undersizing an air-conditioning system rather than oversizing it.

30. **a.** The difference in temperature between the conditioned air and the room air is about 15°F to 20°F.

31. **b.** Evaporator coils must be downstream of gas, oil, or propane furnace heat exchangers.

32. **a.** The compressor is the pump that drives the Freon through the system.

33. **b.** On conventional split-system air-conditioning systems, the compressor is located in the condenser cabinet outdoors or in the attic.

34. **b.** The larger refrigerant line typically carries a cool gas.

35. **b.** The smaller refrigerant line is called the liquid line.

36. **a.** The larger refrigerant line is called the return line or the suction line.

37. **b.** Flexible ducts have far more friction loss than rigid ducts do.

38. **c.** One Btu is the amount of heat required to raise one pound of water one Fahrenheit degree.

39. **b.** Induction is not a primary heat transfer method.

40. **a.** It takes about 15 cubic feet of air to burn one cubic foot of gas.

41. **c.** A typical furnace room needs two openings, one near the bottom and one near the top. In this case, each one should be 100 square inches (one square inch for every 1,000 Btus).

42. **a.** Natural gas is lighter than air.

43. **c.** An inactive flame is not a problem.

44. **b.** Flashback or flame rollout is not caused by a cracked heat exchanger.

45. **a.** Heat exchangers separate the combustion air from the house air.

46. **d.** When one burner won't ignite, it is usually a crossover igniter problem.

47. **d.** If the flame touches the heat exchanger, the burner is probably misaligned.

48. **b.** The fan/limit switch typically turns the blower on at 150°F. In some modern systems it can be considerably lower (as low as 120°F).

49. **b.** The high limit setting is typically 200°F.

50. **b.** The anticipator stops the furnace before it is quite heated up to reduce overshoot (overheating of the house).

51. **d.** The best location for a thermostat is on an interior dining room wall close to a light switch. The light switch is not a heat source.

52. **b.** The house air fan should not come on before the gas valve opens or the burner ignites.

53. **b.** The seasonal efficiency is less than the steady state efficiency.

54. **c.** Corrosion in the draft hood and on the access cover indicates back drafting.

55. **b.** Heat exchanger failure may lead to spillage but not soot buildup on burner side of heat exchanger.

56. **a.** The temperature of exhaust products from conventional gas furnaces is about 300°F to 350°F.

57. **b.** Duct location does not affect the amount of air delivered to each room.

58. **d.** It is not a common problem to find house air fans installed backwards.

59. **b.** Filter problems do not include installing the filter upstream of the blower. That is where the filter should be.

60. **c.** If the supply and return are too close together, the return will simply pull the supply air back in, short-circuiting the system.

61. **a.** The supply plenum is too close to the wood.

62. **c.** The best place for supply registers is low on exterior walls.

63. **d.** Uninsulated ducts will not result in poor air flow.

64. **a.** A vent damper stuck open is not a life safety problem. The chimney will vent properly.

65. **c.** Off-cycle losses are roughly 20 percent.

66. **c.** Induced draft fans most often do not have standing pilots.

67. **d.** Thermocouples are not usually found in midefficiency gas furnaces.

68. **c.** Reverse draft is not a draft mechanism.

69. **c.** If the furnace vent pressure is positive, the water heater may not be able to draft properly. This may cause backdrafting through the draft hood of the water heater.

70. **a.** Midefficiency gas-fired furnaces can be side-wall vented.

71. **c.** Induced draft fans do not condense the exhaust gases.

72. **b.** You won't normally have a draft hood with an induced-draft fan on a midefficiency furnace.

73. **c.** High-efficiency furnaces condense exhaust gases and reduce the temperature rise across the heat exchanger.

74. **b.** A typical temperature rise on a high-efficiency furnace is 35°F to 65°F or 40°F to 70°F.

75. **d.** Corrosion inside a high-efficiency gas furnace blower compartment may indicate humidifier leakage, condensate line blockage, or an induced-draft fan failure.

76. **a.** Direct vent heating systems take combustion air from outside the dwelling. That is the definition.

77. **a.** The condensation is the result, not the goal. The goal is to collect the latent heat of vaporization.

78. **c.** Supply and return duct insulation is usually provided for the first few feet moving away from the furnace. However, the insulation is on the interior, not the exterior, of the duct.

79. **c.** Efficiencies of over 90 percent have been claimed.

80. **b.** The temperature of the condensate is 100°F to 150°F.

81. **d.** Because the gases are cool, the combustibility of the deck isn't a problem. Because there is a lot of moisture, rot is the issue.

82. **d.** A pulse furnace does not have an induced-draft fan.

83. **b.** Vent damper problems won't be common with high-efficiency furnaces, because they don't have vent dampers.

84. **c.** Vibration is not a common heat exchanger problem.

85. **b.** Condensate lines do not need an automatic air vent.

86. **b.** Sidewall vents should be at least one foot off the ground.

87. **b.** Improper slope on a high-efficiency furnace exhaust flue may result in frost closure at the discharge.

88. **d.** No combustible clearances are required for a high-efficiency furnace exhaust flue.

89. **b.** Flame sensors are used to detect combustion in a direct-spark ignition furnace.

90. **c.** Combination furnaces use a single burner to heat both the house space and the domestic hot water.

91. **a.** A conventional gas furnace is expected to last 20–25 years.

92. **c.** One gallon of #2 heating oil contains approximately 140,000 Btus.

93. **d.** Oil furnace burners are very different from gas furnace burners as gas burners do not have blast tubes.

94. **c.** If the entire outside of the oil tank is rusting, this could well be the clothes dryer venting into the tank area. The warm, moist air may condense on the cool metal.

95. **b.** A failed fire pot will not prevent a burner from operating.

96. **b.** A ragged, black-edged, yellow flame is normal on a conventional oil burner. More modern burners have a smoother flame.

97. **a.** A ceramic felt combustion chamber that is brown and stained is probably saturated with oil.

98. **a.** The primary control senses combustion in an oil furnace.

99. **b.** The primary control is on the burner on a retention head system.

100. **c.** The barometric damper is on the exhaust flue.

101. **a.** If atmospheric pressure were greater than the flue pressure, the barometric damper would open. (This is a normal operating condition.) Most likely damper is seized.

102. **d.** The required clearance from combustibles for an oil furnace vent connector is 9 inches on modern systems. On some older systems, it is 18 inches. Because the 18-inch answer is not available, the most correct answer is 9 inches.

103. **c.** Loose fittings at plastic connections are not an issue on oil furnaces. Plastic connections would not be used on vent connectors for oil furnaces.

104. **b.** A high-static burner uses higher air and oil pressure.

105. **d.** The maximum steady state efficiency for an oil burner is about 87 percent.

106. **d.** Aluminum tubing is not used for heat exchangers.

107. **a.** Heat is transferred through the heat exchanger by conduction.

108. **d.** Heat is transferred from the radiator into the room by both convection and radiation.

109. **c.** Piping in boiler systems is rarely made from galvanized steel.

110. **c.** Boilers get make-up water from the house plumbing system.

111. **c.** The pressure-relief valve prevents the formation of superheated water.

112. **c.** Superheated water is above 212°F at higher than atmospheric pressures and can cause steam explosions.

113. **a.** Superheated water, when released, will not turn to liquid. It is already liquid. The problem is that it will turn to steam.

114. **d.** A boiler that has a cracked heat exchanger will periodically leak.

115. **b.** Fresh water will cause rusting in the pipes because it contains fresh oxygen.

116. **b.** Copper tube boilers should always have the pump running when the burner is firing, so that the heat exchanger does not overheat.

117. **d.** The common high temperature limit setting is 210°F.

118. **b.** The outdoor air thermostat may fire the burner as it gets colder outside.

119. **d.** A pipe extension that is clogged is not going to cause a pressure-relief valve to drip.

120. **c.** Tall houses need higher pressure settings.

121. **b.** The normal operating cut in temperature for a circulator on a cast iron boiler is anywhere from 110°F to 140°F.

122. **c.** Circulators should not be mounted at the lowest point in the piping.

123. **a.** Zone control can be achieved with multiple circulators or multiple flow control valves.

124. **b.** The expansion tank in an oil system is typically located above the highest radiator.

125. **c.** A closed expansion tank is typically at about the same elevation as the boiler.

126. **a.** A reverse-return system yields more evenly distributed heat than a single-pipe system.

127. **c.** Heat distribution can be balanced by adjusting the valves at each radiator.

128. **b.** A waterlogged expansion tank may cause the pressure-relief valve to drip. That is because pressure builds up and may exceed 30 psi.

129. **b.** The typical pressure in a boiler at rest is 10–15 psi.

130. **c.** The typical pressure for a boiler at rest in a three story house is also 10–15 psi. It is likely to be close to 15 psi. It isn't usually above that, because that is the maximum setting on most pressure-reducing valves.

131. **c.** Circulators are not controlled by pressure-relief valves.

132. **a.** Radiators deliver the greatest amount of heat-per-length.

133. **b.** The radiators should be on exterior walls below windows.

134. **c.** The radiator has to be high in the room if it is a basement and an open system. Otherwise heat will never flow to that radiator.

135. **d.** Nickel is not used for radiant piping systems.

136. **b.** Tankless coil boilers require that the main house boiler be kept hot all year round.

137. **a.** The problem in designing a high-efficiency boiler is that the return water temperature is too high.

138. **c.** The prepurge system removes any unburned fuel from the combustion chamber.

139. **d.** Cast iron boilers have a life expectancy of 35–50 years.

140. **c.** Back flow preventers keep the boiler water out of the drinking water.

141. **b.** Pressure-reducing valves are typically connected to the supply plumbing.

142. **c.** Air vents are sometimes called air eliminators.

143. **a.** A stack relay does not keep water hot on standby.

144. **d.** Flow-control valves prevent circulation of hot water when system is at rest.

145. **a.** Circulator pumps are sometimes noisy.

146. **b.** A common problem with radiators is when they are on the same system with convectors. A combination of radiators and convectors (baseboards) can result in uneven, uncomfortable heating, because these components heat up and cool down at different rates.

147. **c.** It is not common or proper for a tankless coil to be in direct contact with boiler water.

148. **c.** In older homes, which are more drafty and poorly insulated, 30–60 Btu-per-square-foot of heat is required.

149. **a.** It is not a disadvantage that there is no fan or pump to move heat through the system.

150. **c.** There is no such thing as a two-pipe, reverse-flow steam system.

151. **b.** You would find a pressure gauge on a steam system.

152. **b.** Boilers, piping, and radiators are most commonly cast iron.

153. **a.** A water temperature and pressure gauge would be found on a hot water boiler.

154. **a.** A typical steam pressure in a single family residential steam boiler would be 0.5 psi to 5 psi.

155. **c.** When the system is at rest, you will find air and water in the boiler.

156. **b.** When the heating system is at work, you would expect to find steam and condensed water in the radiators.

157. **b.** An equalizer pipe helps to equalize the steam pressure on the supply and return sides of the boiler.

158. **a.** A pressure-relief valve will not shut off the boiler.

159. **c.** A Hartford Loop prevents water from leaking out of the boiler if the wet return leaks.

160. **d.** An appropriate slope in a two-pipe system is 1-inch-in-20-feet.

161. **d.** The air vents in a one-pipe parallel flow system are typically located at the radiators and at the end of the return mains.

162. **d.** Steam traps are typically located on the return pipe from each rad on a two-pipe system, and at the end of the supply mains on two-pipe systems.

163. **b.** An F & T trap is a float and thermostatic trap.

164. **a.** Condensate pumps are used on one-pipe and two-pipe systems.

165. **c.** Pressure-relief valve on steam systems are normally set at 15 psi.

166. **c.** A blowdown valve is used to test and flush the low water cutout.

167. **a.** Electric furnaces do not necessarily have greater input capacity than gas or oil furnaces.

168. **d.** An electric heating system has an overcurrent protection device.

169. **c.** A 20-kilowatt electric furnace would draw approximately ($P = VI$, $I = P/V$, $I = 20,000$), ($20,000/240$) = 83.3 amps.

170. **b.** A 20-kilowatt electric furnace would have an output capacity of $3,412 \times 20 = 68,640$ Btus-per-hour.

171. **c.** Duct heaters are not space heaters.

172. **a.** Space heaters may be forced-air or convection systems.

173. **c.** Electrical receptacles installed beside heaters are not a problem. Receptacles installed above heaters are a problem.

174. **d.** Drapes should be hung eight inches above baseboard heaters.

175. **b.** We don't want receptacles above heaters because an electric cord resting on the heater is a fire hazard.

176. **d.** Electric fans should not stay on after the thermostat is satisfied.

177. **d.** A 120-volt heater powered by 240 volts is likely to overheat.

178. **b.** A sequencer on an electric furnace ensures that individual elements do not all come on at the same time.

179. **a.** A staged electric furnace activates only the elements that are required to meet the heat loss.

180. **d.** Ducts for electric furnaces typically are larger than ducts for gas or oil furnaces.

181. **c.** Electric boilers will not have a draft hood.

182. **a.** Flex Heat radiant panels are unsafe and should be removed from houses.

183. **b.** Wire embedded in lightweight concrete is not a common radiant ceiling heating system. Wires can be embedded in concrete or mortar under tile floors, but not usually in ceilings.

184. **d.** Wall and floor furnaces and space heaters are not designed to be connected to duct systems under most circumstances.

185. **d.** Wall furnaces use BW vents.

186. **a.** As long as the ceiling is at least 18 inches above the furnace, there is no problem.

187. **c.** A 2-inch clearance is insufficient. The grate for a floor furnace should be at least 12 inches from doors, drapes, etc.

188. **d.** Mounting the thermostat within six feet of the furnace is not a problem.

189. **c.** Room heaters may be installed in masonry fireplaces.

190. **b.** Gas fireplaces can be rated as space heaters.

191. **b.** Gas logs must be vented either through a chimney or a direct vent system.

192. **d.** A common problem with gas fireplaces and gas log installations is the damper in the existing fireplace not being fixed open.

193. **d.** It is acceptable to have a gas-fired room heater without outdoor combustion air supply.

194. **c.** For the purposes of inspection, fireplace inserts should be treated as wood stoves.

195. **b.** Heat pumps are designed to capture heat from the outdoors and bring it into the home.

196. **d.** When a heat pump is in the heating mode, the indoor coil is the condenser.

197. **c.** Heat pumps may have two expansion devices.

198. **d.** The reversing valve changes the direction of the refrigerant flow.

199. **a.** The capacity of the heat pump is usually determined by the cooling load.

200. **b.** If the heat pump is sized for the heating load, it may be oversized for the cooling load.

201. **a.** The coefficient of performance is variable with outdoor temperature.

202. **b.** If the backup heat is electric, the heat pump should shut off when the COP is below 1.0.

203. **d.** If the backup heat is electric, the electric heat should be shut off when the system is operating above the balance point.

204. **c.** The balance point is the point at which the heat pump can just keep up with the heat loss from the building.

205. **d.** Frost on the outdoor coil is a normal operating condition.

206. **a.** A water source heat pump can be an open or closed system.

207. **c.** A reversing valve is found on a heat pump but not an air conditioner.

208. **b.** An emergency heat switch would be found on a heat pump but not on an air conditioner.

209. **b.** The purpose of the outdoor air temperature sensor on a heat pump is to shut down the heat pump when the outdoor temperature is too low.

210. **b.**   A two-stage thermostat activates the backup heat when needed.

211. **a.**   An accumulator is a storage spot for excess liquid Freon.

212. **c.**   Roughly 1,350 cubic feet of air should move past a three-ton heat pump coil every minute.

213. **c.**   You should not test a heat pump in the heating mode when the outdoor temperature is above 65°F.

214. **d.**   You should not test a heat pump in the cooling mode when the outdoor temperature is below 65°F.

215. **b.**   The best location for an outdoor coil on a heat pump may be on the east side of the house. The other choices listed are situations where airflow to the heat pump may be obstructed or the heat pump may be exposed to moisture.

216. **a.**   If the outdoor temperature is 47°F, the heat pump should be operative.

217. **d.**   Weak air flow is not caused by a low refrigerant charge.

218. **d.**   The backup heat is typically controlled by the second stage of a two-stage thermostat.

219. **a.**   If the compressor has been turned off, it should not be turned back on for five minutes because the refrigerant pressure on the discharge side of the compressor is too high.

220. **b.**   The most expensive and important component of the heat pump is the compressor.

221. **a.**   A water-to-water heat pump system is not a common residential type.

222. **c.**   Operating the heat pump in the heating mode when the outdoor temperature is above 65°F may damage the compressor.

223. **c.**   There may be a risk of damaging the compressor if the heat pump is operated in the cooling mode when the temperature is below 65°F.

224. **b.**   The Emergency Heat switch bypasses the heat pump.

225. **b.**   The heat pump should go into the defrost mode if an ice build-up is more than ⅛-inch thick.

226. **b.**   Ice builds up on the outdoor section of the heat pump because the cold outdoor air has a relatively high humidity. When cooling this outdoor air by passing it over the cold evaporator coil, the outdoor air is saturated, raising its relative humidity to 100 percent.

227. **b.**   The electric backup heating system on a heat pump should be downstream of the indoor coil.

228. **b.**   A bivalent heat pump has a gas burner.

229. **c.**   When the heat pump is operating in 35°F weather, the liquid refrigerant line upstream of the expansion device will typically be at 105°–115°F.

230. **a.**   When a heat pump is operating in 35°F weather, the liquid refrigerant line downstream of the expansion device may be below 30°F.

231. **d.**   When a heat pump is operating in 35°F weather, the refrigerant line temperature immediately downstream of the compressor may be over 140°F.

232. **b.**   Central air-conditioning systems also help to dehumidify the home.

233. **d.**   Freon is not a liquid at atmospheric temperature and pressure.

234. **a.**   Freon heats up as it turns from a liquid to a gas in the evaporator.

235. **b.**   The refrigerant cools as it changes from a gas to a liquid in the condenser.

236. **d.**   The refrigerant heats up as it is squeezed in the compressor.

237. **b.**   The warm liquid changes to a cool liquid in the metering device.

238. **a.**   The latent heat of vaporization is the energy consumed when converting water at 212°F to steam at 212°F.

239. **c.**   Lower humidity levels in the home are more comfortable because it is easier for moisture on the skin to evaporate.

240. **c.**   The function of a compressor is to warm up the cool gas.

241. **c.**   The crankcase heater on a compressor boils the refrigerant out of the lubricating oil.

242. **a.** A compressor should stay off for five minutes before restarting to allow the pressures on the suction and discharge side of the compressor to equalize.

243. **d.** Overcooling the Freon in the condenser is not a common problem with a compressor.

244. **c.** The condenser is in an outdoor cabinet near the compressor.

245. **a.** It is not a problem to have the condenser exposed to the direct sun.

246. **c.** Water from the swimming pool should not be circulated through a water-cooled air-conditioning system.

247. **c.** Evaporator coils are not located outside.

248. **d.** A dirty coil is not likely to cause damage to the expansion device.

249. **b.** A dirty filter may cause frost on the evaporator coil.

250. **c.** A thermostatic expansion valve is the most precise expansion device.

251. **a.** It is not a problem if the condensate goes into a ¾-inch drain line.

252. **a.** A trap in the condensate line is more important on pans upstream of the house air fan.

253. **b.** The liquid refrigerant line runs from the condenser to the expansion device.

254. **b.** Central air-conditioning and refrigerators operate on the same principle and use similar components to remove heat and dump it outside.

255. **c.** The condenser fan is outside, adjacent to the compressor.

256. **c.** The condenser fan cools the refrigerant by turning it into a liquid.

257. **a.** The evaporator fan should move 400–450 CFM of air for each ton of air conditioning.

258. **b.** Air-conditioning systems can use flexible ducts.

259. **c.** The ideal (but rare) location for a supply register on an air-conditioning system is at or near ceiling level on an exterior wall.

260. **d.** The ideal location for a return air grill is at or near ceiling level on an interior wall.

261. **d.** An oversized duct system is not a common problem.

262. **c.** The thermostat should not be located in the warmest room of the house.

263. **b.** Evaporative coolers do not use a recirculating duct system.

264. **c.** An air gap should be provided for the water reservoir on an evaporative cooler.

265. **c.** There is no condensate trap on an evaporative cooler.

266. **d.** The fan operation is not interlocked with the house heating thermostat.

6. INSULATION AND VENTILATION SYSTEMS

Practice Questions

1. Basement wall insulation is necessary.
   a. True
   b. False

2. All crawl spaces should be vented.
   a. True
   b. False

3. The vapor barrier should be on the warm side of the wall assembly.
   a. True
   b. False

4. Power roof vents should be operated continuously for best results.
   a. True
   b. False

5. Soffit vents typically make up about 25 percent of roof ventilation.
   a. True
   b. False

6. Heat recovery ventilators are usually located in conditioned spaces.
   a. True
   b. False

7. The attic access hatch does NOT need to be insulated.
   a. True
   b. False

8. It is considered good practice to place a vapor barrier on an earthen crawl space floor.
   a. True
   b. False

9. The best way to check that an exhaust fan is moving air adequately is to make sure that air is being pulled into the fan, using your hand or a piece of tissue to check for airflow.
   a. True
   b. False

10. An air barrier performs a different function depending on whether the climate is warm or cool.
    a. True
    b. False

11. Degree-days are
    a. days when the temperature is above 0°F.
    b. the day's average temperature plus 65°F.
    c. the day's average temperature subtracted from 65°F.
    d. the number of days in a year when the heating system is not required.

12. Which statement about heat is *FALSE?*
    a. Heat is the amount of thermal energy in a body.
    b. Heat is measured in degrees Fahrenheit.
    c. Sensible heat is one type of heat.
    d. Heat always moves from an area of high energy to an area of low energy.

13. All the following are mechanisms of heat transfer *EXCEPT*
    a. conduction.
    b. radiation.
    c. convection.
    d. absorption.

14. Which statement about thermal insulators is *FALSE?*
    a. Thermal resistance is the inverse of thermal conductivity.
    b. Good insulators have low R-values.
    c. Good insulators have very low thermal conductivity.
    d. Good insulators are typically low-density.

15. Pick the *FALSE* statement about air leakage in houses. Air leakage
    a. allows heat to escape from the house.
    b. is necessary to provide fresh air.
    c. depends on the wind.
    d. out of a house always exceeds air leakage into a house.

16. All of the following are moisture sources *EXCEPT*
    a. people washing themselves.
    b. drying clothes in a vented clothes dryer.
    c. people breathing.
    d. drying firewood inside a house.

17. Which of the following statements about humidity are *TRUE?*
    a. Relative humidity indicates the amount of moisture in the air relative to the amount it could potentially hold.
    b. Relative humidity indicates the amount of humidity inside the house relative to the humidity outside.
    c. Warm air can hold a lot less moisture than cold air.
    d. Relative humidity over three grams per cubic liter is excessive.

18. Which statement about relative humidity is *TRUE?*
    a. Relative humidity is always greater than absolute humidity.
    b. Relative humidity is always less than absolute humidity.
    c. Relative humidity drops as air temperature rises.
    d. Air at 80 percent relative humidity is considered saturated.

19. Condensation in buildings can cause all the following *EXCEPT*
    a. increased air leakage.
    b. expanding and shrinking wood.
    c. rusting steel.
    d. reduced thermal resistance of insulation.

20. These are all common forms of insulation *EXCEPT*
    a. liquid.
    b. batt.
    c. loose-fill.
    d. foamed-in-place.

21. Which of the following is *NOT* a common residential insulation material?
    a. Cellulose fiber
    b. Mineral wool
    c. Polyvinyl chloride
    d. Polystyrene

22. Which insulation is controversial with respect to health issues?
    a. Polyurethane
    b. Urea formaldehyde
    c. Phenolic board
    d. Vermiculite

23. Air barriers
    a. are only important in warm climates.
    b. help control heat and moisture flow.
    c. help control heat flow only.
    d. help control moisture flow only.

24. Which statement about vapor barriers is *FALSE?*
    a. A vapor barrier is a vapor diffusion retarder.
    b. A vapor barrier has a perm rating of more than one.
    c. A vapor barrier does not have to be continuous to be effective.
    d. We do not want vapor barriers on both the inside and outside of the wall.

25. Which statement about venting roofs is *FALSE?*
    a. Venting roofs helps indoor air quality.
    b. Venting roofs helps cool homes in summer.
    c. Venting roofs helps prevent ice dams.
    d. Venting roofs lowers the attic temperature.

26. All of the following are types of attic vents *EXCEPT*
    a. soffit vents.
    b. ridge vents.
    c. louver vents.
    d. roof vents.

27. Which statement about power vents is true?
    a. They should operate in the winter.
    b. They should be thermostatically controlled to operate below 65°F.
    c. They can depressurize the attic.
    d. They cannot be controlled with a manual switch.

28. Venting the house living space during the winter in climates where heating is required does all the following *EXCEPT*
    a. adding moisture to the house.
    b. reducing odors.
    c. bringing fresh air into the home.
    d. reducing carbon monoxide.

29. Which of the following is *NOT* a house ventilation method?
    a. Exhaust-only
    b. Supply-only
    c. Balanced ventilation system
    d. Direct-vent furnace

30. The average efficiency of an HRV is
    a. 10 percent
    b. 50 percent
    c. 70 percent
    d. 90 percent

31. The appropriate number of air-changes-per-hour in an average house is roughly
    a. 0.3 air-changes-per-hour.
    b. 0.5 air-changes-per-hour.
    c. 1.5 air-changes-per-hour.
    d. 3.0 air-changes-per-hour.

32. Which statement about flow measuring stations on HRVs is *FALSE?*
    a. There should be two flow-measuring stations.
    b. They should be at least 12 inches away from the balancing dampers.
    c. They should be on the insulated ductwork.
    d. They should be connected to gauges to balance the system.

33. Which of the following is *NOT* a defrost system for heat recovery ventilators?
    a. Recirculating the exhaust through the fresh air side
    b. Running house air through the fresh air side
    c. Shutting off the fresh air fan
    d. Directing furnace air to the HRV

34. Common attic access-hatch problems include all the following *EXCEPT*
    a. a lack of insulation.
    b. an oversized access hatches.
    c. a lack of weather-stripping.
    d. missing access hatches.

35. Secondary attics
    a. are often too small to vent.
    b. are common in 1½-story houses.
    c. can only be accessed through ceilings.
    d. are often too small to insulate.

36. Common attic insulation problems include all of the following *EXCEPT*
    a. gaps or voids.
    b. compression.
    c. excess depth.
    d. missing insulation at dropped ceilings.

37. All of the following suggest skylight condensation *EXCEPT*
    a. uniform water accumulation around the perimeter of the light well.
    b. the problem occurs only on the north side of the light well.
    c. the problem occurs only during cold weather.
    d. the problem does not get worse during or after rains.

38. Attic duct problems include all the following *EXCEPT*
    a. oversized ducts.
    b. disconnected ducts.
    c. missing or loose insulation.
    d. missing or damaged air/vapor barriers.

39. Which statement about chimneys and insulation is *TRUE?*
    a. Masonry chimneys can be in contact with any type of insulation.
    b. Masonry chimneys should be in contact with noncombustible insulation only.
    c. Metal chimneys can be in contact with combustible insulation.
    d. Metal vents can be in contact with noncombustible insulation.

40. All of the following are common attic venting problems *EXCEPT*
    a. missing vents.
    b. vents located only at the ridge.
    c. continuous soffit vents with only spot roof vents.
    d. undersized sheathing openings.

41. All of the following are common approaches to insulating flat and cathedral roofs *EXCEPT*
    a. provide no insulation and vent the roof space.
    b. treatment as an attic.
    c. completely fill the roof space with insulation.
    d. provide insulation above the roof sheathing.

42. Which of the following is *NOT* a venting concern with flat roofs?
    a. Vents on all four exposures of the fascia
    b. Vent areas totaling less than ¹⁄₁₅₀ of the roof area
    c. Obstructed vents
    d. Vents on only one side of the roof

43. All of the following suggest possible rot in flat or cathedral roofs *EXCEPT*
    a. sagging or spongy roof surfaces.
    b. sagging plaster or drywall ceilings.
    c. mold or mildew on an interior wall surface.
    d. vents recently added to the roof.

44. Adding fiberglass batt insulation to the exterior surface of uninsulated wood-frame walls is a problem because this may create
    a. convective loops within the stud cavity.
    b. a vapor barrier in the wrong place.
    c. an air barrier in the wrong place.
    d. a double vapor barrier.

45. Rot may occur in wood-frame walls as a result of warm, moist air from the house condensing in the walls. This rot is likely to be most severe
    a. on north walls.
    b. on walls facing prevailing winds.
    c. on walls with lots of windows.
    d. at the bottom of walls.

46. Earthen floors in crawl spaces
    a. should always be vented.
    b. may add considerable moisture to the home.
    c. should be covered with housewrap.
    d. should be treated to prevent animal and pest infestations.

47. All of the following reduce house moisture *EXCEPT*
    a. disconnecting or removing humidifiers.
    b. Operating the furnace blower on low speed.
    c. covering sump pits.
    d. venting the clothes dryer to the outside.

48. All of the following are common exhaust fan problems *EXCEPT*
    a. inoperativeness.
    b. inadequate air movement.
    c. timer control.
    d. missing fan cover.

49. Which of the following is a problem with an HRV?
    a. Warm-side ducts not insulated
    b. No flap on exterior inlet
    c. Inlet and exhaust separated by 12 inches
    d. Balancing dampers provided on warm-side ducts

ANSWERS AND EXPLANATIONS

1. **b.** Insulating the basement will help to reduce heating costs and may improve comfort, but it is not a requirement.

2. **b.** Heated crawl spaces need not be vented. Unheated crawl spaces should be vented to remove warm, moist air in cold climates.

3. **a.** The vapor barrier should be on the warm side of the wall to prevent moisture from moving into the cooler space where it may condense and cause damage.

4. **b.** Power roof vents tend to depressurize the attic in winter, promoting entry of warm, moist air.

5. **b.** Soffit vents typically make up at least 50 percent of the roof ventilation. Ridge, roof, or gable vents make up the balance.

6. **a.** Heat recovery ventilators (HRVs) are balanced ventilation systems that improve energy efficiency. Putting them in unconditioned spaces such as garages or attics is considered poor practice because this reduces the energy efficiency.

7. **b.** The attic access hatch should be insulated, ideally to the same level as the rest of the attic.

8. **a.** Placing a vapor barrier on an earthen crawl space floor keeps moisture in the ground, rather than diffusing it into the air and adding to the moisture levels in the crawl space and house.

9. **b.** The best way to check exhaust fan airflow is at the exhaust point, but this is often difficult to access.

10. **b.** Air barriers have the same purpose regardless of climate. They are designed to stop air movement through the building walls and roof.

11. **c.** Degree days are calculated by subtracting the average temperature for the day from 65°F.

12. **b.** Heat is measured in Btus or joules; temperature is measured in degrees Fahrenheit.

13. **d.** Absorption is not a heat transfer mechanism.

14. **b.** Good insulators have high R-values.

15. **d.** The air leakage out of a house cannot exceed the air leakage into the house, otherwise the house would collapse.

16. **b.** Drying clothes in a clothes dryer actually removes moisture from the house, assuming the clothes dryer is vented outside.

17. **a.** Relative humidity indicates the amount of moisture in the air relative to the amount that it can potentially hold.

18. **c.** Relative humidity drops as temperature rises, assuming there are no other factors at play.

19. **a.** Condensation cannot cause increased air leakage.

20. **a.** Liquid is not a common form of insulation.

21. **c.** Polyvinyl chloride is not a common insulation material.

22. **b.** Urea formaldehyde is a controversial insulation material.

23. **c.** Air barriers help to control heat flow only.

24. **b.** A vapor barrier has a perm rating of less than one.

25. **a.** Venting roofs has no effect on indoor air quality.

26. **c.** Louver vents are not a specific description of a type of roof vent or attic vent.

27. **c.** Power vents can depressurize the attic.

28. **a.** Venting the house living space does not add moisture to the house. It helps to reduce the moisture level.

29. **d.** A direct-vent furnace is not a house ventilation method.

30. **c.** The average efficiency of an HRV is 70 percent.

31. **a.** The appropriate number of air changes in an average house is roughly 0.3 air-changes-per-hour.

32. **c.** The flow measuring stations on HRVs should be on the warm side ducts not the insulated ducts.

33. **d.** Having the furnace air directed to the HRV is not a defrosting method.

34. **b.** Oversized access hatches are not a problem.

35. **b.** Secondary attics are common in one-and-a-half-story houses.

36. **c.** Excess insulation depth is not a problem.

37. **b.** If the problem occurs only on the north side of the light well, this does not suggest condensation as the problem.

38. **a.** Duct problems do not include ducts being oversized.

39. **b.** Masonry chimneys may be surrounded by noncombustible insulation, but not by combustible insulation.

40. **c.** Continuous soffit vents and spot roof vents are acceptable.

41. **a.** It's not common to vent the roof space if there is no insulation provided.

42. **a.** Vents on all four exposures of the fascia are good rather than a problem.

43. **c.** Mold and mildew on interior surfaces do not necessarily suggest rot in the roof space. These suggest high levels of moisture in the home and on cold surfaces.

44. **a.** Convective loops in the stud cavity may develop if insulation is added only to the exterior surface of wood frame walls.

45. **d.** Rot is most likely to be severe at the bottom of the walls because condensation tends to run down and get hung up on the bottom plates.

46. **b.** Earth floors in crawl spaces may add considerable moisture to the crawl space and to the home itself.

47. **b.** Operating the furnace blower on low speed will not reduce the house moisture levels.

48. **c.** Controlling an exhaust fan with a timer is not a problem.

49. **c.** Inlet and exhaust points for HRVs should be separated by several feet, rather than 12 inches.

7. PLUMBING SYSTEMS

Practice Questions

1. A toilet requires a vent.
   a. True
   b. False

2. Evaluating the quality of the water available at a private source is beyond the scope of a standard home inspection.
   a. True
   b. False

3. Plastic piping needs less support than copper piping because it tends to expand more.
   a. True
   b. False

4. A vacuum is necessary to have backflow at a cross-connection.
   a. True
   b. False

5. Vertical pipes at ends of runs are one method of preventing water hammer.
   a. True
   b. False

6. Polybutylene supply piping should NOT be closer than 18 inches to a water heater.
   a. True
   b. False

7. Polybutylene piping can be used on a hot water recirculating loop.
   a. True
   b. False

8. Gas-fired and oil-fired water heaters are *NOT* allowed in sleeping areas.
   a. True
   b. False

9. A waste pipe is intended to carry solids only.
   a. True
   b. False

10. Copper pipe can be connected in drain, waste, and vent systems with compression fittings.
    a. True
    b. False

11. PVC plastic pipe can be connected in drain, waste, and vent systems with solder.
    a. True
    b. False

12. Copper pipe does not rust.
    a. True
    b. False

13. Welded-steel piping is permitted as a material in drain, waste, and vent systems.
    a. True
    b. False

14. Pipe size should always increase as you move downstream and more fixtures join in.
    a. True
    b. False

15. Every trap should be provided with some method of removal or cleaning.
    a. True
    b. False

16. A running trap is a good idea because it provides extra protection.
    a. True
    b. False

17. It's impossible for a trap to be too big.
    a. True
    b. False

18. The vent is typically located upstream of the trap.
    a. True
    b. False

19. Nearly horizontal vent pipes should slope slightly down and away from the trap they are protecting.
    a. True
    b. False

20. The presence of a sump pump may be a requirement of the municipality.
    a. True
    b. False

21. Sump pumps must discharge to a sanitary sewer.
    a. True
    b. False

22. It is possible to find a sump pump running continuously with water in the sump.
    a. True
    b. False

23. The discharge pipe of a sump pump that discharges water outside the building at grade level can create a vicious circle.
    a. True
    b. False

24. Testing for loose, wall-hung basins is best done by putting all your weight on the basin.
    a. True
    b. False

25. Running toilets are less prone to sweating because the water in the tank is constantly replenished.
    a. True
    b. False

26. A toilet needs to have a shutoff valve on the supply line.
    a. True
    b. False

27. Because there is a watertight liner underneath the tiles in a shower stall base, the floor is *NOT* required to slope to drain.
    a. True
    b. False

28. A whirlpool bath requires a ground-fault circuit interrupter.
    a. True
    b. False

29. Potable water is
    a. water people can safely drink.
    b. well water.
    c. water suitable for cooking and washing but not drinking.
    d. water with an e-coli reading of more than 25.

30. Which of the following statements is true about water flow and pressure in regard to pipes in residential plumbing systems?
    a. The pressure is highest when there is no water flowing.
    b. The pressure is highest at the outlet point of the pipe.
    c. As more pressure is applied to a given pipe-length with an open faucet at the end, the flow rate will remain the same.
    d. The flow rate in a pipe is greater close to the source than at the outlet.

31. Pressure loss due to friction
    a. is zero when there is no water flowing.
    b. cannot exceed 20 psi.
    c. is independent of pipe length.
    d. is independent of pipe wall smoothness.

32. How much water flows through a ¾-inch-diameter pipe relative to a ½-inch-diameter pipe with the same pressure-loss?
    a. 150 percent
    b. 200 percent
    c. 250 percent
    d. 270 percent

33. Excess water pressure may lead to
    a. excess water velocity.
    b. excess friction loss.
    c. longer operating periods for clothes washers.
    d. splashing and excessive siphoning as toilets are flushed.

34. If you wanted to fill a bucket, which of the following fixtures with faucets fully opened would fill it the most quickly? (Assume that pipe length, size, and pressure are equal for all of these.)
    a. Bathroom basin
    b. Kitchen sink
    c. Outdoor hose bib
    d. Bathtub fill spout

35. Causes of poor pressure and flow in a house include all of the following *EXCEPT*
    a. undersized piping.
    b. rusted piping.
    c. a gate-valve-type main valve.
    d. leaks.

36. Which of the following ½-inch-diameter pipes would have the lowest pressure and flow characteristics?
    a. A 50-foot pipe with the outlet at the same elevation as the source
    b. A 50-foot pipe with the outlet 20 feet above the source
    c. A 100-foot pipe with the outlet 10 feet above the source
    d. A 100-foot pipe with the outlet 20 feet above the source

37. Which of the following has no effect on water pressure and flow?
    a. How smooth the pipe is
    b. What the static pressure is
    c. How fast the valve closes
    d. How high it is being pushed uphill

38. Bored wells are typically
    a. deeper than 200 feet.
    b. deeper than 400 feet.
    c. shallower than 100 feet.
    d. 12 inches in diameter.

39. A submersible pump in a 200-foot-deep drilled well is under 70 feet of water. The top of the well is 15 feet below the basement of the house. How much static head is present?
    a. 70 feet
    b. 130 feet
    c. 200 feet
    d. 215 feet

40. If you see three pipes at a jet pump in the basement, it means that
    a. the pump is feeding two separate pressure tanks.
    b. the well must be deeper than 50 feet.
    c. the suction line has been replaced because of obstruction.
    d. the venturi is in the well, lake, or river.

41. Which of the following is *NOT* a cause for an inoperative pump?
    a. The motor is burned out.
    b. The discharge line is split.
    c. The control switch for the pump is not working.
    d. There is no electricity at the pump.

42. The purpose of the pressure tank is to
    a. increase the pressure in the system.
    b. prevent the pump from short cycling.
    c. decrease the flow rate through the pump.
    d. prevent over-pressurizing the supply piping system.

43. What would the difference be in static pressure readings on a vertical pipe at zero elevation and at a 20-foot elevation?
    a. 4.5 psi
    b. 9 psi
    c. 17 psi
    d. 20 psi

44. What kind of a flow rate from a well is usually considered acceptable?
    a. 2 gpm
    b. 3 gpm
    c. 5 gpm
    d. 10 gpm

45. Which of the following is the most serious problem with a well supplying water to a house?
    a. Less than optimum water quantity
    b. A piston-type pump on a well
    c. Contaminated well water
    d. A well that is too close to the property line

46. Drilled wells
    a. are up to 100 feet deep.
    b. are often four inches in diameter.
    c. need no well casing.
    d. cannot have submersible pumps.

47. Common well problems include all of the following *EXCEPT*
    a. poor surface grading.
    b. missing casing.
    c. recovery rate of 10–15 gpm.
    d. not enough water.

48. Which of the following pumps definitely does *NOT* need priming?
    a. Jet pump
    b. Submersible pump
    c. Deep well pump
    d. Shallow well pump

49. Typical pump problems include all of the following *EXCEPT*
    a. inoperativeness.
    b. excess noise or vibration.
    c. excess pressure.
    d. running continuously.

50. Common problems with shutoff valves in the house include all of the following *EXCEPT*
    a. missing valves.
    b. leaking valves.
    c. damaged handles.
    d. location in a basement.

51. What is galvanic action?
    a. Corrosion that occurs when two dissimilar metals touch
    b. Connecting ABS and PVC piping together in a plumbing system
    c. Gurgling noise in the drain system
    d. Failure mode peculiar to brass piping

52. The water service line diameter from the street to new houses should be at least
    a. ¼-inch.
    b. ½-inch.
    c. ¾-inch.
    d. 1-inch.

53. The supply water piping diameter inside houses should be at least
    a. ¼-inch.
    b. ½-inch.
    c. ¾-inch.
    d. 1-inch.

54. Supply water pressure inside the house should *NOT* exceed
    a. 40 psi.
    b. 50 psi.
    c. 80 psi.
    d. 150 psi.

55. Horizontal plastic water pipe should be supported every
    a. 4 feet.
    b. 12 feet.
    c. 20 feet.
    d. 1 foot.

56. A water service line with a pressure of 110 psi will require a
    a. reduced-pressure backflow device.
    b. expansion tank.
    c. Extra-heavy pipe and fittings.
    d. pressure regulator.

57. A 40–50-year-old, galvanized-steel water supply system
    a. is the best system available.
    b. should have the water tested for lead.
    c. will probably show reduced water volume and pressure.
    d. is not compatible with PVC drain lines.

58. Galvanized-steel pipe typically fails first at
    a. threaded connections.
    b. elbows.
    c. the top sides of long horizontal runs.
    d. bends in the pipe.

59. Which of the following is *NOT* a backflow prevention device?
    a. Vacuum breaker
    b. Backflow preventer
    c. Isolating valve
    d. Backwater valve

60. Which of the following is *NOT* a common material used for water-entry piping?
    a. Copper
    b. Polyethylene plastic
    c. Welded-steel pipe
    d. CPVC plastic

61. Which type of plastic piping is typically cream-colored and suitable for use on both the hot and cold water system?
    a. PVC
    b. CPVC
    c. Polybutylene
    d. ABS

62. Which of the following suggests failing galvanized-steel supply piping?
    a. Weaker pressure on the hot side than the cold
    b. Weaker pressure on the cold side than the hot
    c. Vertical risers replaced with copper
    d. Green stains on the insides of plumbing fixtures

63. Any brass supply piping you come across will be
    a. ¾-inch diameter.
    b. yellow brass, with many years of service left.
    c. prone to failure at the horizontal soldered connections.
    d. near the end of its life.

64. How can you tell the difference between brass piping and galvanized-steel piping?
    a. Galvanized steel has threaded connections and brass piping is soldered.
    b. Galvanized steel has soldered connections and brass piping is threaded.
    c. Brass piping will always be smaller diameter than galvanized steel.
    d. Galvanized steel will attract a magnet and brass will not.

65. Joining copper and galvanized-steel piping together will produce corrosion unless a(n)
    a. isolation hanger is used.
    b. dielectric connector is used.
    c. tempering valve is used.
    d. brass coupler is used.

66. Which of the following devices protects against backflow?
    a. Double-check valve assembly
    b. Atmospheric vacuum breaker
    c. Pressure-type vacuum breaker
    d. Pressure regulator

67. Gas-fired water heaters and boilers for space heating both have all of the following components *EXCEPT*
    a. gas piping and a gas burner.
    b. a cold water inlet pipe.
    c. a temperature/pressure-relief valve set at 210°F and 150 psi.
    d. a venting system.

68. Gas fired water heaters have
    a. an expansion tank.
    b. potable water.
    c. an operating pressure of 12–15 psi.
    d. operating temperatures of 180°F, typically.

69. Gas-fired and oil-fired water heaters have all of the following *EXCEPT*
    a. dip tubes.
    b. insulated tanks.
    c. sacrificial anodes.
    d. lower recovery rates than electric water heaters.

70. Which water heater has the fastest recovery rate?
    a. Single-element electric heater
    b. Double-element electric heater
    c. Oil-fired water heater
    d. Direct-vent, gas-fired water heater

71. Which of the following is *NOT* a common problem with gas piping?
    a. Threaded connections
    b. Leaks
    c. Rusting
    d. No drip leg

72. Gas meters
    a. must be located outside.
    b. are never undersized.
    c. never leak.
    d. may ice up.

73. Which of the following natural gas piping arrangements is *NOT* permitted in any jurisdiction?
    a. Plastic pipe used underground outdoors
    b. Plastic pipe used indoors
    c. Coated steel piping used outdoors underground
    d. Black steel piping used indoors

74. All of the following are common problems found on gas piping *EXCEPT*
    a. leaks.
    b. excess pressure.
    c. rusting.
    d. improper connections.

75. Which of the following is *NOT TRUE* about indoor oil tanks?
    a. The tank should be 10 feet away from any burner.
    b. Tanks may rust over time.
    c. Rusting of tanks is common at the bottom weld if there is water in the tank.
    d. Outside tanks were never buried.

76. Common problems with oil fill and vent pipes *DO NOT* include
    a. leaks.
    b. oversizing.
    c. missing caps.
    d. abandonment.

77. Oil supply lines that carry the oil from the tank to the burner are typically
    a. copper.
    b. exposed along the floor or wall surface.
    c. 1-inch diameter.
    d. never more than 15 feet long.

78. All of the following are common oil supply line problems *EXCEPT*
    a. leaks.
    b. corrosion or mechanical damage.
    c. undersizing.
    d. excess elevation changes.

79. Oil flows from an above-ground exterior tank, through a 2-inch pipe into the basement. Here it passes a shutoff valve and a union. The ⅜-inch copper line starts here and runs to the burner. The part missing here is a
    a. fuel filter.
    b. fuel pressure reducer.
    c. pump to increase fuel pressure in the exterior line.
    d. manifold to allow oil to be drawn off for other burners.

80. Which is *NOT* a common oil filter problem?
    a. Leaking filter
    b. Dirt
    c. Missing filter
    d. Oversizing

81. Which of the following is *NOT* a cause of inadequate combustion air?
    a. The water heater is in a small enclosure.
    b. The house is extremely airtight.
    c. There are several other pieces of equipment exhausting air from the house.
    d. An air vent to the outdoors from the water heater enclosure.

82. All of the following are common venting problems on gas and oil water heaters *EXCEPT*
    a. rust.
    b. poor slope.
    c. a vent connector that is too long.
    d. vent connector manifolds with vent connector from furnace.

83. The required clearance from combustibles for a single-wall vent connector on a gas water heater is
    a. one inch.
    b. two inches.
    c. six inches.
    d. nine inches.

84. Vent connectors from conventional gas water heaters are commonly
    a. corrugated.
    b. aluminum.
    c. B-vents.
    d. L-vents.

85. The function of a draft hood on a gas fired water heater is to
    a. add air to the venting system to maintain chimney draft.
    b. provide combustion air.
    c. prevent the burner from competing with the furnace for combustion air.
    d. prevent flame rollout at the burner.

86. Which of the following is not a common problem with oil fill and vent pipes on an oil storage tank?
    a. Leaks
    b. Abandoned tank with pipes not sealed
    c. Damage or corrosion
    d. A gooseneck on the vent pipe

87. All of the following are common problems with oil burners *EXCEPT*
    a. draft hood obstruction.
    b. inoperativeness.
    c. incomplete combustion.
    d. excess proximity to combustibles.

88. Refractories on oil burners
    a. are typically located at the top of a water heater.
    b. can be completely inspected during a home inspection.
    c. may be masonry or ceramic fiber.
    d. are located above the burner.

89. If the vent length on a gas-fired water heater is too long, then
    a. the cost of the system is too high.
    b. combustible clearances have to be increased.
    c. there is a possibility of poor drafting and spillage of combustion products.
    d. it may require supports at more frequent intervals.

90. Vent connectors on oil-fired water heaters
    a. should extend 2 inches into the flue of a masonry chimney.
    b. should enter a masonry chimney below a vent for a furnace or boiler.
    c. should reduce in size to accelerate the exhaust products before it joins a masonry chimney.
    d. are prone to corrosion along the bottom.

91. Which of the following statements about electric water heaters is *NOT TRUE?*
    a. They usually have a larger storage capacity than gas or oil tanks.
    b. They have a slow recovery rate.
    c. They sometimes have an energy cutout and pressure-relief valve.
    d. They do not require a sacrificial anode.

92. Which of the following statements about leaking water heaters is *NOT TRUE?*
    a. Water heaters often leak at the bottom first.
    b. The leaks are never a result of rusting.
    c. The life expectancy of a water heater is less than that of a boiler.
    d. The temperature/pressure-relief valve or drain valve may be leaking.

93. Gas-fired water heaters
    a. can typically be installed on combustible floors, including carpeting.
    b. usually require 36 inches of combustible clearance around and above the water heaters.
    c. do not have any insulation in the tank walls.
    d. should not be installed in bedrooms or bedroom closets.

94. Which of the following statements about temperature/pressure-relief valves is *NOT TRUE?*
    a. Temperature/pressure-relief valves protect against steam explosions.
    b. Temperature/pressure-relief valves shut off the water heater if the temperature exceeds 210°F.
    c. Temperature/pressure-relief valves should be connected to a discharge tube.
    d. The Btu rating of the temperature/pressure-relief valve should be at least as big as the water heater Btu rating.

95. Which of the following statements about water heater discharge tubes for temperature/pressure-relief valves is *NOT TRUE?*
    a. The tubes cannot be plastic.
    b. The tubes cannot have any shutoff valves.
    c. The tubes have to extend 6–12 inches above the floor or, outdoors, 6–24 inches above grade.
    d. The tube cannot have threads, fittings or caps on the end.

96. Which of the following is *NOT* a problem with water heaters?
    a. There is no isolating valve on the cold water inlet.
    b. The tank is leaking.
    c. There is no isolating valve on the hot water outlet.
    d. The hot and cold water piping are reversed.

97. Circulating hot water systems
    a. eliminate the wait for hot water after long, idle periods.
    b. require no additional piping.
    c. have a pump that comes on every time water flows through the hot water system.
    d. should never have a check valve in the system, because that may obstruct the flow.

98. Which of the following is a good vent-termination location for a fan-assisted, gas-fired water heater?
    a. Five feet from a mechanical air supply inlet
    b. Two feet from a gas meter regulator
    c. Five feet from a door or window
    d. Two feet from a combustion air inlet for the furnace

99. Which of the following statements is *FALSE* with respect to high-efficiency, gas-fired water heaters?
    a. The tanks are better insulated than conventional water heaters.
    b. The seasonal efficiency is 70–80 percent.
    c. The exhaust gas temperatures are 100°F to 150°F.
    d. They are condensing systems.

100. Which of the following statements about combination domestic hot water and space heating systems is *FALSE?*
    a. They cannot be used with a radiant piping, heat-distribution system.
    b. Potable water is passed through a coil in an air handler with a duct system.
    c. Electric water heaters are not typically used in this application.
    d. The pump may operate even during nonheating seasons to prevent stagnant water accumulations.

101. A tempering valve may be needed on a combination domestic hot water and space heating system. The tempering valve
    a. mixes cool water with the hot water before sending the water to a fan coil.
    b. raises the temperature of the domestic hot water delivered to the house.
    c. reduces the temperature of the water to the domestic hot water side.
    d. protects people from scalding when bleeding radiators or radiant piping systems.

102. Which of the following is a common problem with combination heating systems?
    a. Inadequate combustion air
    b. Inadequate heat and/or hot water
    c. Excess pressure at faucets
    d. Increased fuel consumption and cost

103. Which of the following statements is true of tankless coils?
    a. Tankless coils have a small, high-output burner.
    b. The domestic boiler is left idle during the summer months.
    c. No domestic water heater and tank are necessary.
    d. These coils take up considerable space in a home.

104. Which of the following is *NOT* a drawback to tankless coils?
    a. A tempering valve is usually necessary.
    b. Leaking coils can damage the house boiler.
    c. These coils are prone to clogging with scale and rust.
    d. A separate pump is needed for the coil.

105. A side-arm heater
    a. is a variation on a tankless coil.
    b. is added to the side of a domestic water heater.
    c. is typically located at each fixture requiring hot water.
    d. has a high-efficiency oil burner.

106. Which of the following is *NOT* an advantage of combination systems?
    a. There is only one combustion appliance, rather than two.
    b. It can be a high-efficiency system.
    c. They make use of the domestic hot water in the tank, which is kept at the ready anyway.
    d. These systems are typically oversized for both heating and domestic hot water, so there is a lot of capacity.

107. Venting arrangements on high-efficiency domestic water heaters typically include all of the following *EXCEPT*
    a. CPVC or PVC vent piping.
    b. sidewall venting arrangements.
    c. exhaust gas temperatures of 350°F–400°F.
    d. condensate handling systems.

108. A pressure switch on a power vented water heater
    a. operates the blower if air pressure is too low.
    b. provides adequate combustion air.
    c. senses excess water pressure in the system.
    d. verifies that the blower has started.

109. Common problems with temperature/pressure-relief valves on water heaters include all of the following *EXCEPT*
    a. a missing.
    b. a missing discharge tube.
    c. a discharge tube dripping or leaking.
    d. a discharge tube made of copper.

110. Common problems for pumps with hot water circulating systems include all of the following *EXCEPT*
    a. inoperativeness.
    b. leakage.
    c. excess noise or vibration.
    d. control by an aquastat.

111. Where two water heaters are installed in a single house
   a. they must always be installed in the same area.
   b. they are typically installed in series.
   c. the upstream unit is typically smaller than the downstream unit.
   d. parallel systems should have similar pipe lengths to each water heater.

112. An energy cutoff in a water heater replaces
   a. the thermostat.
   b. the temperature function of the TPR valve.
   c. the barometric damper.
   d. the thermocouple or flame sensor.

113. Each temperature/pressure-relief valve shall have a
   a. discharge tube no longer than 30 inches.
   b. trapped discharge tube.
   c. Full-size discharge tube extended to a safe location.
   d. reducing fitting and threaded end on the discharge tube.

114. All gas water heaters require
   a. a venting system for exhaust product.
   b. enclosed water supply pipes.
   c. temperature/pressure-relief valves.
   d. 12 inches of elevation off of the floor in a garage.

115. All gas meters should be preceded by a
   a. bypass connection.
   b. shutoff valve.
   c. drip leg.
   d. union connection.

116. Conventional gas-fired water heaters may be installed in
   a. bedrooms.
   b. bathrooms.
   c. kitchens.
   d. All of the above

117. Which water heater may have an energy cutout?
   a. Electric
   b. Gas
   c. Oil
   d. Propane

118. Which water heater has the slowest recovery rate?
   a. Electric
   b. Gas
   c. Oil
   d. A heater installed beside a parallel heater

119. Which item is *NOT* essential for the safe operation of a conventional gas-fired water heater?
   a. Thermocouple
   b. TPR valve
   c. Thermostat
   d. Pressure limit switch

120. A building drain is
   a. the lowest pipe in or under a home that carries sewage to the building sewer.
   b. the underground pipe that carries sewage from the building out to the public sewer.
   c. the underground pipe that carries sewage from the building to an on-site sewage disposal system.
   d. the pipes that run along the street and receive the waste from several houses.

121. Soil pipes
   a. carry liquid and solid waste from a toilet.
   b. carry liquid wastes only in a horizontal plane.
   c. carry air only on horizontal runs.
   d. carry solid and liquid waste on vertical runs only.

122. Home inspectors should not turn on plumbing systems that have been turned off for all *EXCEPT* which one of the following reasons?
   a. There may be a leak in the piping.
   b. It is the client's responsibility.
   c. There may be a leak at the fixture.
   d. The system may have been winterized and you will wash antifreeze out of the system.

123. Horizontal drain pipes should have a slope of roughly
   a. ¼-inch-per-foot.
   b. ½-inch-per-foot.
   c. ¾-inch-per-foot.
   d. 1-inch-per-foot

124. Bell and spigot is a
    a. male/female connection method for cast-iron pipe.
    b. sweated lead joint.
    c. brazed copper joint.
    d. tapered threaded joint.

125. Common drainage piping problems include all of the following *EXCEPT*
    a. leaks.
    b. rust.
    c. splits, damage, and crimping.
    d. oversizing.

126. All of the following are common drainage piping problems *EXCEPT*
    a. missing or inaccessible cleanouts.
    b. clay tile piping that is buried in the soil.
    c. combustible piping that is used in multifamily buildings.
    d. nonstandard piping materials.

127. Leaks in drain pipes are commonly caused by all of the following *EXCEPT*
    a. poor joint connections.
    b. damaged piping or traps.
    c. missing air gaps.
    d. clogging.

128. Clogging of drainage piping can be caused by any of the following *EXCEPT*
    a. too little slope.
    b. slopes of 45° or more off horizontal.
    c. foreign materials in the piping.
    d. pipe connections that project into the path of the waste.

129. Cross connections may exist at each of the following *EXCEPT*
    a. supply faucets that are below the flood rims of fixtures.
    b. drain connections from dishwashers.
    c. outside hose bibs with no hoses attached.
    d. lawn sprinkler systems.

130. All of the following are possible cross connection situations *EXCEPT*
    a. extendable faucets on kitchen sinks.
    b. water supply connections to heating boilers.
    c. trap primers.
    d. floor drains with no trap primers.

131. The causes of poor slope on drainage piping include all of the following *EXCEPT*
    a. poor installation.
    b. building settlement or heaving.
    c. hanger problems.
    d. double trapping.

132. Defective ABS piping
    a. occurred in installations after 1990.
    b. occurred throughout North America.
    c. resulted in cracking around the circumference of the pipe joints.
    d. is an issue with a 1¼-inch to 2-inch diameter only.

133. Dishwashers in some areas
    a. require an air gap fitting.
    b. must drain directly into a stack.
    c. cannot discharge into a tailpiece of a sink.
    d. must discharge into a trap arm upstream of the vent.

134. Drain pipes from clothes washers should
    a. have a direct connection to a plumbing stack.
    b. go into a standpipe.
    c. not have a trap in the standpipe for fear of collecting debris and clogging.
    d. have standpipes that discharge into the trap arm of a laundry tub.

135. One of the weaknesses of copper drain, waste, and vent pipe is that
    a. it corrodes easily.
    b. it's combustible.
    c. it's susceptible to acid.
    d. it's hard to work with.

136. A common use for brass as a waste material is
    a. vent piping.
    b. wet venting.
    c. fittings.
    d. waste piping.

137. Horizontal cast-iron piping is prone to
    a. splits on the top.
    b. noise transmission.
    c. sags, when supported at three foot intervals.
    d. rusting, after 15 years.

138. Which of the following drain pipes is typically used below grade?
    a. Galvanized steel
    b. Cast iron
    c. Clay
    d. Copper

139. A trap seal is the
    a. fastener that joins the trap to the tailpiece.
    b. fitting that joins the trap to the trap arm.
    c. another name for the drain stopper.
    d. vertical distance from the trap dip to the weir.
    e. connection from the trap to the vent.

140. The tail piece is the
    a. pipe that joins the fixture to the trap.
    b. pipe that runs from the trap to the vent.
    c. downstream-half of the trap.
    d. upstream-half of the trap.
    e. inside of the lowest part of the trap.

141. The trap arm is the
    a. cleanout at the bottom of the trap.
    b. pipe that runs from the trap to the vent.
    c. fixture outlet pipe.
    d. distance from the trap dip to the trap weir.

142. Which of the following is *NOT* a factor in helping to keep traps from clogging?
    a. Their special shape
    b. Their self-scouring characteristic
    c. The trap size
    d. The avoidance of S-traps

143. Double trapping is a problem because the
    a. water velocity is too great.
    b. water velocity at the second trap is too low.
    c. water velocity at the first trap is too high.
    d. second trap is prone to siphoning.

144. All of the following may cause traps to lose their seal *EXCEPT*
    a. dumping mineral oil down a drain.
    b. indirect siphonage.
    c. backpressure.
    d. evaporation.

145. Trap problems include all of the following *EXCEPT*
    a. slip joints.
    b. missing.
    c. leakage.
    d. double trapping.

146. All of the following indicate leaking traps *EXCEPT*
    a. slow-draining fixtures.
    b. staining or streaking on the trap.
    c. rusting of cleanout plugs.
    d. water damage on the floor or cabinetry below the trap.

147. What are the implications of a tail piece for a fixture that is too long?
    a. Clogging of the trap
    b. Siphoning of the trap
    c. Freeze-up of the trap
    d. Ineffective venting

148. A trap may clog if
    a. the trap is oversized or undersized.
    b. the trap is assembled with slip joints.
    c. the trap arm length is too long.
    d. the vent is oversized.

149. What type of trap is allowed by most plumbing codes?
    a. P-trap
    b. S-trap
    c. Double trap
    d. Bell trap

150. A plumbing trap
    a. provides a flow of air to and from the drainage system.
    b. prevents foreign objects from clogging the drainage system.
    c. provides a liquid seal that prevents the passage of air/gas.
    d. controls the discharge of water or sewage into the sanitary system.

151. Floor drain problems include all of the following *EXCEPT*
    a. missing drains.
    b. backing up.
    c. a missing trap.
    d. a missing backwater valve.

152. All of the following are functions of plumbing vent systems *EXCEPT* that vents
    a. allow air to be pushed out of the waste pipes ahead of slugs.
    b. prevent siphoning of traps.
    c. provide a path for odors to escape from the house.
    d. provide a fresh-air inlet directly to the living space.

153. Crown-vented traps are
    a. recommended on the upper floors of houses.
    b. not permitted in most areas.
    c. always more than two pipe diameters from the trap.
    d. used on drum traps.

154. Why are island sinks difficult to vent?
    a. You don't want a vent pipe running up through the center of the kitchen.
    b. It is difficult to vent double sinks.
    c. Double sinks lead to double trapping and ineffective vents.
    d. There is no room on the counter for an air gap fitting.

155. What is a wet vent?
    a. A hose attached to a sink drain
    b. When the cap is missing from the water heater vent flue
    c. A vent that also serves as a drain
    d. When a clothes dryer is located near a laundry sink

156. What might cause a gurgling sound when draining water out of a sink?
    a. Sewer blockage
    b. No vent pipe
    c. Excessive water pressure
    d. Undersized drain piping

157. What is the minimum recommended height of a plumbing vent stack above the roof?
    a. 30 inches
    b. 24 inches
    c. 6 inches
    d. 1 inch

158. How close can a vent be to a trap?
    a. 1 pipe-diameter after the trap
    b. 2 pipe-diameters after the trap
    c. 6 pipe-diameters after the trap
    d. 4 feet from the trap

159. All of the following are reasons that a sewage pump may not operate *EXCEPT*
    a. a defective switch.
    b. a leak in the outlet line.
    c. a seized pump or burned-out motor.
    d. an undersized vent.

160. Sewage sumps are required for toilets located
    a. below the elevation of the curb at the street.
    b. below the municipal sewer.
    c. in the basement.
    d. in a home with a septic system.

161. Sewage ejector pumps *DO NOT* need
    a. an inlet pipe.
    b. a trap.
    c. a discharge pipe.
    d. a 120-volt electrical supply.

162. Sump pumps
    a. typically operate on 240-volt electrical power.
    b. may be pedestal-type or submersible.
    c. should not have a check valve in the discharge pipe.
    d. should have a hermetically sealed sump lid.

163. All of the following are common sump pump problems *EXCEPT*
    a. inoperativeness.
    b. short cycling.
    c. running continuously.
    d. a discharge point that is above grade level.

164. Laundry tub pumps
    a. should be upstream of the laundry tub trap.
    b. should be downstream of the laundry tub trap.
    c. should be mounted above the laundry tub.
    d. must be automatically activated.

165. Good plumbing fixtures have all of the following features *EXCEPT*
    a. smoothness.
    b. porousness.
    c. durability.
    d. ease of cleaning.

166. Which of the following fixtures does *NOT* require a trap?
    a. Toilets
    b. Basins
    c. Bathtubs
    d. Bidets

167. Floors and walls around toilets, bathtubs, and showers should *NOT* be
   a. smooth surfaced.
   b. pervious.
   c. marble.
   d. tile.

168. The most common problem with plumbing fixtures is
   a. poor pressure.
   b. poor flow.
   c. inoperative isolating valves.
   d. leakage.

169. The fixture in the house that is going to have the weakest flow and drainage is/are
   a. the lowest fixture in the house.
   b. the smallest fixture in the house.
   c. toilets, because they have only cold water supply.
   d. the highest fixture in the house.

170. Causes of slow drains include all of the following *EXCEPT*
   a. missing trap.
   b. a clogged fixture strainer.
   c. a partly clogged drain system.
   d. an undersized drain system.

171. In new construction, you will not normally find basins and sinks made out of
   a. stainless steel.
   b. cast iron.
   c. synthetic marble.
   d. concrete.

172. Faucets or spouts must be above the _____ of the sink or basin.
   a. vent stack
   b. flood rim
   c. supply valve
   d. vacuum breaker

173. Rust on fixtures is typically caused by all of the following *EXCEPT*
   a. failure at welded overflow connections.
   b. corrosive chemicals.
   c. chipped enamel.
   d. condensate from air conditioners draining into fixtures.

174. Overflows should *NOT* be found on
   a. bathtubs.
   b. basins.
   c. kitchen sinks.
   d. whirlpool baths.

175. Washerless faucets are more prone to water hammer problems than compression faucets because
   a. water can be turned off much more quickly.
   b. washers wear enough to be slightly leaky.
   c. packing leakage is common on compression faucets.
   d. compression faucets are typically on older piping systems, which are more accommodating and less likely to suffer water hammer.

176. Water hammer is typically prevented by
   a. pressure-balancing faucets.
   b. thermostat mixers.
   c. single lever faucets.
   d. dead-end risers.

177. Pressure-balancing valves
   a. protect against scalding at showers.
   b. prevent cross connections.
   c. are backflow preventers.
   d. are used with pressure regulators.

178. Common faucet problems include all of the following *EXCEPT*
   a. leaks.
   b. looseness.
   c. cross connections.
   d. a lack of isolating valves.

179. The most common cause of poor pressure and flow at a single fixture is
   a. poor city water pressure.
   b. poor performance of a well pump.
   c. a clogged aerator.
   d. older galvanized-steel supply piping in the house.

180. Common toilet problems include all of the following *EXCEPT*
   a. low water pressure.
   b. looseness.
   c. an inoperative flush mechanism.
   d. obstructions.

181. All of the following are common toilet problems *EXCEPT*
    a. lazy flushing.
    b. floor damage around the toilet.
    c. excess pressure at the tank.
    d. running continuously.

182. A toilet is *NOT* likely to leak at the
    a. wax gasket connection to the floor.
    b. gasket between the tank and bowl.
    c. seat bolt holes.
    d. rubber gasket connection to the floor.

183. Bidets are all of the following *EXCEPT*
    a. self-trapping.
    b. connected to both hot and cold water supplies.
    c. provided with a vacuum breaker.
    d. typically provided with a spray and rim wash and a diverter.

184. Common bidet problems *DO NOT* include
    a. leaks.
    b. missing vacuum breakers.
    c. inoperative spray/rim wash diverters.
    d. damaged seats or lids.

185. Leaks at bidets may be at any of the following locations *EXCEPT*
    a. supply piping connections.
    b. drain piping connections.
    c. tank lids.
    d. vacuum breakers.

186. A tile lip for a bathtub
    a. is part of the drain connection.
    b. provides a mounting plate for fixtures.
    c. provides a support point for the tub to the structure.
    d. supports the tub skirt.

187. Common bathtub problems include all of the following *EXCEPT*
    a. leaks.
    b. rust.
    c. cross connections.
    d. missing vacuum breakers.

188. Testing inaccessible bathtub overflows is *NOT* recommended because
    a. it takes too long to fill the tub to the overflow.
    b. these systems are used regularly and problems would show up below.
    c. overflows often leak when tested.
    d. overflows are integral with drain stoppers and leaks will flow into the tailpiece of the fixture.

189. Enclosures around bathtubs and shower stalls are typically all of the following *EXCEPT*
    a. ceramic tile.
    b. acrylic.
    c. smooth, easy to clean, and nonporous.
    d. unlikely to allow leakage.

190. Appropriate backup materials for a ceramic tile shower stall include all of the following *EXCEPT*
    a. drywall.
    b. moisture resistant drywall.
    c. lightweight concrete panels.
    d. plywood.

191. The most common leakage point in a ceramic shower stall is at the
    a. escutcheon plate.
    b. base.
    c. shower nozzle.
    d. soap dish.

192. Vulnerable spots in shower and bathtub enclosures include all of the following *EXCEPT*
    a. faucet penetrations.
    b. the top of the tile where it joins the conventional wall finish.
    c. soap dishes.
    d. windows.

193. Leaks through tub and shower enclosures may be caused by all of these *EXCEPT*
    a. poor grout work.
    b. poor caulking.
    c. building settlement.
    d. porous ceramic tile.

194. Electrical light switches in bathrooms should be
    a. moved outside the bathroom.
    b. at least three feet away from shower stalls and bathtubs.
    c. as close to the basin as possible.
    d. vapor proof.

195. The lowest quality shower stall base on this list is
    a. one-piece fiberglass.
    b. three-piece fiberglass.
    c. mortar bed ceramic.
    d. metal.

196. Mortar bed shower stalls
    a. should have no slope.
    b. require a drain with holes in the side.
    c. require liners turned up the wall ½ inch.
    d. require plaster of Paris under the tile.

197. A toe tester is
    a. a hose bib outdoors.
    b. a bathtub fill spout.
    c. a faucet spout near the bottom of the shower stall.
    d. a bathtub with a small side recess.

198. Shower stalls should typically be at least
    a. 20 × 40 inches.
    b. 24 × 36 inches.
    c. 30 × 30 inches.
    d. 30 × 36 inches.

199. All of the following statements are true about whirlpool baths EXCEPT that they
    a. are filled and drained with each use.
    b. have a dedicated hot water heating system.
    c. are used for cleaning people.
    d. have a pump.

200. Whirlpool baths are also called
    a. spas.
    b. hot tubs.
    c. whirlpool spas.
    d. hydro-massage bathtubs.

201. All of the following statements about whirlpool baths are true EXCEPT that
    a. there should be an access cover to service and replace the pump.
    b. the pump should have a dedicated 120-volt circuit.
    c. the pump should have a ground fault circuit interrupter.
    d. the pump should be variable speed.

202. All of the following statements are true about whirlpool baths EXCEPT that
    a. whirlpool baths may hold more water than a conventional bathtub.
    b. whirlpool baths may exert a significant load on the floor system.
    c. there are health concerns surrounding whirlpool baths related to stagnant water in the circulation piping system.
    d. whirlpool baths are designed to have the pump operated with no water in the tub.

203. Common whirlpool problems include all of the following EXCEPT
    a. an inoperative pump.
    b. dirty water coming from the jets.
    c. a missing suction cover.
    d. if there are pneumatic switches directly on the tub.

204. What is the most difficult problem to determine in a bathroom?
    a. Low water pressure
    b. The condition of the shower pan under base
    c. Water hammer
    d. Continuously running toilets

205. Which of the following is least likely to have a cross connection?
    a. Outside hose bib
    b. Shower stall
    c. Water softener connection
    d. Extendable faucet at the kitchen sink

206. Which of the following is the inspector NOT required to observe during the plumbing inspection?
    a. The exhaust vent from the gas water heater
    b. Functional drainage at the bathtubs
    c. The on-site water supply quantity
    d. Cross connections

207. Which of the following is the inspector required to do?
    a. Operate temperature/pressure-relief valves on a water heater
    b. Observe private waste disposal systems
    c. Operate the isolating valve at the toilet
    d. Operate the spray feature of the bidet

ANSWERS AND EXPLANATIONS

1. **a.**   A toilet requires a vent.

2. **a.**   Evaluating the quality of the water available at a private source is beyond the scope of a standard home inspection.

3. **b.**   Plastic piping needs more support than copper piping because it tends to expand more.

4. **b.**   A vacuum isn't necessary for backflow to occur.

5. **a.**   Water hammer can be corrected by installing vertical pipes, at the ends of hot and cold runs, that extend up at least 12 inches beyond any fixture.

6. **a.**   Polybutylene connections should be at least 18 inches from water heaters.

7. **b.**   Some authorities say that houses with recirculating loops for hot water piping should not use polybutylene on these loops.

8. **a.**   Gas or oil-fired water heaters should not be located in sleeping areas, including bedrooms and bedroom closets.

9. **b.**   A waste pipe carries liquids only, according to some authorities, or liquids and solids, according to other authorities.

10. **a.**   In addition to compression fittings, solder can be used to connect copper pipe in DWV systems.

11. **b.**   PVC plastic pipe cannot be connected with solder.

12. **b.**   Copper can rust if exposed to acids, a corrosive environment, or contact with dissimilar metals.

13. **b.**   Welded steel piping is not permitted in residential plumbing systems in many areas.

14. **a.**   Pipe size should always increase as you move downstream and more fixtures join in.

15. **a.**   Traps should be provided with a method of removal or cleaning, as they may sometimes get clogged.

16. **b.**   Running traps were found to be unnecessary once effective venting systems were designed.

17. **b.**   A trap can be too big.

18. **b.**   The vent must be on the downstream side of the trap.

19. **b.**   Nearly horizontal vent pipes should slope up slightly, away from the trap they are protecting.

20. **a.**   The municipality may require a sump pump if the storm sewers are higher than the lowest floor level.

21. **b.**   There are several acceptable discharge locations for sump pumps, including a storm sewer, combination sewer, ditch, and French drain.

22. **a.**   A sump pump may run continuously with water in the sump due to an obstructed or disconnected discharge pipe.

23. **a.**   Water discharged adjacent to the building may find its way back into the sump, creating a cycle that doesn't get rid of any water.

24. **b.**   Putting all your weight on a wall-hung sink may result in its sudden collapse.

25. **b.**   Running toilets are more prone to sweating.

26. **a.**   All toilets should have an operable shutoff valve located adjacent to the toilet.

27. **b.**   All shower stalls should have a slope of at least ¼-inch per foot in toward the drain.

28. **a.**   All whirlpool bathtubs should have a dedicated electric circuit protected by a ground-fault circuit interrupter.

29. **a.**   Potable water is water that is safe to drink.

30. **a.**   The pressure is highest when there is no water flowing.

31. **a.**   There is no pressure loss due to friction when there is no water flowing.

32. **d.**   Roughly 270 percent more water will flow through a ¾-inch-diameter pipe than a ½-inch-diameter pipe.

33. **a.**   Excess water pressure may lead to excess water velocity.

34. **d.**   The quickest way to fill a bucket is with the bathtub fill spout.

35. **c.**   A gate valve does not cause poor pressure and/or flow.

36. **d.** The lowest pressure and flow characteristics would belong to the 100-foot pipe with the outlet 20 feet above the source.

37. **c.** How fast the valve closes has no effect on water pressure and flow.

38. **c.** Bored wells are shallower than 100 feet.

39. **a.** The static head for a submersible pump 70 feet under water is 70 feet.

40. **d.** If you see three pipes at a jet pump in the house, this means that the venturi is in the well, lake, river, or whatever the source may be.

41. **b.** A split discharge line is not a cause for an inoperative pump.

42. **b.** The pressure tank helps to prevent the pump from short cycling.

43. **b.** A 20-foot elevation difference would cause a pressure differential of roughly 9 psi.

44. **b.** A 3 gpm flow rate is usually considered acceptable from a private well.

45. **c.** Contaminated well water is the most serious problem you can have because it is a life safety issue. Running out of water is an inconvenience but is not life threatening.

46. **b.** Drilled wells are typically four to six inches in diameter.

47. **c.** A recovery rate of 10 gpm to 15 gpm is not a problem.

48. **b.** Submersible pumps do not need priming because they are always surrounded by water.

49. **c.** Excess pressure is not a pump problem.

50. **d.** Shut off valves are frequently located in basements. This is not a problem.

51. **a.** Galvanic action is corrosion that occurs when dissimilar metals contact each other, in a plumbing system, for example.

52. **c.** The water service line diameter from the street to the house in new construction should be at least ¾-inch.

53. **b.** The supply water piping diameter inside houses should be at least ½ inch.

54. **c.** Supply water pressure inside the house should not be more than 80 psi.

55. **a.** Horizontal plastic water pipes should be supported at least every four feet. Some areas call for supports even closer together.

56. **d.** If the water surface line pressure is 110 psi, a pressure regulator would typically be required.

57. **c.** A 40–50-year-old galvanized-steel water supply system will probably show reduced water volume and pressure.

58. **a.** Galvanized-steel pipe typically fails first at the threaded connections, which are thinner.

59. **c.** An isolating valve is not a backflow prevention device.

60. **c.** Welded steel is not commonly used for water entry piping.

61. **b.** CPVC is typically cream colored and suitable for use on both the hot and cold water system.

62. **a.** Weaker pressure on the hot side than the cold side suggests failing galvanized-steel supply piping.

63. **d.** Any brass piping that you find on the supply system will probably be near the end of its life.

64. **d.** Galvanized-steel piping will attract a magnet; brass piping will not.

65. **b.** Copper and galvanized-steel piping will corrode each other, unless s dielectric connector is used.

66. **a.** A double-check valve assembly protects against backflow.

67. **c.** Boilers and water heaters that are gas-fired typically have all of these components except a temperature/pressure-relief valve set at 210°F and 150 psi. Boilers typically use a pressure-relief valve set at 30 psi.

68. **b.** Gas-fired water heaters see potable water.

69. **d.** Gas-fired and oil-fired water heaters have faster recovery rates than electric water heaters.

70. **c.** An oil-fired water heater has the fastest recovery rate.

71. **a.** Threaded connections are not a problem with gas piping, which is usually steel.

72. **d.** Gas meters may ice up.

73. **b.** Plastic pipe cannot be used indoors.

74. **b.** Excess pressure is not a common problem on gas piping.

75. **d.** Oil tanks outside were often buried.

76. **b.** It isn't common for, nor would it be a problem if, oil fill and vent pipes were oversized.

77. **a.** Oil supply lines are typically copper, although they can be steel or brass as well.

78. **d.** Excessive elevation change is not a common oil supply line problem. A fuel filter is needed in this arrangement.

79. **a.** A fuel filter is needed here.

80. **d.** It is not common for an oil filter to be oversized.

81. **d.** A vent to the outdoors from a water heater enclosure does not cause inadequate combustion air. It might solve a combustion air problem.

82. **d.** A vent connector from a water heater which manifolds with a furnace vent connector is a common arrangement and is not necessarily a problem.

83. **c.** A six-inch clearance is required from a single-wall vent connector from a gas water heater to combustible materials.

84. **b.** Vent connectors from conventional gas water heaters are commonly aluminum.

85. **a.** Draft hoods add air to the venting system in order to maintain appropriate chimney draft.

86. **d.** A gooseneck on a vent pipe is not a problem on an oil fill and vent system.

87. **a.** Oil burners do not have draft hoods.

88. **c.** Refractories on oil burners may be masonry or ceramic fiber.

89. **c.** If the vent length is too long, there is the possibility of poor drafting and spillage of combustion products on gas-fired or oil-fired water heaters.

90. **d.** Vent connectors on oil-fired water heaters are prone to corrosion along the bottom.

91. **d.** Electric water heaters do require a sacrificial anode.

92. **b.** Leaks are often a result of rusting.

93. **d.** Gas-fired water heaters should not be installed in bedrooms or bedroom closets.

94. **b.** Temperature and pressure-relief valves do not shut off the water heater. They simply allow water to discharge through the valve and discharge tube.

95. **a.** Discharge tubes on water heaters can be plastic.

96. **c.** An isolating valve on the hot water outlet is not required or typically provided.

97. **a.** Circulating hot water systems eliminate the wait for hot water at faucets throughout the house after long idle periods.

98. **c.** It's all right for a vent from a fan assisted gas water heater to discharge within five feet of a door or window.

99. **b.** The seasonal efficiency of a high-efficiency gas water heater is more than 70–80 percent.

100. **a.** Combination hot water and space heating systems can have radiant piping-distribution systems.

101. **c.** The tempering valve on a hot water system reduces the temperature of the water to the domestic hot water side.

102. **b.** Inadequate heat and/or hot water is a common problem with combination heating systems.

103. **c.** No domestic water heater and tank are necessary if a tankless coil is used to provide domestic hot water.

104. **d.** A separate pump is not needed with tankless coils.

105. **a.** A side-arm heater is a variation on a tankless coil.

106. **d.** Combination systems are usually not oversized for heating and/or hot water usage.

107. **c.** High-efficiency domestic water heaters have exhaust gas temperatures well below 350°–400° Fahrenheit.

108. **d.** A pressure switch on a power-vented water heater verifies that the blower has started.

109. **d.** Common problems with temperature pressure-relief valves do not include copper discharge tubes. These are acceptable.

110. **d.** It is acceptable for a hot water circulating system to be controlled by an aquastat.

111. **d.** Where two water heaters are installed in a single home, parallel systems should have similar pipe lengths for each water heater.

112. **b.** The energy cut-off in a water heater replaces the temperature function of the temperature/pressure-relief valve.

113. **c.** Each temperature/pressure-relief valve must have a full-size discharge tube extended to a safe location.

114. **a.** All gas-fired water heaters require a venting system for exhaust products.

115. **b.** All gas meters should be preceded by a shut-off valve.

116. **c.** Conventional gas-fired water heaters may be installed in a kitchen.

117. **a.** Many electric water heaters have an energy cutout.

118. **a.** Electric water heaters have the slowest recovery rate.

119. **d.** Conventional gas-fired water heaters do not require a pressure limit switch. They have a temperature/pressure-relief valve.

120. **a.** A building drain is the lowest pipe in, or under, a home that carries sewage to the building sewer.

121. **a.** Soil pipes carry liquid and solid waste from a toilet.

122. **b.** Answers a, c, and d are all reasons why a home inspector should not turn on plumbing systems that have been turned off.

123. **a.** Horizontal drain pipes should have a slope of roughly 1/4-inch-per-foot.

124. **a.** Bell and spigot is a male/female connection method for cast-iron pipe.

125. **d.** Oversizing is not a common problem with drainage piping.

126. **b.** Clay-tile drainage piping can be buried in the ground.

127. **c.** Missing air gaps do not cause leaks in drain pipes.

128. **b.** Slopes of 45° or more do not cause drainage clogging piping.

129. **c.** A cross connection will not exist at outside hose bibs with no attached hoses.

130. **d.** Floor drains with no trap primers are not cross connection situations.

131. **d.** Double trapping is not a cause of poor slope on drainage piping.

132. **c.** Defective ABS piping resulted in cracking around the circumference of the pipe joints.

133. **a.** Dishwashers in some areas require an air gap fitting.

134. **b.** Drain pipes from clothes washers should go into a standpipe.

135. **c.** Copper drain, waste, and vent piping is susceptible to acid.

136. **c.** A common use for brass as a waste material is in fittings.

137. **a.** Horizontal cast-iron piping is prone to splits on the top.

138. **c.** Clay drain pipes are typically used below grade.

139. **d.** A trap seal is the vertical distance from the trap dip to the weir.

140. **a.** The tail piece is the pipe that joins the fixture to the trap.

141. **b.** The trap arm is the pipe that runs from the trap to the vent.

142. **d.** S-traps are a factor in siphoning, not clogging.

143. **b.** Double trapping is a problem because the water velocity at the second trap is too low.

144. **a.** Answers b, c, and d all may cause traps to lose their seal.

145. **a.** Slip joints are not a common trap problem.

146. **a.** Slow-draining fixtures are not an indication of leaking traps.

147. **b.**   A tail piece that is too long may siphon the trap.

148. **a.**   A trap may clog if the trap is oversized or undersized.

149. **a.**   P-traps are allowed by all plumbing codes.

150. **c.**   A plumbing trap provides a liquid seal that will prevent the passage of air/gas.

151. **d.**   The absence of a backwater valve is not a common floor drain problem.

152. **d.**   Providing a fresh-air inlet directly to the living space is not a function of a plumbing vent system.

153. **b.**   Crown-vented traps are not permitted in most areas.

154. **a.**   Island sinks are difficult to vent because people don't want a vent pipe running up through the center of the kitchen.

155. **c.**   A wet vent is a vent that also serves as a drain.

156. **b.**   A missing vent pipe may cause a gurgling sound when draining water out of a sink.

157. **c.**   The minimum recommended height of a plumbing vent stack above the roof is 6 inches.

158. **b.**   A vent can be as close as two pipe-diameters to the trap.

159. **d.**   An undersized vent is not a reason that a sewage pump may not operate.

160. **b.**   Sewage sumps are required for toilets located below the municipal sewer.

161. **b.**   Sewage ejector pumps do not need a trap.

162. **b.**   Sump pumps may be pedestal-type or submersible.

163. **d.**   A discharge point above grade is an acceptable configuration for a sump pump, not a problem.

164. **b.**   Laundry tub pumps should be downstream of the laundry tub trap.

165. **b.**   Good plumbing fixtures should be nonporous, not porous.

166. **a.**   Toilets do not require a trap.

167. **b.**   Floors and walls around toilets, bathtubs, and showers should not be pervious.

168. **d.**   The most common problem with plumbing fixtures is leaks.

169. **d.**   The highest fixture in the house is going to have the weakest flow and drainage.

170. **a.**   Absence of a trap is not a cause of a slow drain.

171. **d.**   In new construction you will not normally find basins and sinks made out of concrete.

172. **b.**   Faucets or spouts must be above the flood rim of the sink or basin.

173. **d.**   Condensate from air conditioners does not commonly cause rust.

174. **c.**   Overflows should not be found on kitchen sinks.

175. **a.**   Washerless faucets are more prone to water hammer problems than compression faucets because water can be turned off more quickly.

176. **d.**   Water hammer is typically prevented by dead-end risers.

177. **a.**   Pressure-balancing valves protect against scalding at showers.

178. **d.**   Answers a, b, and c are common faucet problems.

179. **c.**   A clogged aerator is the common cause of poor pressure and flow at a single fixture.

180. **a.**   Low water pressure is not a common toilet problem.

181. **c.**   Excess pressure at the tank is not a common toilet problem.

182. **c.**   A toilet is not likely to leak at the seat bolt holes.

183. **a.**   Bidets are not self-trapping.

184. **d.**   Bidets do not have seats or lids.

185. **c.**   Bidets do not have tank lids.

186. **c.**   A tile lip for a bathtub provides a support point for the tub to the structure.

187. **d.**   Bathtubs do not have vacuum breakers.

188. **c.**   We do not recommend testing inaccessible bathtub overflows because most overflows leak when they are used.

189. **d.**   Enclosures around tubs and shower stalls are extremely vulnerable to leakage.

190. **d.**   The backup material for a ceramic tile shower stall should not be plywood.

191. **b.**   The most common leakage point in a ceramic shower stall is at the base.

192. **b.**   Answers a, c, and d are all vulnerable spots in a shower and bathtub enclosure.

193. **d.**   Answers a, b, and c may all cause leaks through tub and shower enclosures.

194. **b.**   Electrical light switches and receptacles in bathrooms should be at least three feet away from shower stalls and bathtubs.

195. **d.**   The lowest quality shower stall bases are metal.

196. **b.**   Mortar bed shower stalls require a drain with holes in the side.

197. **c.**   A toe tester is a faucet spout near the bottom of the shower stall.

198. **c.**   Shower stalls should typically be at least 30 × 30 inches.

199. **b.**   Whirlpool baths do not have a dedicated hot water heating system.

200. **d.**   Whirlpool baths are also called hydro-massage bathtubs.

201. **d.**   Not all whirlpool baths have variable-speed pumps.

202. **d.**   Whirlpool baths are designed to have the pump operated only with water in the tub.

203. **d.**   Answers a, b, and c are all common whirlpool problems.

204. **b.**   The most difficult problem to determine in a bathroom is the condition of the shower pan.

205. **b.**   A shower stall is least likely to have a cross connection.

206. **c.**   The inspector is not required to observe the on-site water supply quantity.

207. **d.**   The inspector is required to operate the spray feature of the bidet.

8. INTERIOR SYSTEMS

Practice Questions

1. Skylights can cause ice damming on roofs.
   a. True
   b. False

2. Dehumidifiers are an effective way to correct wet basement problems.
   a. True
   b. False

3. The percentage of basements that get wet at some point is roughly 75 percent.
   a. True
   b. False

4. If you see evidence of water damage on the floor, but the area is dry, you can tell your client the problem has been corrected.
   a. True
   b. False

5. The most common place for home inspectors to see problems with party walls is in the attic.
   a. True
   b. False

6. Truss uplift is a serious ceiling problem with structural consequences for the house.
   a. True
   b. False

7. Best practice calls for lighting in stairs and hallways to include three-way switches.
   a. True
   b. False

8. Cabinets are prone to cosmetic problems only.
   a. True
   b. False

9. Stairway landings must be at least 24 inches long and the same width as the stairwell.
   a. True
   b. False

10. French doors have a tendency to be leaky and drafty.
    a. True
    b. False

11. As you inspect the interior of a home you will also typically inspect components of all these systems, *EXCEPT*
    a. heating.
    b. electrical.
    c. plumbing.
    d. footings.

12. All of the following may limit your inspection, *EXCEPT*
    a. carpet.
    b. storage.
    c. furniture.
    d. drapes.

13. All of the following are common floor materials, *EXCEPT*
    a. concrete.
    b. glass block.
    c. wood.
    d. ceramic tile.

14. All of the following are common wood flooring types, *EXCEPT*
    a. pine.
    b. oak strip.
    c. parquet.
    d. particleboard.

15. All of the following are common flooring problems, *EXCEPT*
    a. water damage.
    b. trip hazard.
    c. mechanical damage.
    d. paint or stain needed.

16. Which of the following flooring problems is a safety issue?
    a. Cracking
    b. Mechanical damage
    c. Trip hazard
    d. Absorbent materials in wet areas

17. Which of the following is *NOT* a problem with concrete flooring?
    a. Cracking
    b. Missing grout
    c. Settling
    d. Hollowing below

18. Which of the following is *NOT* a wood flooring problem?
    a. Rot
    b. Warping
    c. Exposed tongues
    d. Diagonal nailing

19. Which of the following is *NOT* a common carpet problem?
    a. Rot
    b. Odors
    c. Missing underpad
    d. Buckling

20. The difference between ceramic wall tile and ceramic floor tile is
    a. thickness.
    b. strength.
    c. surface durability.
    d. moisture-resistance.

21. All of the following are common wall materials, *EXCEPT*
    a. plaster.
    b. acrylic.
    c. drywall.
    d. wood paneling.

22. All of the following are features of plaster and drywall, *EXCEPT*
    a. durability.
    b. fire-resistance.
    c. moisture-resistance.
    d. inexpensiveness.

23. Wall finishes around wet areas such as bathtubs and showers should have all of the following features *EXCEPT*
    a. smoothness.
    b. hardness.
    c. resilience.
    d. non-absorbency.

24. The optimum spacing between two panes in a double-glazed window is roughly
    a. ⅛-inch.
    b. ¼-inch.
    c. ⅝-inch.
    d. ⅞-inch.

25. The implications of shadow effect on a wall are
    a. failed lathing.
    b. wall racking.
    c. cosmetic only.
    d. an inability to hold nails and screws.

26. All of the following are common party wall problems, *EXCEPT*
    a. ice dams.
    b. discontinuity.
    c. construction from wood.
    d. incompleteness in attics.

27. Garage wall problems include
    a. construction from wood.
    b. finishing with drywall.
    c. lack of fireproofing.
    d. adjacency to bedrooms or other sleeping areas.

28. The most serious problem you may encounter in removing wallpaper is that
    a. the plaster or drywall may come off with the wallpaper.
    b. the moisture used in applying the wallpaper may damage the plaster or drywall behind.
    c. the wallpaper may not have been a strippable type.
    d. removing vinyl wallpaper removes the vapor barrier.

29. All of the following are functions of ceilings, *EXCEPT*
    a. decoration.
    b. addition of rigidity to roof structure.
    c. support for wall structures.
    d. support for insulation.

30. Common ceiling materials include all of the following, *EXCEPT*
    a. plaster.
    b. acoustic tile.
    c. wood.
    d. PVC.

31. Sagging drywall on ceilings may be caused by all of the following, *EXCEPT*
    a. a lack of collar ties in attic.
    b. drywall that is too thin.
    c. roof framing that is spaced too far apart.
    d. winter construction allowing condensation before insulation is installed.

32. All of the following are plaster or drywall problems, *EXCEPT*
    a. shadow effect.
    b. exposed tongues.
    c. crumbling or powdery plaster/drywall.
    d. poor joints.

33. Common problems with wood ceilings include all of the following, *EXCEPT*
    a. rot.
    b. nail pops.
    c. buckling.
    d. cracking or splitting.

34. Which statement about ceiling stains is *FALSE?*
    a. If the stain is wet to the touch, it is probably an active leak.
    b. If the stain shows elevated moisture with a moisture meter, it is probably an active leak.
    c. The best time to check a stain is after running the plumbing fixtures above.
    d. Stains may indicate intermittent leaks.

35. Which statement about lighting is *FALSE?*
    a. Lighting is required in each hall.
    b. Lighting must be overhead.
    c. Lighting in halls should be controlled by three-way switches.
    d. Room lighting should be controlled by a wall switch close to the entrance.

36. All of the following are common trim components, *EXCEPT*
    a. baseboard.
    b. quarter round.
    c. window casings.
    d. muntins.

37. Cornice moldings are commonly made of any of the following materials, *EXCEPT*
    a. wood.
    b. plaster.
    c. polystyrene.
    d. plastic laminate.

38. All of the following are common countertop materials, *EXCEPT*
    a. cork.
    b. plastic laminate.
    c. marble.
    d. granite.

39. Trim problems include all of the following, *EXCEPT*
    a. missing trim.
    b. rot.
    c. inoperativeness.
    d. looseness.

40. All of the following are common counter problems, *EXCEPT*
    a. the entire top being loose.
    b. lack of backsplash.
    c. staining.
    d. mechanical damage.

41. The most important safety issue with respect to cabinets is
    a. water damage.
    b. not being well secured to wall.
    c. rust.
    d. shelves that are not well supported.

42. Common stair materials include all of the following, *EXCEPT*
    a. factory-built wood.
    b. waferboard.
    c. metal.
    d. concrete.

43. Tread problems on stairs include all of the following, *EXCEPT*
    a. tread that is too wide.
    b. wear.
    c. sloping.
    d. looseness.

44. Minimum stair tread widths are roughly
    a. 5¼ inches.
    b. 7¼ inches.
    c. 9¼ inches.
    d. 11¼ inches.

45. The minimum average tread width for curved stairs is required to be roughly
    a. 7 inches.
    b. 8 inches.
    c. 9 inches.
    d. 10 inches.

46. How many sets of winders are typically allowed in one staircase?
    a. One
    b. Two
    c. Three
    d. None

47. The minimum stairwell width is roughly
    a. 29 inches.
    b. 31 inches.
    c. 32 inches.
    d. 35 inches.

48. Handrails on open stairs in the United States should typically be
    a. 20 to 24 inches high.
    b. 22 to 26 inches high.
    c. 30 to 36 inches high.
    d. 34 to 38 inches high.

49. Handrails are usually installed
    a. on balconies.
    b. on decks.
    c. on staircases.
    d. at landings that form mezzanines.

50. Guardrails should be how tall, at a minimum?
    a. 28 inches
    b. 32 inches
    c. 36 inches
    d. 42 inches

51. Which statement about balusters is *FALSE?*
    a. They should be vertical only.
    b. They should have minimum four-inch-wide spaces between them.
    c. They are also called spindles.
    d. They are safety devices.

52. The function of windows includes all of the following *EXCEPT*
    a. allowing light in.
    b. reducing heating costs.
    c. adding ventilation.
    d. allowing for emergency exit.

53. Window frames and sashes are typically of any of the following materials, *EXCEPT*
    a. vinyl.
    b. fiberglass.
    c. fiberboard.
    d. aluminum.

54. All of the following are common window types, *EXCEPT*
    a. double hung.
    b. single hung.
    c. pocket.
    d. horizontal slider.

55. All of the following are common window types, *EXCEPT*
    a. awning.
    b. bifold.
    c. hopper.
    d. jalousie.

56. All of the following are common glazing materials, *EXCEPT*
    a. glass.
    b. acrylic.
    c. laminated glass.
    d. fiberglass.

57. All of the following are common muntin materials, *EXCEPT*
    a. wood.
    b. lead.
    c. acrylic.
    d. brass.

58. A mullion is
    a. a material used to divide glass into individual panes in windows.
    b. the interior part of the sill.
    c. a vertical rail separating two windows in a group.
    d. the part of the window that supports the edge of the glass.

59. The "edge effect," with respect to windows, causes
    a. frame deformation.
    b. difficult operation.
    c. condensation around the perimeter.
    d. lost seals on double glazed and triple glazed units.

60. A thermal break in a window is
    a. the point where the two sashes meet in a double hung window.
    b. an insulating shutter or curtain on a window.
    c. an insulating material between inner and outer halves of a sash or frame.
    d. the separation usually maintained by weatherstripping between the fixed and operable parts of a window.

61. Which of the following windows is most likely to suffer condensation and leakage problems? (Assume that all are single glazed.)
    a. Double hung wood
    b. Double hung vinyl
    c. Vinyl casement
    d. Steel casement

62. Which of the following windows is most likely to suffer air and water leakage?
    a. Sashless horizontal sliders
    b. Awning
    c. Hopper (outward-opening)
    d. Fixed

63. Missing window lintels cause
    a. air leakage.
    b. sagging openings.
    c. water leakage.
    d. mold and mildew.

64. Common window frame problems include all of the following, *EXCEPT*
    a. rot.
    b. frame deformation.
    c. drain hole blockage or lack.
    d. inoperability.

65. Which of the following is *NOT* a common problem with exterior trim?
    a. Rot
    b. Reverse sill slope
    c. Excessive sill projection
    d. Deteriorated caulking

66. All of the following are common window sash problems, *EXCEPT*
    a. inoperability.
    b. stiffness.
    c. inability to stay open.
    d. no drip edge.

67. Which of the following is *NOT* an interior trim problem?
    a. Rot
    b. Cracking
    c. Poor fit
    d. Reverse sill slope

68. All of the following are common glass problems, *EXCEPT*
    a. thermally broken.
    b. lost seal.
    c. excess condensation.
    d. deteriorated glazing compound.

69. All of the following are common window hardware problems, *EXCEPT*
    a. rust.
    b. breakage.
    c. interior mounting.
    d. inoperability.

70. Where in the home might low window sills be a problem?
    a. Basement
    b. Living room
    c. Kitchen
    d. Stairwell

71. Under what circumstances would the size of the window be an issue?
    a. In a room where lighting is important
    b. In a room where ventilation is important
    c. In a room where emergency exit is important
    d. In an area where excess heat loss could be a problem

72. The R-value of a conventional double glazed window is roughly
    a. one.
    b. two.
    c. three.
    d. five.

73. The functions of exterior doors include all of the following, *EXCEPT*
    a. security.
    b. weather-tightness.
    c. gas/fire protection.
    d. ventilation.

74. The functions of interior doors include all of the following, *EXCEPT*
    a. security.
    b. privacy.
    c. sound barrier.
    d. fire protection.

75. All of the following are operating types for doors, *EXCEPT*
    a. hinged.
    b. casement.
    c. bifold.
    d. sliding.

76. All of the following are common door surfaces, *EXCEPT*
    a. pebbled.
    b. flush.
    c. paneled.
    d. louvered.

77. The R-value of a solid wood exterior door is roughly
    a. one.
    b. two.
    c. four.
    d. five.

78. All of the following are common problems with doors and frames, *EXCEPT*
    a. rot.
    b. rust.
    c. low R-value.
    d. delamination.

79. Dark paint on a metal door
    a. reduces the life expectancy of the door.
    b. reduces the R-value of the door.
    c. may become very hot if exposed to the sun.
    d. typically requires frequent repainting.

80. Interior door trim problems include all of the following, *EXCEPT*
    a. floors stained below.
    b. ineffective or missing doorstops.
    c. guides and stops damaged.
    d. backwards installation.

81. Exterior hinges on doors
    a. reduce security.
    b. improve the appearance of interior trim.
    c. are used with doors that have to open inward.
    d. must be self-closing.

82. Self-closers on doors are recommended at, in, and on
    a. the tops of staircases.
    b. bathrooms.
    c. garages.
    d. doors with storms.

83. Chronically-wet basements are most often the result of
    a. ground water.
    b. surface water.
    c. sweating plumbing.
    d. leaking appliances.

84. Other water sources in homes include all of the following, *EXCEPT*
    a. heating leaks.
    b. siding leaks.
    c. sewer backup.
    d. dripping faucets.

85. The implications of wet basement problems include all of the following, *EXCEPT*
    a. odors.
    b. frost heaving of floors.
    c. health hazards, in the form of molds.
    d. structural deterioration.

86. All of the following may be signs of surface water penetration into basements and crawl spaces, *EXCEPT*
    a. water on the floor.
    b. efflorescence.
    c. rot at the bottom of stair stringers.
    d. check valves on floor drains.

87. All of the following are signs of water problems in basements, *EXCEPT*
    a. rust at the base of steel columns.
    b. loose floor tiles.
    c. basement storage kept off the floor.
    d. window wells extending below windows.

88. Roof water runoff is best controlled with
    a. good grading.
    b. catch basins.
    c. gutters and downspouts.
    d. dampproofing.

89. All of the following statements about mold in cold rooms are true, *EXCEPT*
    a. that it's usually caused by condensation.
    b. weatherstripping the door will help.
    c. opening or providing a vent to the exterior will help.
    d. the cold room should be sealed off and abandoned.

90. All of the following are common foundation flaws, *EXCEPT*
    a. excessive height above grade.
    b. cracks.
    c. holes at form ties.
    d. cold pours.

91. Which of the following can effectively patch cracks in concrete-block foundation walls from the inside?
    a. Asphalt-based products
    b. Epoxy
    c. Mastic
    d. None of the above

92. All of the following statements about foundation drainage membranes are true, *EXCEPT* that they
    a. should not be installed on older foundation walls.
    b. can be installed below grade.
    c. provide an air space between the earth and the foundation.
    d. are typically sealed at the top.

93. Bentonite clay injections
    a. are a positive cure for wet basements.
    b. are used only on concrete-block foundations.
    c. rely on perimeter drainage.
    d. are often ineffective.

94. All of the following are limitations to your wet-basement investigation *EXCEPT*
    a. wall finishes may cover evidence.
    b. there may be a raised floor.
    c. storage may be kept off the floor.
    d. there may have been no rain for some time before the inspection.

ANSWERS AND EXPLANATIONS

1. **a.** Skylights can cause ice damming on roofs.

2. **b.** Dehumidifiers don't solve leaking basement problems.

3. **b.** Virtually all (98 percent) basements get wet at some point.

4. **b.** If the water-damaged area is dry, you should not assume the problem has been corrected. There may be an inactive or intermittent leak.

5. **a.** Party walls should be continuous to the underside of the roof sheathing and should fit tightly there. There should be no openings in the party wall at the attic level.

6. **b.** Truss uplift is a cold weather problem that is not terribly serious from a structural standpoint, although it can cause considerable cosmetic disruption.

7. **a.** Three-way switches allow for lights to be turned on and off from either end of a stairway or hallway.

8. **b.** Cabinet problems can be serious and safety-related, including cabinets that are loosely secured to the wall and may fall on people.

9. **b.** Stairway landings must be at least 36 inches long and the same width as the stairwell. No stairwell is needed if the door at the top of the stairs opens away from the stairs.

10. **a.** True French doors meet at the center, with no middle mullion or frame to close against, so they can be leaky, drafty, and less secure than other types of doors.

11. **d.** You can't inspect the footings because they are typically not visible.

12. **d.** Drapes can be pulled back out of the way, so they do not limit the inspection.

13. **b.** Glass block can be a floor material, but it is not a common one.

14. **d.** Particleboard is not a common wood flooring material.

15. **d.** The need for paint or stain is not a common flooring problem.

16. **c.** A trip hazard is a safety issue.

17. **b.** Grout is not a component of concrete flooring.

18. **d.** Diagonal nailing is common with tongue-and-groove wood flooring. It is not a problem.

19. **c.** Missing underpad is not a problem with carpet. Carpet does not require underpad.

20. **c.** The primary difference between wall tile and floor tile is surface durability. Ceramic floor tile stands up much better to foot traffic than wall tile.

21. **b.** Acrylic is not a common wall material.

22. **c.** Plaster and drywall are not very moisture resistant, unfortunately.

23. **c.** Wall finishes around bathtubs do not have to be resilient.

24. **c.** The optimum space between two panes in a double glazed window is about ⅝ of an inch.

25. **c.** Shadow effect is a cosmetic issue only.

26. **c.** Party walls can be constructed of wood in most cases.

27. **c.** In the United States, garage walls and ceilings require fireproofing.

28. **a.** When removing wallpaper, plaster or drywall may come off with the paper.

29. **c.** Ceilings do not support wall structures.

30. **d.** PVC is not a common ceiling material.

31. **a.** Missing collar ties will not cause sagging drywall.

32. **b.** Exposed tongues are not a problem with plaster or drywall. These materials do not have tongues.

33. **b.** Nail pops are not a common problem with wood ceilings.

34. **c.** If the stain is dry, this does not necessarily mean that the leak is not active. It may only mean that the plumbing fixture above hasn't been used recently, or that the roof has not leaked because there has not been any rain for some time.

35. **b.** Room lighting does not have to be overhead. Lighting in living rooms, for example, is rarely overhead.

36. **d.** Muntins are not trim components; they are an integral part of windows.

37. **d.** Plastic laminate is not typically used for cornice moldings because it cannot be painted easily.

38. **a.** Cork is not a common countertop material because it is quite absorbent.

39. **c.** Inoperative trim is not a problem because trim is not supposed to go anywhere.

40. **b.** Counters do not need backsplashes, although they are a good idea.

41. **b.** The big safety issue with cabinets is whether or not they are well-secured to the wall.

42. **b.** Waferboard is not a common stair material.

43. **a.** Stair treads cannot be too wide.

44. **c.** Minimum stair tread widths are roughly 9¼ inches.

45. **c.** The minimum average tread width for curved stairs is roughly 9 inches.

46. **a.** Only one set of winders is typically allowed per stair case.

47. **d.** The minimum stairwell width is roughly 35 inches.

48. **d.** Handrails on open stairs in the United States should be 34–38 inches high.

49. **c.** Handrails are usually installed on staircases. These other structures have guardrails.

50. **c.** Guardrails should be at least 36 inches tall.

51. **b.** Ballisters should have maximum 4-inch-wide spaces between them.

52. **b.** Windows do not help reduce heating costs. They typically increase heating costs relative to walls.

53. **c.** Window frames and sashes are not made of fiberboard; however, they are made out of vinyl, fiberglass, steel, and aluminum.

54. **c.** There are pocket doors but no pocket windows.

55. **b.** There are bifold doors, but no bifold windows.

56. **d.** Fiberglass is not a common glazing material.

57. **c.** Acrylic is not used for window muntins.

58. **c.** A mullion is a vertical rail between two windows.

59. **c.** The edge effect with respect to windows is condensation around the perimeter, caused by the thermal bridging of the sash or frame.

60. **c.** A thermal break is an insulating material between the inner and outer halves of a sash or frame. This is usually found on vinyl and metal frames.

61. **d.** The steel casement window is most likely to suffer condensation and leakage.

62. **a.** The sashless horizontal sliders are the lowest quality window in this group.

63. **b.** Missing lintels result in sagging openings.

64. **d.** Inoperable window frames are not a problem because the frames should not operate.

65. **c.** Excessive sill projection is not a problem. Usually there is too little sill projection.

66. **d.** Window sashes do not have drip edges.

67. **d.** Reverse sill slope is not a problem with interior trim. It doesn't matter what the slope is on an interior sill.

68. **a.** A thermally broken window is not a problem with the glass. It is a separation in the frame designed to reduce thermal bridging and heat loss.

69. **c.** Window hardware should be mounted on the interior of the window.

70. **d.** Low window sills might be a problem on a stairwell because if someone tripped, they might fall out the window.

71. **c.** The size of the window may be an issue if the window is an emergency exit.

72. **b.** The R-value of a conventional double glazed window is roughly two.

73. **d.** The function of exterior doors does not include ventilation in most cases.

74. **a.** Interior doors are not generally designed to provide security.

75. **b.** Casement is a type of window but not a type of door.

76. **a.** Pebbled is not a common door surface.

77. **b.** The R-value of a solid wood exterior door is roughly two.

78. **c.** Low R-value is not a problem with doors and frames. It is a fact of life, but it does not affect the door performance as the other items on this list do.

79. **c.** Dark paint on a metal door may become very hot if exposed to the sun.

80. **d.** Interior door trim problems do not include backwards installation.

81. **a.** Exterior hinges on doors reduce security.

82. **c.** Self-closers on doors are recommended for garages that are attached to homes.

83. **b.** Chronically-wet basements are most often a result of surface water.

84. **d.** Dripping faucets do not cause water problems in houses because the water runs into the fixture and down the drain.

85. **b.** Wet basement problems do not typically result in frost heaving.

86. **d.** Check valves on floor drains may indicate sewer back up problems but do not indicate surface water penetration problems.

87. **d.** Window wells extending below windows is a normal and good arrangement. This is not an indicator of basement water problems.

88. **c.** Roof water run off is best controlled with gutters and downspouts.

89. **d.** There is no need to seal off and abandon a cold room simply because there is mold. It is better to eliminate the conditions that allow the mold to develop.

90. **a.** Foundations that extend above grade are not a problem. It doesn't matter how far above grade they extend.

91. **d.** Concrete block foundation walls can not be effectively patched from the inside.

92. **a.** Foundation drainage membranes can be installed on older foundation walls.

93. **d.** Bentonite clay injections are often ineffective.

94. **c.** Storage kept off the floor is a clue, rather than a limitation.

9. FIREPLACE AND CHIMNEY SYSTEMS

Practice Questions

1. Chimneys may have multiple flues.
   a. True
   b. False

2. Masonry chimneys usually help support wood frame structures.
   a. True
   b. False

3. You can tell whether a chimney is lined by looking for a liner extending above the top.
   a. True
   b. False

4. Any B-vent can be installed running up the outside of a house.
   a. True
   b. False

5. Metal chimneys often have several flues.
   a. True
   b. False

6. Sections of metal chimneys are typically welded together on site.
   a. True
   b. False

7. Wood stoves typically do *NOT* have ductwork.
   a. True
   b. False

8. Convective stoves can usually be closer to combustibles than can radiant stoves.
   a. True
   b. False

9. All wood stoves have firebrick in the combustion chamber.
   a. True
   b. False

10. Fireplaces can be built-in or free-standing
    a. True
    b. False

11. Fireplaces are designed as a primary heating source in most cases.
    a. True
    b. False

12. Factory-built fireplaces do *NOT* have a smoke shelf.
    a. True
    b. False

13. Zero-clearance fireplaces typically do *NOT* require any clearance from combustibles at the top of the firebox.
    a. True
    b. False

14. A home inspection includes an analysis of the quality of chimney draw for a fireplace.
    a. True
    b. False

15. Soot or smoke deposits on a mantel always indicate a poorly drafting fireplace.
    a. True
    b. False

16. If the fireplace is raised, the hearth extension should be extended.
    a. True
    b. False

17. Metal fireboxes should be mortared tightly to the masonry of the fireplace.
    a. True
    b. False

18. Clay tile liners should be supported on metal fireboxes.
    a. True
    b. False

19. Lintels should be mortared tightly into place.
    a. True
    b. False

20. Zero-clearance fireplaces do *NOT* require footings and foundations.
    a. True
    b. False

21. The floor of the ashpit should be 12 inches below the bottom of the cleanout door.
    a. True
    b. False

22. Glass doors are designed to replace fireplace dampers.
    a. True
    b. False

23. Heat-circulator systems always require a fan that is thermostatically controlled.
    a. True
    b. False

24. The characteristics of a good chimney include all of the following *EXCEPT*
    a. enhancing the draft from appliances.
    b. prevention of exhaust gases from entering the house.
    c. providing combustion air.
    d. helping to keep water out of the house.

25. A vent connector is
    a. a chimney.
    b. a flue.
    c. an exhaust flue.
    d. clay tile.

26. Chimneys are designed to support
    a. satellite dishes.
    b. television antennas or towers.
    c. roof framing (but not floor framing) members.
    d. their own weight.

27. The temperature that a wood-burning fireplace chimney might commonly see is
    a. 350°F.
    b. 600°F.
    c. 800°F.
    d. 1,000°F.

28. All of the following can affect the chimney draft *EXCEPT*
    a. the number of flues.
    b. the chimney height.
    c. the flue size.
    d. whether the chimney is interior or exterior.

29. Which of the following is NOT considered in determining the size of a chimney flue?
    a. Fuel that is used
    b. Flue material
    c. Appliance size
    d. Chimney height

30. In masonry chimneys, adjacent flues are usually separated by
    a. a clay tile liner.
    b. an air space.
    c. a wythe of brick.
    d. noncombustible insulation.

31. Which of the following is *NOT* an integral component of a masonry chimney?
    a. Rain cap
    b. Footing and foundation
    c. Chimney wall
    d. Flue liner

32. Masonry chimneys typically require bracing if
    a. they are on a roof with a slope of more than 10 in 12.
    b. the unsupported tops are taller than 12 feet.
    c. they are single flue.
    d. there is a tall structure nearby that may create wind turbulence.

33. Firestopping
    a. should be provided at every floor level.
    b. is only required on masonry chimneys.
    c. cannot be accomplished with noncombustible insulation.
    d. is not required on multiple flue chimneys.

34. Liners for masonry chimneys may *NOT* be made of
    a. clay tile.
    b. steel.
    c. asbestos cement.
    d. fiberglass.

35. Which of the following statements is NOT true of chimney liners?
    a. Chimney liners help exhaust gases flow quickly up the chimney.
    b. Liners help prevent combustion products from getting into the house.
    c. Liners should extend at least eight inches above the chimney cap.
    d. Liners help chimneys withstand chimney fires.

36. Which of the following statements about clay tile liners in masonry chimneys is true?
    a. The bottom piece of a clay tile liner should rest on stainless-steel nails.
    b. Liners may be round or rectangular.
    c. Liners should be firmly and continuously supported by brick around their perimeter.
    d. Adjacent pieces of clay tile liner should be joined with a high-temperature caulking.

37. All of the following are characteristics of good concrete chimney caps *EXCEPT* that they
    a. are four inches thick.
    b. are sloped to drain water away from the flue.
    c. are poured tightly against the clay tile liner.
    d. have a capillary break.

38. Masonry chimneys may settle or lean for any of the following reasons, *EXCEPT*
    a. undersized footings.
    b. frost heave.
    c. absence of clay tile liner.
    d. excessive corbelling.

39. The implications of settling and leaning include all of the following *EXCEPT*
    a. collapse of the chimney.
    b. fire hazard.
    c. water leakage into the house.
    d. loss of drip edge on cap.

40. Spalling is
    a. typically caused by exposure to high temperatures.
    b. typically caused by exposure to acid.
    c. crumbling or flaking of brick or concrete surfaces.
    d. a common problem where metal liners are used.

41. Masonry chimneys should extend above the roof
    a. 3 feet higher than anything within 5 feet.
    b. 1 foot higher than anything within 10 feet.
    c. 3 feet higher than the roof where it penetrates the roof.
    d. 3 feet higher than any point in the roof.

42. A masonry chimney serving a wood fireplace should be at least
    a. 8 feet tall.
    b. 12 feet tall.
    c. 15 feet tall.
    d. 18 feet tall.

43. Clay tile liners became common in masonry chimneys around
    a. 1920.
    b. 1935.
    c. 1950.
    d. 1960.

44. Where a clay tile liner is found in a masonry chimney, the most likely place to find a gap in this liner is
    a. at the cleanout door.
    b. where multiple appliances are connected.
    c. between the top and second liner sections.
    d. at the midpoint of the chimney.

45. The main function of a chimney cap or crown is to
    a. protect the top of the chimney from water penetration.
    b. deflect downdrafts.
    c. prevent burning embers from leaving the chimney and igniting the roof.
    d. keep birds and animals out of the chimney.

46. Which of the following statements about creosote is *NOT* true?
    a. Creosote is a major cause of chimney fires.
    b. Burning hardwoods generates more creosote than softwoods.
    c. Slow-burning fires deposit more creosote than roaring fires.
    d. Black, shiny creosote is more of a problem than brown, flaky creosote.

47. All of the following are vent connector problems *EXCEPT* the vent connector
    a. run from the appliance to the chimney is too short.
    b. is loose at the chimney.
    c. is obstructed.
    d. is two inches above the cleanout.

48. Why are abandoned flue connections a problem with masonry chimneys?
    a. They can adversely affect draft.
    b. They can allow moisture into the chimney.
    c. They may allow exhaust gases to escape from the chimney.
    d. They can allow excessive cooling of the chimney.

49. Which of these situations definitely constitutes too many appliances in one flue?
    a. Two gas appliances on different floors
    b. Two oil appliances on the same floor
    c. A wood stove and an oil furnace on the same floor
    d. Two wood fireplaces on the same floor

50. For metal systems, what is one convention that is used to differentiate a vent from a chimney?
    a. Vents are found on water heaters, and chimneys are found on all other appliances.
    b. Vents typically serve oil or gas appliances and chimneys serve wood.
    c. Vents are screwed together and chimneys are assembled with locking bands.
    d. Vents are used indoors and chimneys run up the outside of buildings.

51. B-vents are used with
    a. wood stoves.
    b. wood fireplaces.
    c. oil and gas appliances.
    d. gas appliances.

52. B-vents
    a. are insulated, double-wall systems.
    b. are all suitable for use outdoors.
    c. require a one-inch clearance from combustibles.
    d. are designed to be tied in to masonry chimneys.

53. L-vents are used with
    a. gas appliances.
    b. oil appliances.
    c. wood stoves.
    d. gas and oil appliances.

54. All of these statements about factory built chimneys are true *EXCEPT* that they
    a. are also called 650° chimneys.
    b. are not designed for solid fuels.
    c. typically have two-inch-thick walls.
    d. are tested for up to 2,000°F.

55. Bracing metal chimneys is necessary
    a. in high wind areas.
    b. if the chimney penetrates the roof at the peak.
    c. if the chimney is more than five feet above the roof.
    d. if the chimney is larger than six inches in interior diameter.

56. A factory-built chimney designed for use with a wood fireplace requires how much clearance from combustibles?
    a. 1 inch.
    b. 2 inches.
    c. 3 inches.
    d. 18 inches.

57. Problems with rain caps include all of the following *EXCEPT* when the rain cap
    a. has a spark arrester with ½-inch screening.
    b. is not there.
    c. sits too low on the chimney.
    d. is obstructed by a bird's nest.

58. Spark arresters
    a. are installed at the bottom of most wood-burning chimneys.
    b. are not permitted on masonry fireplaces.
    c. are often built into rain caps on metal chimneys.
    d. should be ¼-inch screening or less.

59. Metal chimney walls may warp or buckle because of
    a. improper assembly.
    b. a lack of bracing.
    c. a missing cap.
    d. a chimney fire.

60. Rusting or pitting of metal chimney walls may be related to
    a. acid rain.
    b. water combining with insulation to form acid.
    c. combining a water heater and furnace in the same flue.
    d. running the vent through more than five feet of unheated attic space.

61. A B-vent should extend at least
    a. 2 feet above the roof at its point of penetration.
    b. 3 feet above anything within 10 feet horizontally of the vent.
    c. 3 feet above the roof at its point of penetration.
    d. 4 feet above any part of the roof within 10 feet horizontally.

62. Blistering and discoloring of chimney walls indicates
    a. corrosion.
    b. poor maintenance.
    c. multiple appliances in one flue.
    d. poor support.

63. A B-vent for a gas furnace should have a total height of not less than
    a. 12 feet above the draft hood.
    b. 10 feet above the draft hood.
    c. 8 feet above the draft hood.
    d. 5 feet above the draft hood.

64. A metal chimney should not connect to a masonry chimney partway up a building because of all of the following *EXCEPT*
    a. a galvanic reaction will be set up.
    b. inspection is more difficult.
    c. cleaning is more difficult.
    d. overheating or leakage may occur at the joint.

65. Looking up from the basement around a metal chimney for a wood-burning fireplace, you should see
    a. a metal roof flashing at the shingles.
    b. a neoprene roof flashing at the chimney.
    c. the floor framing cut back 1 inch from the chimney.
    d. a metal firestop spacer.

66. From an energy-efficiency standpoint, which is the least-efficient appliance?
    a. Wood stoves
    b. Wood-burning fireplaces
    c. Wood-burning furnaces
    d. Oil furnaces

67. Which of the following helps to make a good wood fire?
    a. The use of softwood
    b. Lots of combustion air
    c. The use of driftwood
    d. The use of manufactured logs

68. Which statement is *FALSE?*
    a. Creosote is noncombustible.
    b. Creosote can be shiny and black.
    c. Creosote can be brown, fluffy, and flaky.
    d. Creosote becomes a liquid at high temperatures.

69. Which of the following is *NOT* a component of a wood-burning furnace?
    a. Combustion chamber
    b. Burner
    c. Vent connector
    d. House air fan

70. All of the following are components of wood furnaces *EXCEPT*
    a. combustion air control.
    b. safety controls.
    c. thermocouple.
    d. duct system.

71. All of the following are common cabinet problems for wood furnaces *EXCEPT*
    a. inadequate combustible clearances.
    b. obstructed air intakes.
    c. scorching.
    d. a missing heat shield.

72. Which of the following would *NOT* affect the amount of air available for combustion in a wood furnace?
    a. Closing all of the doors and windows
    b. Turning on the dishwasher
    c. Turning on the clothes dryer
    d. Turning on the central-vacuum system

73. All of the following are typical combustion chamber problems in wood furnaces *EXCEPT*
    a. poor sealing at the door.
    b. a dirty combustion chamber.
    c. a missing catalytic combustor.
    d. deteriorated brick.

74. A combustion air fan on a wood furnace
    a. replaces the house air fan.
    b. replaces the barometric damper.
    c. works with the combustion air damper.
    d. is controlled by the thermostat.

75. The combustion chamber in a wood furnace
    a. is located downstream of the heat exchanger.
    b. must be made of brick.
    c. has a tight-fitting door.
    d. must be a single-combustion chamber.

76. Which of the following statements about heat exchangers in wood furnaces is *FALSE?*
    a. They are similar to the heat exchangers in oil furnaces.
    b. They are typically made of heavy-gauge steel.
    c. They are larger than oil furnace heat exchangers to improve heat transfer.
    d. They shouldn't have any sharp turns or elbows that could collect debris.

77. All of the following are vent connector problems on wood furnaces *EXCEPT* that
    a. there is less than five feet of distance from furnace to chimney.
    b. the combustible clearance is less than 18 inches.
    c. it is made of galvanized steel.
    d. the male end is at the upper end of each section.

78. Which of the following is a problem with a vent connector on a wood furnace?
    a. The near horizontal sections slope up away from the furnace at ¼-inch per foot.
    b. Individual sections are friction-fit together.
    c. The seams are at the top of nearly horizontal sections.
    d. The vent connector is the same diameter as the flue collar on the furnace.

79. The high-temperature limit on a wood furnace should be set at
    a. 235°F.
    b. 265°F.
    c. 295°F.
    d. 325°F.

80. The first six feet of supply duct from a wood furnace typically has to be how far from combustible materials?
    a. 1 inch
    b. 2 inches
    c. 6 inches
    d. 9 inches

81. Wood stoves are also called
    a. zero clearance fireplaces.
    b. wood furnaces.
    c. add-on furnaces.
    d. space heaters.

82. When talking about a wood stove, the word "airtight" means that
    a. the chimney is sealed to prevent downdrafts.
    b. air for combustion can only enter the stove through controlled openings.
    c. this is an advanced-combustion stove.
    d. this stove has a catalytic combustor.

83. Which of the following does *NOT* improve the efficiency of wood stoves?
    a. Secondary combustion chambers
    b. Catalytic combustors
    c. Outdoor combustion air supply
    d. Open doors on stoves

84. All of the following are typical of pellet stoves *EXCEPT*
    a. catalytic combustors.
    b. hoppers.
    c. exhaust fans.
    d. sidewall venting.

85. A wood stove should have a pad under it that prevents sparks or embers from igniting a combustible floor. How far should this pad extend out in front of the stove?
    a. 12 inches
    b. 16 inches
    c. 18 inches
    d. 20 inches

86. A wood stove on a combustible floor should rest on
    a. ceramic tile.
    b. a metal plate.
    c. two rows of bricks or blocks.
    d. one-inch spacers and a metal plate.

87. A wood stove has no data plate that indicates combustible clearances. What clearance should you be looking for from the rear and sidewalls?
    a. 24 inches
    b. 36 inches
    c. 48 inches
    d. 60 inches

88. An unlisted wood stove should have what clearance from the top of the stove to combustibles?
    a. 36 inches
    b. 48 inches
    c. 60 inches
    d. 72 inches

89. All of the following are common cabinet problems with wood stoves *EXCEPT*
    a. a cabinet not sitting solidly on floor.
    b. gaps that are visible in the cabinet.
    c. a door that fits poorly.
    d. metal plates that are secured to the side and rear of the stove.

90. All of the following are vent connector problems on wood stoves *EXCEPT*
    a. the seams on horizontal sections are at the bottom.
    b. a heat reclaimer has been provided.
    c. the vent connector runs through a closet.
    d. the vent connector is eight feet long.

91. Backpuffing on a wood stove is
    a. using bellows to ignite a wood fire.
    b. reigniting a fire that has burning down to embers by restoking it.
    c. heat flowing backwards through the ductwork.
    d. smoke escaping through the door of a stove when it is opened.

92. Masonry wood-burning fireplaces with steel fireboxes
    a. do not have a damper.
    b. typically are single-walled.
    c. operate at lower temperatures than other masonry fireplaces.
    d. are factory-built fireplaces.

93. The basic components of a wood-burning fireplace include all of the following *EXCEPT*
    a. footings.
    b. hearth.
    c. firebox.
    d. glass doors.

94. All of the following are basic components of a masonry wood-burning fireplace *EXCEPT* a
    a. damper.
    b. throat.
    c. smoke shelf.
    d. heat circulator.

95. Pyrolysis is a
    a. method of improving the efficiency of wood stoves.
    b. method of improving the efficiency of wood-burning fireplaces.
    c. by-product of creosote.
    d. lowering of the autoignition temperature of wood.

96. All of the following are common fireplace footing and foundation problems *EXCEPT*
    a. settling.
    b. heaving.
    c. scorching.
    d. mortar deterioration.

97. A wood-burning masonry fireplace has a hearth extension that is flush with the hearth. The fireplace opening is five square feet. The hearth size should be
    a. 16 inches in front and 8 inches to the sides of the opening.
    b. 20 inches in front and 12 inches to the sides of the opening.
    c. 24 inches in front and 12 inches to the sides of the opening.
    d. 24 inches in front and 16 inches to the sides of the opening.

98. The steel lintel at the face of a wood-burning fireplace
    a. should be mortared tightly into place.
    b. should be able to expand without cracking the masonry.
    c. is not prone to rusting.
    d. would never cause cracking in the face of the fireplace.

99. Common metal firebox problems in wood-burning fireplaces include all of the following *EXCEPT*
    a. rustout.
    b. burnout.
    c. buckling.
    d. poor support.

100. Which of the following statements about wood-burning fireplace dampers is *FALSE?*
    a. Dampers are usually hinged at the middle or back.
    b. Dampers help prevent cold air from entering the house when the fireplace is idle.
    c. Dampers should be 50 percent of the cross-sectional area of the flue.
    d. Dampers are typically made of cast iron or, at least, 12-gauge steel.

101. Which of the following statements about smoke shelves and smoke chambers is *NOT* true?
    a. Masonry fireplaces have a smoke shelf and a smoke chamber.
    b. Factory-built fireplaces do not have a smoke shelf.
    c. The back of the smoke chamber should never be vertical.
    d. The walls of the smoke chamber should never slope at more than 45 degrees.

102. Problems with the chimney face or breast in a masonry wood-burning fireplace include all of the following *EXCEPT*
    a. settling.
    b. inadequate combustible clearances.
    c. excess thickness.
    d. location too far below the damper.

103. How far away from a cleanout door on an ashpit should combustible materials be kept?
    a. One inch
    b. Two inches
    c. Three inches
    d. Six inches

104. All of the following are components of an outdoor combustion air supply for a wood-burning fireplace *EXCEPT*
    a. insulation.
    b. a damper near the outlet.
    c. a hood and/or screen near the outlet.
    d. a 12-inch-clearance from combustibles for the duct.

105. All of the following statements are true about glass doors on wood-burning fireplaces *EXCEPT* the
    a. glass may be cracked or broken.
    b. doors may not open and close.
    c. doors may obstruct cooling-air inlets.
    d. doors should never be closed when the fireplace is operating.

106. Gas igniters for masonry fireplaces have
    a. an automatic gas valve.
    b. pilot ignition.
    c. a variable firing rate.
    d. to be shut off manually.

ANSWERS AND EXPLANATIONS

1. **a.**   Masonry chimneys may have several flues.

2. **b.**   Chimneys are not intended to support other building components.

3. **b.**   The presence of a liner extending above the top of the chimney does not necessarily mean that the chimney is completely lined.

4. **b.**   Not all B-vents can be installed on the exterior of the house for their entire length.

5. **b.**   A metal chimney typically has one flue.

6. **b.**   Sections of metal chimneys typically are connected mechanically through a twist-lock mechanism or locking bands.

7. **a.**   Wood stoves do not have duct systems or pipes connected to them.

8. **a.**   Convective stoves are cooler than radiant stoves and are often permitted to have reduced combustible clearances.

9. **b.**   Not all wood stoves have firebrick liner in the combustion chamber.

10. **a.**   Fireplaces can be built into a wall or as freestanding units.

11. **b.**   Fireplaces are basically entertainment devices. They are not designed to serve as a primary heating source.

12. **a.**   Factory-built fireplaces usually do not have a smoke shelf or smoke chamber above the damper.

13. **b.**   Zero-clearance fireplaces do not require any clearance from combustibles at their sides and back. However, a common problem with zero-clearance fireplaces is inadequate clearance from combustibles at the top of the firebox.

14. **b.**   An analysis of the quality of the chimney draw is beyond the scope of a standard home inspection.

15. **b.**   Soot or smoke on a mantel is not always an indication of poor draft.

16. **a.**   If the fireplace is raised above floor level, it is good practice to extend the hearth further.

17. **b.**   Metal fireboxes should be ½-inch to 1 inch away from masonry.

18. **b.**   Clay tile lines should not rest directly on metal fireboxes.

19. **b.**   The lintel will expand and contract as the fireplace is in use, so it should not be mortared too tightly into place.

20. **a.**   Zero clearance fireplaces do not require footings and foundations.

21. **b.**   It is considered good practice to have the cleanout at the bottom of the ashpit.

22. **b.**   Glass doors are not intended to replace dampers.

23. **b.**   Some heat circulators rely on natural convection flow.

24. **c.**   A chimney does not provide combustion air under normal circumstances.

25. **c.**   A vent connector is an exhaust flue.

26. **d.**   Chimneys are designed to support only their own weight.

27. **c.**   A wood burning fireplace chimney will commonly see temperatures of 800°F.

28. **b.**   The flue material is not considered in determining the diameter of a chimney flue.

29. **a.**   The number of flues does not affect the chimney draft.

30. **c.**   In masonry chimneys, adjacent flues are usually separated by a wythe of brick.

31. **a.**   A rain cap is not an integral component of a masonry chimney.

32. **b.**   Masonry chimneys typically require bracing if they are taller than 12 feet above their highest support (the roof, wall, or ceiling structure).

33. **a.**   Firestopping should be provided at every floor level.

34. **d.**   Liners for masonry chimneys may not be made of fiberglass.

35. **c.**   Liners should not extend at least eight inches above the chimney cap.

36. **b.**   Clay tile chimney liners may be round or rectangular.

37. **c.**   Ideally, concrete chimney caps should not be poured tightly against the clay tile liner.

38. **c.** The absence of a clay tile liner is not likely to cause a chimney to settle or lean.

39. **d.** The loss of a drip edge on the cap is not one of the typical implications of settling and leaning in a masonry chimney.

40. **c.** Spalling is crumbling or flaking of brick or concrete surfaces.

41. **c.** Masonry chimneys should extend above the roof three feet higher than the point where they penetrate the roof.

42. **c.** A masonry chimney serving a wood fireplace should be at least 15 feet tall.

43. **c.** Clay tile liners became common in masonry chimneys around 1950.

44. **c.** The most common place to find a gap in a clay tile liner in a masonry chimney is between the top and second liner sections.

45. **a.** The main function of a chimney or crown is to protect the top of the chimney from water penetration.

46. **b.** Burning hardwoods does not generate more creosote than soft woods.

47. **a.** A short vent connector is not a problem, assuming that is it properly connected to the chimney.

48. **c.** Abandoned flue connections may allow exhaust gases and heat to escape from the chimney.

49. **d.** Two wood fireplaces on the same floor connected to a single flue would be too many.

50. **b.** One convention used to differentiate a vent from a chimney is to say that vents typically serve oil or gas appliances and chimneys serve wood-burning appliances.

51. **d.** B-vents are used with gas appliances.

52. **c.** B-vents require a one-inch clearance from combustibles.

53. **d.** L-vents are used with gas and oil appliances.

54. **b.** Factory-built chimneys are designed for solid fuels.

55. **c.** Bracing metal chimneys is necessary if the chimney is more than five feet tall from the point where it passes through the roof.

56. **b.** A factory built chimney designed for use with a wood fireplace typically requires two inches of clearance from combustibles.

57. **a.** A rain cap with a spark arrester having ½-inch screening is not a problem.

58. **c.** Spark arresters are often built into raincaps on metal chimneys.

59. **d.** Metal chimney walls may warp or buckle because of a chimney fire.

60. **b.** Water combining with insulation to form acid can cause rusting or pitting of metal chimney walls.

61. **a.** A B-vent should extend at least two feet above the roof at its point of penetration.

62. **a.** Blistering and discoloration of chimney walls indicate corrosion.

63. **d.** A B-vent for a gas furnace should have a total height of not less than five feet above the draft hood.

64. **a.** A galvanic reaction is not likely to be set up because a masonry chimney is connected to a metal chimney.

65. **d.** From the basement you should see the metal firestop spacer.

66. **b.** Wood-burning fireplaces are the least-efficient appliance on this list.

67. **b.** Providing lots of combustion air helps to make a good wood fire.

68. **a.** Creosote is combustible.

69. **b.** A wood-burning furnace does not have a burner.

70. **c.** A wood furnace does not have a thermocouple.

71. **d.** A missing heat shield is not a common cabinet problem on wood furnaces.

72. **b.** Turning on the dishwasher would not affect the amount of air available for combustion in a wood furnace.

73. **c.** A missing catalytic combustor is not a typical combustion chamber problem on a wood furnace.

74. **d.** A combustion air fan on a wood furnace is controlled by the thermostat.

75. **c.** The combustion chamber on a wood furnace has a tight fitting door that can be opened to add wood.

76. **c.** It is not true that the heat exchangers on wood furnaces are larger than oil furnaces to improve heat transfer.

77. **a.** A vent connector that is less than five feet long is not too short, provided that it reaches the chimney, of course. The vent connector length should be kept as short as possible.

78. **b.** Individual sections should be screwed together rather than friction fit on a vent connector for a wood furnace.

79. **b.** The high temperature limit on a wood furnace should may be set at 250° to 280°F (the higher setting is typical of add-on furnaces).

80. **c.** The first six feet of supply duct on a wood furnace typically has to be about 6 inches from combustibles.

81. **d.** Wood stoves are also called space heaters.

82. **b.** An airtight wood stove has combustion air that can only enter through controlled openings.

83. **d.** Doors on wood stoves that can be kept open do not improve the efficiency.

84. **a.** Pellet stoves do not typically have a catalytic combustor.

85. **c.** The pad under a wood stove should extend 18 inches out in front of the stove.

86. **c.** A wood stove on a combustible floor should rest on two rows of bricks or blocks.

87. **c.** The appropriate rear and side wall clearance for a wood stove that has no data plate is 48 inches.

88. **c.** An unlisted wood stove should have 60 inches of clearance from the top of the stove to combustible materials.

89. **d.** Metal plates secured to the side and rear of the stove are not a problem.

90. **d.** An eight-foot-long vent connector is not a problem.

91. **d.** Backpuffing is smoke escaping through the door of a wood stove when the door is opened.

92. **c.** Masonry fireplaces with steel fireboxes operate at lower temperatures than other masonry fireplaces.

93. **d.** The basic components of a wood-burning fireplace do not include glass doors.

94. **d.** A heat circulator is not a basic component of a masonry fireplace.

95. **d.** Pyrolysis is a lowering of the autoignition temperature of wood.

96. **c.** Scorching is not a common fireplace footing and foundation problem.

97. **a.** The hearth extension for a fireplace with a five-square-foot opening should extend 16 inches in front and eight inches to the sides of the opening.

98. **b.** The steel lintel at the face of the fireplace should be able to expand without cracking the masonry.

99. **d.** Poor support is not a common metal firebox problem.

100. **c.** Dampers on wood burning fireplaces should open to approximately the same cross sectional area as the flue.

101. **c.** The back of the smoke chamber should be vertical.

102. **d.** A chimney face or breast that is too far below the damper is not a common problem.

103. **d.** Combustibles should be kept six inches from a cleanout door on an ashpit.

104. **d.** A 12-inch clearance from combustibles for the duct is not a criteria for an outdoor combustion air supply for a fireplace.

105. **d.** Glass doors can typically be closed when wood burning fireplaces are operating.

106. **d.** Gas igniters for masonry fireplaces typically have to be shut off manually.

10. REPORTING AND PROFESSIONAL PRACTICE

Practice Questions

1. The inspection must determine the cause of a problem.
   a. True
   b. False

2. One advantage of clients attending the home inspection is that showing is better than telling.
   a. True
   b. False

3. Leaving the heat turned up is a common mistake that home inspectors make.
   a. True
   b. False

4. Home inspectors shouldn't be concerned about delivering good news about a house; the client only cares about problems.
   a. True
   b. False

5. The average home inspection fee is around $500.
   a. True
   b. False

6. A written report is *NOT* necessary if your client accompanies you throughout the home inspection and you tell them all of the necessary information.
   a. True
   b. False

7. Limitations to the inspection must be listed in the contract document.
   a. True
   b. False

8. The purpose of a home inspection is to determine the fair market value of a property.
   a. True
   b. False

9. A required component of the home inspection report is recommended actions.
   a. True
   b. False

10. Home inspection reports must include
    a. recommendations to correct or monitor deficiencies.
    b. life expectancy of components and systems.
    c. causes of need for major repair.
    d. cost of repairs.

11. A home inspection must include an evaluation with respect to
    a. compliance or noncompliance with codes.
    b. market value of the property.
    c. advisability of purchase of the property.
    d. the condition of the inspected components.

12. Inspections must include
    a. design analysis.
    b. a written report.
    c. calculations of strength and adequacy of structural members.
    d. calculation of capacity and efficiency of heating and cooling systems.

13. Home inspectors must inspect
    a. humidifiers and dehumidifiers.
    b. central air-conditioning.
    c. window air conditioners.
    d. household appliances.

14. The advantages of sending a report later may include all of the following *EXCEPT* that
    a. the seller will be happier.
    b. the report presentation can be better.
    c. you can do some research.
    d. you have an opportunity to proofread the report.

15. Which below is the *FALSE* statement?
    a. The home inspection profession has been around since the 1930s.
    b. Home inspection started in the eastern United States.
    c. Home inspection in North America is unregulated in most areas.
    d. It is estimated there were 20,000–25,000 home inspectors in North America as of the year 2000.

16. All of the following are types of inspections that home inspectors typically perform *EXCEPT*
    a. prepurchase home inspection.
    b. prelisting home inspection.
    c. prerenovation home inspection.
    d. mortgage inspection.

17. The home inspector's ultimate obligation is to
    a. the buyer.
    b. the seller.
    c. the listing agent.
    d. the home itself.

18. All of the following phrases apply to home inspection *EXCEPT*
    a. neutral and unbiased.
    b. paid, whether or not transaction completed.
    c. a simple practice and business.
    d. a performance.

19. The typical length of time for an inspection of a standard home is
    a. one and a half hours.
    b. two and a half hours.
    c. three and a half hours.
    d. four and a half hours.

20. The characteristics of a home inspector include all of the following *EXCEPT*
    a. specialist.
    b. technical wizard.
    c. great communicator.
    d. diplomat.

21. It is important that a home inspector's shoes
    a. are aesthetically compatible with his or her clothing.
    b. have steel toes.
    c. have rubber soles.
    d. are slip-on so they can be easily removed when going into a home.

22. All of the following are components of a home inspection *EXCEPT*
    a. preinspection routine.
    b. introductory discussion.
    c. inspection itself.
    d. review of house plans.

23. An important advantage in arriving early at an inspection is that
    a. you are more likely to find a parking spot close to the home.
    b. you can evaluate the neighborhood topography and homes.
    c. your client can't accuse you of not doing a complete job because you arrived late.
    d. you'll be able to finish up earlier and get to your next inspection or get home earlier.

24. The seller introduction
    a. is typically done after the introductory discussion with the client.
    b. should be done by the listing agent.
    c. should be done by the selling agent.
    d. is typically done before anyone else arrives.

25. The introductory discussion with the client
    a. should never be done in front of the listing or selling agents.
    b. should never be done in front of the seller.
    c. should include setting out your goals for the inspection.
    d. should never include questions to the client because this will put them on the spot.

26. If asked questions about the home that are outside your scope you should
    a. give clients a vague answer, because you don't want to damage your credibility.
    b. indicate that you haven't gotten to that part of the inspection yet and, in most cases, the client will forget to ask the question a second time.
    c. suggest where the client may get an answer to that question.
    d. explain to the client that you are making a presentation, not answering questions.

27. The inspection
    a. should include signing of the contract at the end.
    b. should save all of the technical explanation for the end of the inspection.
    c. may include two tours of certain parts of the building.
    d. should never include a discussion of implications, because of increased liability.

28. The inspection should
    a. be done without the client present, if possible.
    b. start with the bad news about the house, in order to get it out of the way.
    c. focus on the actions that people must take.
    d. include a detailed description of deteriorated or inoperative systems, and how they got that way.

29. The home inspection
    a. includes descriptions and recommendations.
    b. should never actually show the client the problem, for fear of scaring him or her off.
    c. should only be done if the client accompanies you through the entire inspection, except for the roof and attic.
    d. should never compare the subject home against other properties for fear of confusing the client.

30. The inspection
    a. should rely on humor, at least to some extent.
    b. should include watching and evaluating clients' reactions to your comments.
    c. should be done as quickly as possible.
    d. should be done with the client in the lead asking questions.
    e. should include copious note-taking.

31. Which of the following helps to avoid getting overwhelmed by homes?
    a. Go through as many open houses as you can so you can make sure you've seen every kind of home.
    b. If the home is more than 3,000 square feet, bring two inspectors.
    c. Break the home down into small inspection chunks.
    d. On complicated homes, just check some items and extrapolate from those.

32. The macro/micro approach refers to
    a. learning to inspect big houses as well as small.
    b. using a visual technique and a testing technique.
    c. looking at the house from a distance, passively and up close, using a checklist approach.
    d. focusing on big problems and ignoring small ones.

33. Common home inspector mistakes include all of the following EXCEPT
    a. going back and checking things you may have overlooked.
    b. leaving the heat turned up.
    c. leaving appliances turned on.
    d. leaving clothes on a bed.

34. If you see something in a house you don't recognize and understand
    a. don't mention it in your discussion or written report.
    b. explain to the client it's beyond your scope.
    c. advise the client you don't know, but will try to find out.
    d. ask the listing or selling agent what it is.

35. If there is an argument about whether or not the inspection should proceed
    a. explain the benefits of a home inspection to all parties.
    b. offer to reduce your fee.
    c. offer to perform the inspection without the client.
    d. stay out of the discussion.

36. The closing discussion should include
    a. a detailed description of every problem in the home.
    b. an opportunity for clients to ask questions.
    c. cost estimates.
    d. a recommendation to buy, or not buy, the home.

37. The closing discussion should
    a. focus on the area that you know the most about.
    b. reiterate the limitations of the inspection.
    c. never take place inside the home.
    d. introduce the contract.

38. A listing agent is
    a. a person who shows prospective buyers a number of homes.
    b. an agent who can only work through a Multiple Listing Service.
    c. typically hired by the seller.
    d. typically hired by the buyer.

39. The selling agent is the person who
    a. receives the entire commission.
    b. typically holds the open house.
    c. owns the real estate company.
    d. draws up the offer for the buyer.

40. A conditional offer
    a. means that a price has been agreed on, as long as one or more conditions are satisfied.
    b. is an initial proposal that is conditional upon the seller signing it.
    c. is a sign back offer which will only become valid if the prospective buyer signs it.
    d. is illegal in some areas.

41. It is recommended to avoid all of these types of body language *EXCEPT*
    a. shifting your weight.
    b. speaking quickly.
    c. avoiding eye contact.
    d. being at the same eye level as your listener.

42. All of the following help improve communications *EXCEPT*
    a. being empathetic to the receiver.
    b. remaining in motion while talking.
    c. encouraging trust.
    d. creating an effective listening environment.

43. The advantages of on site reports include all of the following *EXCEPT*
    a. a more customized presentation.
    b. faster reporting.
    c. you can check what you may have missed while still in the house.
    d. there is no time spent proofreading reports or remembering houses.

44. Optional report items include all of the following *EXCEPT*
    a. the contract.
    b. scope of work.
    c. limitations.
    d. description of components.

45. Common report components include all of the following *EXCEPT*
    a. the plan review.
    b. the body of the report.
    c. an evaluation of physical conditions.
    d. a recommendation of action.

46. Common report elements include all of the following *EXCEPT*
    a. cost estimates.
    b. filing systems.
    c. a scope of work.
    d. appraisal.

47. All of the following contain scope statements *EXCEPT*
    a. the home inspection was performed for the seller.
    b. the inspection included the heating and air-conditioning systems at the request of the client.
    c. the inspection addressed only those issues requested in the attached letter from the client.
    d. the house and garage were inspected, but the coach house was not.

48. All of the following contain description statements *EXCEPT*
    a. the asphalt shingle roof is 10–15 years old.
    b. the poured concrete block foundations are bowing inward.
    c. the aluminum siding is dented in several areas.
    d. the crawl space was not accessible.

49. All of the following contain cause of condition statements *EXCEPT*
    a. the central air-conditioning system was not inspected, due to the outdoor temperature.
    b. the cracked heat exchanger is a result of the leaking humidifier above the furnace.
    c. the inadequate rise of the stairs is an original design problem.
    d. the soffit vents have been obstructed by the blown-in insulation.

50. All of the following contain implication statements *EXCEPT*
    a. the oversized fuses should be replaced to reduce the hazard of fire.
    b. the polarity of the receptacles in the living room should be changed to protect against electrical shock.
    c. the faucet below the rim of the tub is a cross connection.
    d. the lack of roof drains will shorten the life of the flat roof membrane.

51. All of the following contain action recommendations *EXCEPT*
    a. the chimney should be swept before use.
    b. a recommendation to further investigate the soil and footings under the northwest corner of the building.
    c. the galvanized-steel chimney flashings should be painted to extend their life.
    d. the undersized gutters may result in wet basement problems.

52. The most overused recommended action by home inspectors is recommending
    a. that clients provide something that is missing.
    b. further evaluation.
    c. that things be improved without giving specifications.
    d. monitoring of suspect systems.

53. All of the following are limitation statements *EXCEPT*
    a. access was not gained to the roof.
    b. the attic was inspected from the access hatch.
    c. the swimming pool is beyond the scope of this inspection.
    d. the cover on the electrical panel was not removed due to inadequate access.

54. You should avoid using all of the following words or phrases *EXCEPT*
    a. satisfactory.
    b. good condition.
    c. sound.
    d. no deficiencies noted.

55. Building code references
    a. enhance your credibility.
    b. reduce your liability.
    c. should be avoided.
    d. are straightforward.

56. All of the following are examples of prevention strategies for limiting liability *EXCEPT* to
    a. perform a competent inspection.
    b. ensure clients' expectations are realistic.
    c. describe limitations specific to the home in your report.
    d. inspect in greater depth areas where clients have concerns.

57. If verbal communication is vague or incomplete, clients will often
    a. ignore the message.
    b. fill in the gaps.
    c. reject the message.
    d. oversimplify the message.

ANSWERS AND EXPLANATIONS

1. **b.** Home inspectors do not have to indicate the cause of a problem.

2. **a.** When you find a significant problem or condition, it's much easier to help clients understand by showing them as you tell them about it.

3. **a.** Leaving the heat turned up is an easy mistake to make after checking the heating system, but one that annoys homeowners. Remember to turn it down!

4. **b.** Good news about the house—such as a new, high-quality roof or high-efficiency furnace—is valuable information to the prospective homebuyer. Even if you don't record this information in your written report, you should share it with your client.

5. **b.** The average home inspection fee is around $300.

6. **b.** A written report is a required element of a home inspection.

7. **b.** Limitations must be reported, but they can be recorded either in the contract or the written report.

8. **b.** The purpose of a home inspection is to establish the physical condition of the house.

9. **a.** The home inspection report should tell people what corrections and improvements need to be made.

10. **a.** Reports must recommend what to do about any conditions found. There is no comment herein on life expectancy, causes of problems, methods and materials for repairs, or cost of repairs.

11. **d.** You must comment on the condition of inspected components.

12. **b.** Home inspection must include a written report.

13. **b.** We have to inspect central air-conditioning.

14. **a.** Sellers are not usually happier if you send a report later because the buyer may not make a final decision until he or she sees the written report. This slows down the transaction and keeps the house off the market.

15. **a.** The home inspection profession has not been around since the 1930s.

16. **d.** Home inspectors do not typically perform mortgage inspections.

17. **d.** In the opinion of some/many, the home inspector's ultimate obligation is to the home itself.

18. **c.** Home inspection is not a simple practice and business.

19. **b.** The average home inspection is about two and half hours.

20. **a.** Home inspectors are generalists rather than specialists.

21. **c.** Shoes should have rubber soles so that you are not likely to slip.

22. **d.** Home inspections do not typically include a review of the house plans. This has very little impact on the performance. Also, house plans are often not accurate with respect to how the house was/is built.

23. **b.** The most important reason for arriving early at an inspection is the opportunity to evaluate the neighborhood topography and homes.

24. **d.** The seller introduction is usually conducted before your client or agents arrive.

25. **a.** The introductory discussion can help adjust client's expectations.

26. **c.** If you receive questions that are outside the scope of the home inspection, you can direct the client to another source for the information they are looking for.

27. **c.** The inspection may include two tours of parts of the building.

28. **c.** The inspections should focus on recommended actions.

29. **a.** The inspection includes descriptions and recommendations.

30. **b.** The inspection should include watching and evaluating client's reactions.

31. **c.** Breaking the home down into smaller chunks helps to avoid getting overwhelmed.

32. **c.**   The macro/micro approach refers to looking at the house from a distance passively and up close using a checklist approach.

33. **a.**   It is not a mistake to go back and check things that you may have overlooked.

34. **c.**   If you see something in the house you do not recognize or understand, you should advise clients that you will try to find out about it and give them a source of information.

35. **d.**   Home inspectors should stay out of discussions between agents, buyers, and sellers even if the discussion is about whether or not the inspection should proceed.

36. **b.**   The closing discussion should include an opportunity for clients to ask questions. This is a time where feedback from clients is helpful to ensure that they understand the home.

37. **b.**   The closing discussion should reiterate limitations to help ensure the client's expectations have been appropriately adjusted.

38. **c.**   The listing agent is typically hired by the seller.

39. **d.**   The selling agent typically draws up the offer for the buyer.

40. **a.**   A conditional offer means a price has been agreed on if one or more conditions are satisfied.

41. **d.**   You should be at the same eye level as your listener.

42. **b.**   Remaining in motion while talking does not help improve communications.

43. **a.**   A customized presentation is not an advantage of an on-site report. It's an advantage of a report prepared after the inspection.

44. **d.**   Description of components is a mandatory part of the report.

45. **a.**   Plan review is not a common report component.

46. **d.**   An appraisal is not a common element in a home inspection report.

47. **a.**   The client identification is not part of the scope.

48. **d.**   There is no description in the statement about the crawl space.

49. **a.**   The statement about the air-conditioning system is a limitation statement rather than a condition statement.

50. **c.**   The statement about the cross connection does not explain the implication.

51. **d.**   The statement about the gutters is an implications statement only.

52. **b.**   Recommending further evaluation is the most overused action by home inspectors.

53. **c.**   The swimming pool statement is a scope statement rather than a limitation statement, because swimming pools are not part of any inspection.

54. **d.**   You should say that no deficiencies were noted, rather than say that things were satisfactory, in good condition, operable, or sound.

55. **c.**   Building code references should be avoided, for liability reasons.

56. **d.**   You should not inspect in greater depth in areas where clients have concerns. This upsets the balance of your inspection and may expose you to greater liability because of the depth of inspection in one area was not matched in other areas.

57. **b.**   Clients often fill in the gaps if verbal communication is incomplete.

11.   APPLIANCES
Practice Questions

1. Soaking the electric elements of a range in water is a good cleaning practice.
   a. True
   b. False

2. Gas hoses are *NOT* permitted for connecting a gas range to the gas line.
   a. True
   b. False

3. If a gas leak is detected in a home, the power should be shut off immediately.
   a. True
   b. False

4. Wall ovens typically have a lower volume than freestanding ovens.
   a. True
   b. False

5. Homeowners should be encouraged to service their microwave themselves on an annual basis.
   a. True
   b. False

6. It is acceptable for cooktop exhaust vents to discharge into the attic, provided that a charcoal filter is employed.
   a. True
   b. False

7. Central vacuum systems equipped with a filter in the canister *MUST* be discharged directly to the exterior of the building.
   a. True
   b. False

8. The proper operation of a doorbell will not have a major influence on whether a prospective home-buyer will buy the home.
   a. True
   b. False

9. Most household appliances will outlast a conventional forced-air gas furnace.
   a. True
   b. False

10. Aluminum foil should be used to line the drip bowls for the elements of an electric range in the event of water spilling over a pot.
    a. True
    b. False

11. A limiter is a safety device found on coil elements to prevent them from overheating in the event that an element is left on.
    a. True
    b. False

12. Appliance connectors found on gas ranges should *NOT* be longer than six feet.
    a. True
    b. False

13. Electric ranges take longer to heat up and cool down than gas burners.
    a. True
    b. False

14. Some ovens have the ability to operate at temperatures close to 1,000°F, provided that the oven door has the ability to lock at these high temperatures.
    a. True
    b. False

15. The flame on a gas range burner should be a bright yellow, similar to a campfire, when the stove is operating.
    a. True
    b. False

16. Charcoal-type filters should be used on exhaust fans that do *NOT* discharge to the outside.
    a. True
    b. False

17. Batch feed waste disposers have a power switch near the unit, allowing it to be turned on and off very quickly.
    a. True
    b. False

18. An indirect plumbing connection that transfers wastewater from a washing machine to the waste plumbing system through a trap is referred to as a standpipe.
    a. True
    b. False

19. The typical lifespan of most major appliances is
    a. 5–15 years.
    b. 10–20 years.
    c. 15–25 years.

20. A difference between a gas range and an electric range is that electric ranges
    a. are typically wider.
    b. are typically deeper front-to-back.
    c. require a 240-volt electrical supply.

21. What feature on range-control knobs helps prevent children from turning them on?
    a. The knobs are difficult to turn.
    b. The knobs have to be pushed in before turning them.
    c. The knobs are too large for a child's hand to grasp.

22. Cooktops with down-draft vents should be vented
    a. into the basement.
    b. into the return air ductwork.
    c. outdoors.

23. Gas ranges can be connected to gas pipe by
    a. flexible metal piping.
    b. plastic piping.
    c. rubber hoses.

24. If a gas leak is detected in a home, you should
    a. turn off the power immediately.
    b. phone the gas company from the house.
    c. leave the house without operating anything.

25. An electric oven uses which element for baking?
    a. Upper element
    b. Lower element
    c. Both elements

26. A convection oven is different from a conventional oven in that
    a. a convection oven uses microwaves.
    b. a convection oven has the boiler on all the time.
    c. a convection oven has a fan that circulates hot air.

27. How hot will an electric self-cleaning oven get during the cleaning process?
    a. 500°F
    b. 700°F
    c. 900°F

28. The typical life of a dishwasher is
    a. 5–10 years.
    b. 8–15 years.
    c. 10–20 years.

29. A dishwasher may *NOT* drain properly because the
    a. timer may be faulty.
    b. door and the lock may be defective.
    c. heating element may be burned out.

30. A noisy dishwasher is usually the result of a
    a. defective door and lock.
    b. sprayer arm.
    c. door spring.

31. Which food waste is compatible with a waste disposal system?
    a. Bones
    b. Cornhusks
    c. Celery

32. Central-vacuum systems with a filter in the canister should discharge
    a. outside only.
    b. inside only.
    c. either inside or outside.

33. Weak suction in the central vacuum system is *NOT* typically the result of a
    a. faulty motor.
    b. full canister.
    c. dirty filter.

34. A waste standpipe for a washing machine connection should extend
    a. 2–4 inches above the trap.
    b. 12–20 inches above the trap.
    c. 18–30 inches above the trap.

35. The main difference between waste disposers and trash compactors is that trash compactors
    a. cannot be located in kitchens.
    b. cannot be located under counter tops.
    c. do not take the waste out of the house.

ANSWERS AND EXPLANATIONS

1. **b.** Soaking an electric element in water can damage it.

2. **a.** Gas hoses are not permitted indoors.

3. **b.** If a gas leak is noted, all occupants should leave the house immediately and contact the gas company from a neighbor's house.

4. **a.** Wall ovens typically have less capacity than freestanding ovens.

5. **b.** Microwaves are not intended to be serviced by the homeowner. Any operational failures typically require a service technician.

6. **b.** Vents should not discharge into attics, crawl spaces, or chimneys.

7. **b.** Central-vacuum systems equipped with a filter in the canister may discharge to the exterior or interior.

8. **a.** Repairs to doorbells generally are simple and inexpensive, not a major influence on a home-buying decision.

9. **b.** Most major household appliances have life spans of 10–20 years.

10. **b.** Aluminum foil can become an electrical shock hazard and should never be used to line drip bowls.

11. **b.** Limiters are only found on solid disks to reduce wattage and prevent overheating and pot meltdown.

12. **a.** Connectors should be less than six feet, should not pass through walls, floors, or ceilings, and should be immediately preceded by a shutoff valve.

13. **a.** The biggest advantage of gas ranges is their ability to heat up and cool down very quickly.

14. **a.** Self-cleaning ovens must operate at very high temperatures during the cleaning cycle to turn spills into ash.

15. **b.** The flame should be blue. A yellow flame indicates a poor fuel/air mixture.

16. **a.** Charcoal filters are preferred on recirculating-type exhaust fans because they help remove odors.

17. **b.** Batch feed disposers are controlled with a switch built into the drain stopper.

18. **a.** Standpipes are common on laundry facilities to carry water from the washing machine hose into the waste plumbing system.

19. **b.** The typical lifespan of most major appliances is 10–20 years. This is how long the average major house appliance is expected to last.

20. **c.** Electric ranges require a 240-volt electrical supply. Gas ranges only require 120-volts.

21. **b.** The knobs have to be pushed in before turning them. This is a common safety feature on many ranges, where the knobs are at the front and accessible to children.

22. **c.** Cooktops with down-draft vents should be vented outdoors. You do not want cooking fumes to stay in the house or be distributed through the heating system.

23. **a.** Gas ranges can be connected to gas pipe by flexible metal piping. The other materials are not considered durable and safe.

24. **c.** If a gas leak is detected in a home you should leave the house without operating anything. If you activate any switch, use the telephone, or doorbell, a spark might ignite the gas in the house, causing an explosion.

25. **b.** An electric oven uses the lower element for baking. The lower element is used for baking and roasting; the upper element is used for broiling.

26. **c.** Unlike a conventional oven, a convection oven has a fan that circulates hot air. The fan helps cook food more quickly and evenly, and uses less energy than a conventional oven.

27. **c.** The best answer choice is 900°F. Temperatures of 850°F to 1,000°F are maintained for roughly two hours during the self-cleaning process.

28. **b.** The typical life of a dishwasher is 8–15 years. Dishwashers do not last as long as some other household appliances.

29. **a.** A dishwasher may not drain properly if the timer is faulty. The electronic controls may not activate the drain solenoid valve.

30. **b.**   A noisy dishwasher usually is the result of a sprayer arm. If the sprayer arm is not straight or not well seated, it may vibrate or contact dish racks or the interior of the cabinet.

31. **a.**   Bones are compatible with a waste disposal system. Cornhusks, celery, and other fibrous waste can pose problems for disposals.

32. **c.**   If the canister has a filter, the central vacuum system may discharge to the interior or the exterior.

33. **a.**   Weak suction in a central-vacuum unit is usually not the result of a faulty motor. Motors tend to operate or not operate. It is unusual for them to operate at a diminished capacity.

34. **c.**   A waste standpipe for a washing machine connection should extend 18–30 inches above the trap. You do not want the fast moving water to siphon out of the trap. This drop allows the water to slow down.

35. **c.**   Unlike waste disposal systems, trash compactors do not take the waste out of the house. They merely compress it.

PART

C

SAMPLE EXAM

This sample exam contains 200 multiple-choice questions covering the following topics:

- Inspection methods
- House systems (exterior, structural, roofing, electrical, heating and cooling, insulation and ventilation, plumbing, interior, fireplace and chimney)
- Reporting
- Professional practice

To best simulate the exam experience, you should answer all the questions in one uninterrupted, four-hour session. Then, check your answers against those provided and calculate your score. Different exams use different scoring systems, but in general you should aim to answer 70–80 percent of the questions correctly in order to pass.

SAMPLE EXAM QUESTIONS

1. A home inspection must include a
   a. report on all components, whether observed or not.
   b. report on the presence of termites, rodents, or insects.
   c. report stating which systems and components were not inspected, and why.
   d. report on cosmetic items, underground items, or items not permanently installed.

2. Replacing 50 feet of a 100-foot-long pipe with larger-diameter pipe will
   a. increase the static pressure.
   b. only make a difference if it is the upstream section of pipe that is replaced.
   c. only make a difference if it is the downstream section of pipe that is replaced.
   d. make no difference regardless of which 50 feet of pipe is replaced.

3. Knob-and-tube wiring was in common use from
   a. 1920–1950.
   b. 1850–1880.
   c. 1940–1970.
   d. 1890–1910.

4. Which roofing material lasts the longest?
   a. Slate
   b. Wood
   c. Fiber-cement
   d. Roll roofing

5. A common flow control valve problem on a boiler is
   a. that it is set incorrectly.
   b. leakage.
   c. poorly located.
   d. obstructed air flow.

6. Where you have found evidence of footing settlement, how can you predict whether there will be further settlement?
   a. You can count the number of planes of movement.
   b. You can determine the type of foundation material.
   c. You cannot predict settlement from a single inspection.
   d. You can determine the depth of the footing.

7. You typically identify a Freon leak
   a. as an oil stain.
   b. as refrigerant coming out of the Freon line in the form of a cold mist.
   c. by the strong odor.
   d. by looking for evidence of ice along the refrigerant lines.

8. Typical wood frame wall assemblies include all of the following components *EXCEPT*
   a. studs.
   b. bridging.
   c. sheathing.
   d. siding.

9. All of the following are common approaches to improving chimney draft *EXCEPT*
   a. adding a draft inducer fan.
   b. adding a rain cap.
   c. extending the chimney upwards.
   d. resloping the cap.

10. All of the following statements are true of shrinkage cracks *EXCEPT* that
    a. shrinkage cracks do not typically go into the footings.
    b. shrinkage cracks do not necessarily have corresponding cracks elsewhere in the building.
    c. vertical shear is associated with shrinkage cracks.
    d. shrinkage cracks are common with poured-concrete foundation walls.

11. Which of the following is *NOT* typically a component of a private water supply system?
    a. Foot valve
    b. Pump
    c. Pressure regulator
    d. Pressure tank

12. Split-system, air-cooled, central air-conditioning systems have how many fans?
    a. None
    b. One
    c. Two
    d. Four

13. Insulated metal exterior doors with storm doors should be avoided because they may
    a. increase heat loss.
    b. increase air leakage.
    c. overheat.
    d. have poor architectural appeal.

14. You plug your circuit tester into an outlet that has a washing machine plugged into it. Your tester shows that the outlet is properly wired and grounded. How could you improve this inspection process?
    a. Use a voltage tester
    b. Use a circuit tester with a GFI test button
    c. Unplug the washing machine
    d. Turn the washing machine on before doing your test

15. Home inspectors
    a. must disclose an interest in a business which may affect the client.
    b. having disclosed any interest in a business which may affect the client, must decline to perform the inspection.
    c. may waive the home inspection fee if a repair contract on the home is subsequently signed between the client and home inspector.
    d. may collect separate fees from two interested parties, as long as at least one party is aware of it.

16. All of the following are clues that excess humidity may be a problem in the house *EXCEPT*
    a. window condensation.
    b. mold in bathrooms.
    c. excessive drafts.
    d. nackdraft of combustion appliances.

17. A common temperature rise across a conventional furnace is
    a. 30°F to 60°F.
    b. 50°F to 85°F.
    c. 70°F to 100°F.
    d. 100°F to 150°F.

18. Given a foundation wall that is cracked due to horizontal force
    a. you will not be able to determine whether the wall has also moved inward.
    b. if the wall has moved inward, the cracks would typically be wider on the inside face.
    c. if the wall has moved inward, cracks will typically be wider on the outside face.
    d. you should not be concerned unless the crack is at least ¼-inch in width.

19. On most steep roofs, exposed fasteners are
    a. used for anchorage against wind.
    b. a sign of poor installation.
    c. a sign of good installation.
    d. used to prevent ice dams.

20. Common problems with expansion tanks on well and pump systems include all of the following *EXCEPT*
    a. rust.
    b. leaking.
    c. waterlogging.
    d. undersizing.

21. Which of following steam systems is commonly converted to hot water?
    a. A one-pipe, upfeed system
    b. A one-pipe, downfeed system
    c. A two-pipe system
    d. A one-pipe, parallel flow system

22. All of the following are slab-on-grade construction techniques *EXCEPT*
    a. monolithic slab.
    b. floating slab.
    c. inverted slab.
    d. reinforced slab.

23. Masonry chimneys should have a clearance from combustible framing members of
    a. 1 inch.
    b. 2 inches.
    c. 4 inches.
    d. 12 inches.

24. All of these are common closet lighting problems *EXCEPT*
    a. a light that is above a shelf.
    b. a light that is mounted on a wall above the door.
    c. a light in which bare bulbs are used.
    d. installation of the light above, and toward one end of, the shelf.

25. Conventional gas boilers in boiler rooms, drawing combustion air from indoors, require *HOW MUCH* total combustion and dilution air?
    a. 1 square inch net vent space for each 1,000-btu/hr input
    b. 2 square inches net vent space for each 1,000-btu/hr input
    c. 5 square inches net vent space for each 1,000-btu/hr input
    d. 10 square inches net vent space for each 1,000-btu/hr input

26. Efflorescence
    a. is associated with water moving through masonry walls.
    b. can only appear on the cold side of a wall.
    c. only occurs in freezing climates.
    d. is an organic growth.

27. On a conventional split-system air-conditioning system, the high-pressure side is the portion of the refrigerant line from the
    a. compressor to the expansion device.
    b. metering device to the evaporator coil.
    c. expansion device to the compressor.
    d. evaporator to the compressor.

28. In a multiwire branch circuit, with the red-and-black wire improperly tapped from the same bus, if the red wire carries 10 amps, and the black wire carries 12 amps, the neutral wire will carry
    a. 10 amps.
    b. 22 amps.
    c. none because the 15A breaker will trip.
    d. 12 amps.

29. The presence of step flashing on an asphalt shingle roof can typically be verified by
    a. looking at the counter flashing.
    b. knowing the age of the shingles on the roof.
    c. knowing the number of layers of shingles on the roof.
    d. lifting the shingles adjacent to the chimney or wall.

30. Which material is not an air barrier?
    a. Polyethylene
    b. Housewraps
    c. Plywood
    d. Fiberglass

31. Why are you more likely to see a house with a full basement in cold northern climates than in warm southern climates?
    a. People in cold climates have snow removal equipment to store.
    b. Having to excavate below the frost line for the footings makes a basement cost effective.
    c. Homes with basements need heat. In southern climates, it is a waste of energy to heat the basement.
    d. There is a lot of bedrock in the southern climates—blasting would be required to make a basement.

32. All of the following are advantages to having clients attend inspections *EXCEPT*
    a. an opportunity for better communication.
    b. you can charge a premium for allowing clients to attend.
    c. that showing is better than telling.
    d. you have the opportunity to adjust expectations.

33. The flame of the left burner in a two-burner conventional efficiency furnace touches the heat exchanger only when the blower is running. What is likely to be the problem?
    a. The heat exchanger is cracked on the left side.
    b. The heat exchanger is cracked on the right side.
    c. The left burner is dirty.
    d. The left burner is misaligned.

34. What would you do if you saw that a roof truss had been cut?
    a. Advise client to sister a 2 × 4 piece over the cut. The sistered piece should extend at least three feet on either side of the cut.
    b. Advise client that cuts in trusses are not a problem.
    c. Look for other signs of distress and, if none, do nothing.
    d. Advise further evaluation by a specialist.

35. Common problems with chimney caps include all of the following *EXCEPT*
    a. cracks.
    b. oversizing.
    c. inadequate slope.
    d. a lack of drip edge or drip groove.

36. CPVC water pipe may not be used for hot and cold supply lines
    a. in single-family residences.
    b. in multifamily residences.
    c. inside a building.
    d. below grade.

37. Garage door problems include all of the following *EXCEPT*
    a. a seven-inch step down into garage.
    b. poor weatherstripping.
    c. that it has no self-closer.
    d. if it opens into a bedroom.

38. If you used a multimeter to measure the current in a 3,000W electric water heater that uses both of the ungrounded ("hot") service conductors, it would read
    a. 25A.
    b. 240V.
    c. 12.5A.
    d. 120V.

39. Which of the following statements is *TRUE?*
    a. Uniform settlement is most often the result of building on undisturbed soils.
    b. Expansive soils expand as they dry.
    c. Lowering the basement floor to the top of the footing can cause settlement where there was no settlement initially.
    d. Uniform settlement may stress utility pipes.

40. Foundation irrigation is
    a. a method of stabilizing expansive clay soils.
    b. a method of strengthening the foundation concrete—the concrete is kept damp for a couple of days.
    c. a foundation-drainage technique.
    d. used to prevent basement leakage.

41. A horizontal fracture in the foundation
    a. is a shrinkage crack.
    b. is not as serious as a vertical crack.
    c. reduces the foundation's ability to resist soil pressure.
    d. cannot be caused by adfreezing.

42. Which of the following is *NOT* a common service amperage?
    a. 60A
    b. 100A
    c. 175A
    d. 400A

43. The purpose of the condenser coil in an air-conditioning system is to
    a. cool the outdoor air.
    b. help deliver cooler Freon to the compressor.
    c. dissipate heat from the Freon downstream of the compressor.
    d. absorb heat from the house air.

44. Splashing sounds are heard when the thermostat is turned up and the induced-draft fan starts to run on a high-efficiency furnace. What is a likely concern?
    a. The heat exchanger passages are blocked with soot.
    b. The condensate lines are blocked.
    c. The duct system is too small for the furnace.
    d. The exhaust vent is disconnected inside the house.

45. Water hammer can be solved or greatly reduced by
    a. installing modern, quick-closing faucets.
    b. using 12-inch vertical extensions at ends of lines.
    c. avoiding long, vertical rises in the pipe.
    d. avoiding long, horizontal runs of pipe.

46. Piers may move because the
    a. footings are oversized.
    b. piers are not adequately loaded.
    c. soil below is disturbed.
    d. beams are undersized.

47. Attic insulation may be wet as a result of any of the following *EXCEPT*
    a. insulation that is too close to chimneys.
    b. a roof leak.
    c. condensation.
    d. an exhaust fan discharging directly into the insulation.

48. These products are all asphalt based *EXCEPT* for
    a. roofing cement.
    b. asphalt cement.
    c. plastic cement.
    d. caulking.

49. All of the following are true with EIFS *EXCEPT* that
    a. it is typically applied directly to a polystyrene insulation board.
    b. it is typically a two-coat process.
    c. a fiberglass mesh replaces wire lath.
    d. the finish coat is thicker than with traditional stucco.

50. Which of the following suggests an improperly supported service drop?
    a. Water in the service panel
    b. No seal on meter
    c. Missing drip loop
    d. PVC conduit bulging between the meter and the elbow at the base

51. Which of the following is *NOT* a component of a heat recovery ventilator?
    a. Burner
    b. Heat exchanger
    c. Fans
    d. Air filter

52. The introductory discussion should
    a. help to adjust the expectations of the client.
    b. establish your credibility with the use of a number or technical terms.
    c. include instructions for your clients to avoid questions since this will pull you from your routine.
    d. include questions about the clients' preferred order for inspecting the components of the home.

53. If a conventional gas-fired, forced-air furnace has an input rating of 100,000 Btu and an output rating of 80,000 Btu, its
    a. seasonal efficiency is 80 percent.
    b. steady state efficiency is 80 percent.
    c. steady state efficiency is 60 percent.
    d. steady state efficiency is 20 percent.

54. Rising damp is
    a. a flooded crawlspace.
    b. leakage through foundation walls.
    c. capillary wicking of water into masonry units.
    d. associated with expansive soils.

55. Which of the following statements is *FALSE* with respect to electric water heaters?
    a. Most water heaters have two elements.
    b. The upper element usually comes on first.
    c. The upper element has priority.
    d. It can be difficult to tell if one of the two elements is burned out.

56. Sills not properly anchored are most likely to allow the house to move off its foundations
    a. during winter months.
    b. during construction.
    c. if the house is located on the side of a hill.
    d. if the live loads exceed the design load within the house.

57. If you drilled a hole through a properly laid asphalt-shingle roof, how many shingles would you go through?
    a. One
    b. Two
    c. Three
    d. Four

58. A panel is servicing an indoor pool area, and is in a mechanical room next to the pool. You should be looking for
    a. stranded wires.
    b. rust problems.
    c. minimum 20A breakers.
    d. wires rated at 12 gauge.

59. Metal chimneys with excessive offsets from the vertical are prone to all of the following *EXCEPT*
    a. draft problems.
    b. localized high temperatures.
    c. moisture entry problems.
    d. inadequate height overall.

60. Most concrete foundation cracks occur at
    a. wall/floor intersections.
    b. window corners.
    c. beam pockets.
    d. changes in foundation height.

61. Common problems with water-cooled air-conditioning coils include
    a. clogging.
    b. icing up.
    c. leakage.
    d. running dry.

62. Columns see mostly
    a. tension loads.
    b. racking loads.
    c. shear loads.
    d. compression loads.

63. Which phrase does *NOT* describe a home inspection?
    a. Field review of performance
    b. Evaluation of physical condition
    c. Visual inspection of readily accessible, installed components
    d. Appraisal inspection

64. All of the following statements about hardboard siding are true except one. Which statement is *FALSE?*
    a. Hardboard is a type of fiberboard.
    b. Hardboard is non-combustible.
    c. Common thicknesses are ⁵⁄₁₆–½ inch.
    d. It is denser than conventional wood siding.

65. Clamp-on amp meters may be used on electric furnaces to check
    a. the fuse or breaker sizing.
    b. the wire sizing.
    c. that all the elements come on.
    d. the data-plate information.

66. Columns may settle because the
    a. footing is undersized.
    b. footing is below the basement floor.
    c. footing is too thick.
    d. beams are oversized.

67. There is a chimney protruding through a roll roofing valley flashing on the roof. You report that there may be leakage here because the
    a. chimney height is insufficient.
    b. chimney obstructs valley drainage.
    c. nails from the chimney flashing penetrate the valley flashing.
    d. roofer used roll roofing, rather than metal.

68. Exhaust flues on gas-fired or oil-fired water heaters should
    a. have a minimum length of 10 feet.
    b. slope down away from the water heater to allow for condensation.
    c. have a slope of ¼-inch per foot up away from the heater.
    d. be friction fit together.

69. Assuming copper, standard wire type, and normal temperature rating, what is the typical conductor size (in AWG) for a 100A service?
    a. #6
    b. #4
    c. #3
    d. #2

70. The most serious implication of any insulation, air/vapor barrier, or ventilation deficiency is
    a. excess heat loss.
    b. excess heat gain (in summer).
    c. reduced comfort levels.
    d. rot.

71. The top of a column should be
    a. bonded to a beam with adhesive.
    b. at least as wide as the beam above it.
    c. nailed to at least two joists.
    d. supported by a diagonal bridging or blocking.

72. Which of the following statement about home inspectors' liability is *TRUE?*
    a. As long as you provide written reports, you have no liability.
    b. Your liability is greater if your buyers' expectations are not realistic.
    c. Home improvement contractors play no part in home inspector liability.
    d. The last-one-in syndrome helps to reduce liability.

73. Beams transfer loads directly from
    a. walls to walls.
    b. roofs to walls.
    c. floors to columns.
    d. floors to footings.

74. The condensate drain pan or tray on a split-system air conditioner is typically located below the
    a. compressor.
    b. condenser coil.
    c. evaporator coil.
    d. expansion device.

75. Which of the following is the accepted way for a home inspector to check for a loose connection of a wire to a fuse or breaker?
    a. Measure the temperature of the bare end of the wire.
    b. See if the connection screw can be tightened any more.
    c. Look for signs of overheating on the end of the wire and at the connection point.
    d. Turn the breaker off or remove the fuse to find an outlet that it serves, then turn it back on and measure the voltage at the outlet.

76. The most serious implication of a leaking humidifier is
   a. flooding.
   b. rusting of the furnace cabinet.
   c. rusting of the heat exchanger.
   d. shorting out the furnace wiring.

77. For a galvanized-steel roof
   a. the surface should be coated with mastic to extend the useful life.
   b. painting the surface is one acceptable way of protecting the surface.
   c. the metal should be held down with copper nails or screws to prevent corrosion.
   d. both a and c are true.

78. You smell fuel oil when you walk in the door of a house. Which of the following is *NOT* a likely cause?
   a. The tank is leaking.
   b. The barometric damper is stuck closed.
   c. The fuel supplier has overfilled the tank.
   d. The burner is inoperative.

79. It's important to stay in control of the inspection for all of the following reasons *EXCEPT*
   a. you want to stay on schedule.
   b. you want to stay within your scope.
   c. some agents can show you up if you let them talk.
   d. helps make sure you'll leave things as you found them.

80. Joists are like
   a. small beams.
   b. ledger boards.
   c. ribbon boards.
   d. collar ties.

81. The main service fuses have been installed with the labels facing backward, such that you cannot read their rating. No other markings are visible. You should
   a. turn off the house power and remove a fuse to check its rating.
   b. measure the diameter of the fuse body to determine its rating.
   c. report that the main service fuse rating was not determinable.
   d. carefully insert your inspection mirror until the label is visible, then read the rating from the label.

82. Fiber-cement shingles
   a. are flexible, like asphalt shingles.
   b. don't last as long as asphalt shingles.
   c. are lighter than slate.
   d. are typically installed on battens.

83. After you turn an electric baseboard heater on, how long should it take for the heater to get warm?
   a. Less than 10 seconds
   b. Less than 1 minute
   c. Less than 5 minutes
   d. Less than 10 minutes

84. Which statement about crawlspaces is *FALSE?*
   a. Crawlspaces can be heated or unheated.
   b. The floor will be more comfortable if the crawlspace floor is insulated.
   c. It's typically easier to insulate the walls than the crawlspace ceiling.
   d. Insulating the walls can be done on the inside or outside.

85. Probing the ends of beams with a screwdriver is a good way to check for
   a. rot.
   b. end bearing.
   c. sag.
   d. rotation.

86. Home inspectors
   a. must typically pay real estate agents commissions in order to have business referred to them.
   b. typically receive commissions from real estate agents for providing appropriate reports.
   c. receive commissions from others only with the clients' permission.
   d. can't accept or pay commissions to other parties working with the client.

87. Overlapping joists that extend 12 inches past the support beam
   a. are prone to failure by collapse.
   b. are likely to cause a floor hump.
   c. should be extended to the opposite exterior wall.
   d. indicate a beam that is too narrow.

88. An auxiliary drain pan is needed on a split-system air conditioner when
    a. the condensate cannot be drained by gravity.
    b. there is no trap in the condensate line.
    c. leakage in the primary pan may damage interior finishes.
    d. a high volume of condensate is anticipated.

89. Engineered wood
    a. includes wood I-joists and open web steel joists.
    b. cannot use joist hangers.
    c. do not require rim joists.
    d. often need more end bearing than conventional lumber joists.

90. A midefficiency gas furnace has an electronic ignition system. The safety device that ensures that the pilot or burner is on is the
    a. flame sensor.
    b. thermocouple.
    c. hot surface igniter.
    d. primary control.

91. What are the I (current) and R (resistance) values for a circuit with four 60-watt light bulbs and a 360-watt television?
    a. I = 5A, R = 600 ohms
    b. I = 12A, R = 72 ohms
    c. I = 24A, R = 5 ohms
    d. I = 5A, R = 24 ohms

92. You inspect a 4-year-old asphalt shingle roof. It seems well insulated and the attic is properly ventilated. Roughly 25 percent of shingles show irregular cracks in the surface. You report that
    a. the shingles are suffering freeze-thaw damage.
    b. this is a common cosmetic condition that does not affect performance or life expectancy.
    c. there is a possible manufacturing defect and life expectancy may be shortened.
    d. this is a result of expansion and contraction of waferboard sheathing as a result of changes in humidity.

93. Common problems with power vented or fan assisted water heaters include all of the following *EXCEPT*
    a. a clogged condensate collection system.
    b. an inoperative blower preventing startup.
    c. an obstructed blower intake.
    d. poor vent termination points.

94. Common problems with clay or slate shingles include all of the following *EXCEPT*
    a. missing shingles.
    b. loose shingles.
    c. buckled shingles.
    d. broken shingles.

95. Walls may perform all of these functions *EXCEPT* to
    a. support roofs.
    b. support masonry chimneys.
    c. support other walls.
    d. resist wind loads.

96. The closing discussion
    a. should take place before you compile your reports.
    b. should never take place in front of the agents.
    c. should never take place in front of the seller.
    d. is a brief summary of the key points.

97. On which roof are exposed fasteners most likely to be acceptable?
    a. Metal
    b. Clay
    c. Concrete
    d. Asphalt

98. Newer conventional-efficiency, copper-tube boilers have a life expectancy of
    a. 5 to 10 years.
    b. 10 to 15 years.
    c. 15 to 25 years.
    d. 25 to 35 years.

99. Masonry walls may be prone to leaning outward at the top if
    a. joists are fire-cut.
    b. the wall is taller than the highest ceiling joists.
    c. the building is two stories or more.
    d. the arches are undersized.

100. How thick (maximum) should a creosote deposit in a wood stove be before it is removed?
    a. ¼ inch
    b. ½ inch
    c. ¾ inch
    d. 1 inch

101. The grounded plugs (three-prong plugs) became standard for all branch circuits in the
    a. 1930s.
    b. 1940s.
    c. early 1950s.
    d. early 1960s.

102. Spalling and mortar damage near the bottom of an exterior masonry column would likely be the result of
    a. eccentric loads.
    b. frost heave.
    c. soil erosion.
    d. freeze/thaw cycles.

103. Gas water heaters will *NOT* have
    a. a water supply shutoff valve.
    b. a discharge pipe extended from the pressure-relief valve.
    c. an 18-inch raised platform if installed in the garage.
    d. a barometric damper.

104. All of the following are common HRV problems *EXCEPT*
    a. missing filters.
    b. dirty heat exchanger core.
    c. lack of a trap in the condensate drain.
    d. flow measuring stations located on warm-side ducts.

105. Recommendations to a client regarding brick cracks may include all of these *EXCEPT* to
    a. caulk them.
    b. ignore them.
    c. monitor them.
    d. call in a specialist for further advice.

106. Squeaking subflooring is an indication of
    a. overspanned joists.
    b. undersized beams.
    c. poor fastening of subfloors.
    d. undersized subfloors.

107. Obsolete service boxes typically have
    a. rusted covers.
    b. black covers.
    c. exposed terminals.
    d. undersized fuses.

108. You are examining the side flashing for a masonry chimney. Where the asphalt shingles meet the counter flashing, roofing cement has been applied. Your report should include which of the following?
    a. "It is difficult to say if proper step flashings were installed."
    b. "Roofing cement should only be considered a temporary repair."
    c. "This is not a good building practice."
    d. It should include all of the above.

109. Common drainage piping problems include all of the following *EXCEPT*
    a. clogging.
    b. cross connections.
    c. undersizing.
    d. slopes of ¼-inch to ½-inch per foot.

110. Which wood is *NOT* commonly used in studs in a wood frame wall?
    a. Pine
    b. Fir
    c. Cedar
    d. Larch

111. High-efficiency gas furnaces installed in old ductwork tend to have
    a. higher maintenance requirements.
    b. excess temperature rise across the heat exchanger.
    c. shorter life spans.
    d. All of the above

112. Common refrigerant problems in a split-system air conditioner include all of the following *EXCEPT*
    a. leaking.
    b. missing insulation on lines.
    c. lines too warm or too cold.
    d. lines too far from each other.

113. A landing may *NOT* be needed for exterior steps
    a. when it is a secondary entrance and there are three or fewer risers.
    b. where there are three or fewer risers, regardless of which entrance it is.
    c. where there are fewer than six steps.
    d. when the door opens inward.

114. A 1,500-square-foot house has an electric stove, electric dryer, central air-conditioning (FLA = 18 amps), and a recent basement renovation that included the installation of a 3,000-watt sauna. If it has a 60A service, you should report that
    a. the existing service is adequate.
    b. the existing service will support additional loads.
    c. the service should be upgraded.
    d. additional loads should be upgraded, otherwise the service is okay.

115. If the backup heat system for a heat pump is a gas furnace
    a. an emergency heat switch is not required.
    b. the indoor coil requires a vent.
    c. the indoor coil must be downstream of (or after) the furnace heat exchanger.
    d. the furnace is typically located in the outdoor unit.

116. Jack studs
    a. support lintels.
    b. are full-length studs.
    c. support window sills.
    d. support beams.

117. Double tapping is
    a. an approved method of extending a service panel's capacity.
    b. the term for attaching two wires to a single fuse or breaker terminal.
    c. the term for connecting two wires in a wire nut before connecting them to a fuse or breaker.
    d. not acceptable unless the same number of taps occur on one bus as the other.

118. Wood deterioration is typically discovered during a home inspection by
    a. probing with an awl or similar tool.
    b. visual observation.
    c. tapping with a hammer.
    d. both a and b.

119. Wood frame walls with wood siding should be
    a. at least 6 inches above grade.
    b. just barely above grade.
    c. at least 12 inches above grade.
    d. at least 8 inches above grade.

120. Common and dangerous cracks in the hearth of a wood-burning fireplace are often found
    a. at the back of the hearth.
    b. between the hearth and hearth extension.
    c. at the front of the hearth extension.
    d. at the sides of the hearth extension.

121. Galvanized iron or steel drain piping should *NOT* be installed
    a. in an attic.
    b. in the ground.
    c. in crawlspaces.
    d. as stacks (vertical pipes) that serve as waste and vent stacks.

122. There are two layers of shingles on the roof, with the most recent installation less than two-years-old. At the chimney, the original steel flashings are rusted. The shingles are sealed to the older metal with asphalt cement. The roofer should have
    a. used caulking instead of asphalt cement.
    b. installed new flashings.
    c. stripped off the old shingles first.
    d. replaced only the flashings that are rusted through.

123. Masonry veneer walls are
    a. supported with header courses.
    b. hung on studs.
    c. watertight.
    d. brittle.

124. The induced-draft fan makes grinding noises when you turn up the thermostat. This is likely
    a. indicative of dirt on the fan.
    b. failure of the fan bearings.
    c. decomposition of the plastic vent piping.
    d. condensate water trapped in the fan.

125. You can check the thickness of the flooring and the subfloor material by
    a. referring to building plans.
    b. lifting out a supply air register.
    c. measuring the overall floor thickness and subtracting the joists.
    d. drilling a small pilot hole in an inconspicuous spot.

126. You notice a wooden post as the support for the service drop. You should
    a. recommend replacing it right away with a steel mast.
    b. check for rot, damage, or movement.
    c. assume that you'll find obsolete equipment inside the house.
    d. tug on the service drop wires to make sure the mast doesn't give.

127. Rope wicks in veneer walls
    a. are better than weep holes.
    b. are often used in place of weep holes.
    c. replace brick ties.
    d. are used with plastic screens.

128. Third party liability means that
    a. the seller is liable if you hurt yourself during the inspection.
    b. you are liable if your client hurts himself or herself during the inspection.
    c. there are people other than your client relying on your report.
    d. a report has to be addressed to more than one person (husband and wife, for example).

129. Wood lintels need
    a. wood preservative.
    b. 6 inches of endbearing.
    c. flashing.
    d. 1½ inches of endbearing.

130. Which of the following are the most appropriate deck fasteners?
    a. Roofing nails
    b. Hot-dipped galvanized nails
    c. Drywall screws
    d. Electroplate galvanized nails

131. A trap primer
    a. is used on every trap.
    b. requires an air gap.
    c. prevents traps from freezing.
    d. prevents traps from siphoning.

132. To determine if a beam is sagging
    a. use a plumb bob.
    b. sight along the underside of the beam along its length.
    c. check for crushing at the bearing points.
    d. look for cracks on the bottom side of the beam near the midpoint.

133. The evaporator fan in a split-system air conditioner is usually located
    a. near the compressor.
    b. near the condenser coil.
    c. outdoors.
    d. near the expansion device.

134. Heat circulators for fireplaces
    a. do not improve the efficiency of fireplaces.
    b. are used only on factory-built fireplaces.
    c. may use fans to promote air flow.
    d. can safely have their intakes and outlets obstructed.

135. At roof-to-wall flashings, where wood siding is the counter-flashing, the siding should be kept
    a. less than one inch above the roof.
    b. one to two inches above the roof.
    c. two to three inches above the roof.
    d. four to five inches above the roof.

136. Which statement about suspended ceilings is *FALSE?*
    a. Home inspectors should not lift the tiles because they can be difficult to get back in.
    b. They reduce the ceiling height.
    c. They are also called acoustic tile.
    d. They are often installed below damaged plaster ceilings.

137. Which statement is *CORRECT?*
    a. Neutral and ground wires should be connected at subpanels and separated at the main panel.
    b. Ground and neutral wires should always be connected.
    c. Hot and neutral wires should always be the same color.
    d. Neutral and ground wires should be connected at the main panel and separate at subpanels.

138. The best way to determine if the automatic vent damper is operating correctly is to
    a. turn up the thermostat and check for spillage at the draft hood.
    b. turn the thermostat up and get up on the roof to feel the chimney flue for heat.
    c. check for the presence of corrosion on the exhaust flue downstream of the damper.
    d. turn up the thermostat and listen for a loud grinding noise from the vent damper.

139. If a building is 16 feet wide with a roof peak in the middle and collar ties at the midpoint of each rafter, the rafter span is
    a. 4 feet.
    b. impossible to determine unless we know the height from the ceiling joists to the ridge board.
    c. 8 feet.
    d. 16 feet.

140. In the service box, the ungrounded service entrance wires should be connected
    a. to the "load" side of the main switch.
    b. to the "line" side of the main switch.
    c. one to the switch and the other to the grounding terminal.
    d. one to the switch and the other to the neutral.

141. Most radiant heating systems are located
    a. in the ceiling.
    b. in the floors.
    c. on exterior walls below windows.
    d. in lightweight concrete panels.

142. The main difference between a laundry tub pump and a sump pump is
    a. laundry tub pumps can handle lint.
    b. sump pumps are larger capacity.
    c. laundry tub pumps operate on 120-volt, and sump pumps operate on 1,240-volt electrical power.
    d. sump pumps are automatic, and laundry tub pumps must be manual.

143. What would you do if you saw metal ductwork from a forced-air heating system for a house passing through a garage?
    a. Suggest that it be insulated to the level required in the area
    b. Recommend that it be removed
    c. Recommend covering the ductwork with drywall, as this is the only acceptable method to gas-proof a garage
    d. Recommend a supply air register to help heat the garage

144. Where trusses are used for a roof in a snowy region
    a. your roofing structure inspection should include a careful look at upper roof areas adjacent to lower roofs.
    b. no special attention is required for any part of the roof structure inspection.
    c. where there are two roof levels, snow may drift onto the lower roof adjacent to a wall extending above the roof. This concentrated load may cause sagging or even break truss members.
    d. snow drifting is common where there are two different roof levels, but trusses are "over-designed" such that no problems are likely to occur.

145. Which group of terms does *NOT* go together?
    a. Pier, column, truss
    b. Rafter, truss, purlin
    c. Joist, beam, girder
    d. Stud, header, sill

146. Abandoned wires should be
    a. terminated in junction boxes.
    b. secured tightly against joists or studs.
    c. capped with wire nuts and tape.
    d. removed.

147. The minimum head room for stairs in a home is roughly
    a. 72 inches.
    b. 80 inches.
    c. 84 inches.
    d. 88 inches.

148. Where a steeply pitched shingle roof meets a lower-pitched shingle roof, the valley may be especially vulnerable to
     a. unusually rapid deterioration.
     b. water penetration under the shingles, on the lower-pitched side.
     c. excessive shingle wear adjacent to the valley on the steeper-pitched side.
     d. buckling of the flashing material.

149. Gravity, warm-air furnaces are different from forced-air furnaces in each of the following respects *EXCEPT* that
     a. there is no fan.
     b. there is no high temperature limit switch.
     c. the furnace is always located in the center of the house.
     d. the supply and return duct systems are large, round, and sloped up from the furnace.

150. If clients want to discuss changes to a home, you should
     a. tell them that this is beyond your scope, and you are not allowed to do it.
     b. refer them to a municipal inspector.
     c. ask the listing and selling agents whether the changes would affect the market value of the home.
     d. discuss the changes away from the seller.

151. Common problems with sinks and basins include all of the following *EXCEPT*
     a. leaks.
     b. excess pressure.
     c. rust.
     d. cross connections.

152. Rafter spread can be visually identified by
     a. soffits pulling away from the house wall.
     b. cracking of interior wall finishes below and parallel to the ceiling joists.
     c. cracks in the rafters.
     d. buckling collar ties.

153. A dirty evaporator fan in a split-system air conditioner may result in all of the following *EXCEPT*
     a. reduced airflow.
     b. an unbalanced fan.
     c. vibration.
     d. Freon leaks.

154. To check the connections of the wires inside the service box, you should
     a. measure the amperage in the neutral.
     b. pull on the wire.
     c. measure the voltage between the neutral and the ground.
     d. look for melting, charring, or damage to the wire and insulation.

155. Pyrolysis is
     a. a phenomenon where the autoignition temperature of the wood is reduced.
     b. a phenomenon where chronic condensation on the underside of sheathing causes the sheathing to sag between the rafters.
     c. a phenomenon where cellulose insulation can spontaneously ignite when in contact with roof sheathing that does not have the FRT rating.
     d. premature corrosion of sheathing nails due to contact with acids in some types of waferboard.

156. Good skylight inspections include all of these *EXCEPT*
     a. looking from inside the home below the skylight.
     b. looking at the flashings.
     c. standing on the glazed section.
     d. tapping on the glazing.

157. You notice that the service drop and service entrance conductors are bare at the splice. You should
     a. report this as a safety hazard.
     b. wrap them in tape, if you carry any.
     c. consider this acceptable, if the conductors are secure.
     d. do none of the above.

158. Sweating toilets
     a. are unusual.
     b. are worse if the toilet runs continuously.
     c. should be fed with hot water.
     d. will rust the flush mechanism and flush valve.

159. A heat pump in the defrost cycle
     a. has the outdoor fan running.
     b. is working at maximum efficiency.
     c. may have the system operating in the cooling mode.
     d. will shut down the backup heat.

160. Which of the following statements applies to notching or putting holes in truss members?
    a. Holes should be no more than ⅓ of the depth of the member.
    b. Neither holes nor notches are permitted anywhere on a truss.
    c. Holes are permitted only in the middle-third of the bottom chord of a truss.
    d. Holes and notches are not permitted in the top or bottom chord but are permitted in the webs.

161. Home inspectors typically check the exterior grading
    a. with a level.
    b. with a plumb bob.
    c. by visual examination only.
    d. by observing whether a soccer ball rolls down away from the building when placed against the wall.

162. When you come across an oil furnace that has a tripped primary control, you should
    a. reset the primary controller and attempt to fire the burner.
    b. not reset the primary control, and attempt to view the firepot for pooling oil.
    c. not reset the primary control, and attempt to view the heat exchanger for pooling oil.
    d. reset the primary control, but do not attempt to fire the burner.

163. Which solariums would be most prone to condensation?
    a. Solarium in San Diego
    b. Wood frame solarium
    c. Solarium off a kitchen
    d. Solarium facing south

164. A flashlight can be used during wall inspections to
    a. be rolled across the wall surface to feel for irregularities.
    b. shine parallel to the wall to look for irregularities.
    c. shine at the wall, section by section, to ensure all areas are scanned.
    d. identify condensation on walls by reflection and refraction of light.

165. The most common cross connection on a bathtub is
    a. a pressure-balancing faucet set.
    b. a tub fill spout below the tub flood rim.
    c. a tub drain interconnected with the cold water supply.
    d. a faulty shower diverter.

166. Whole-house fans should
    a. never have insulating covers over them in the winter, because they obstruct airflow.
    b. not be operated during the winter months if there are combustion heating appliances.
    c. never be operated with windows or doors open.
    d. have an outlet area that is roughly 50 percent of the inlet area.

167. Which of the following aluminum wire installations is most likely to overheat?
    a. A receptacle that powers a television and a stereo
    b. A receptacle with a computer
    c. A receptacle with a washing machine
    d. A receptacle with an electric heater

168. All of the following are appropriate response strategies limiting home inspectors' liability, *EXCEPT*
    a. responding to complaints as quickly as possible.
    b. never admitting that there is a problem with the home.
    c. refusing to accept as fact anything you are told.
    d. refusing to argue with the client over the phone on the initial call.

169. Where ceiling joists or rafters are cut to make an opening (skylight, dormer, etc.) the load from the cut members must be transferred to adjacent members. The framing installed to do this is called a
    a. trimmer.
    b. swale.
    c. strut.
    d. header.

170. Which of the following is a simple test on an operating conventional gas-fired, forced-air furnace that should always be performed?
    a. Test the exhaust for carbon monoxide
    b. Test for spillage at the draft hood
    c. Test for excessive vibration of the house air fan by touching the fan
    d. Measure the pressure differential across the house air fan

171. The exterior sides and bottom of the service box are rusting. The interior of the service box is not affected. There is a water stain on the foundation wall below the service box. The box is below grade. Your *BEST* conclusion from these clues is
    a. plumbing leakage; check for a pipe above.
    b. no sealant between the wires and the inside of the conduit.
    c. defective service cap (weatherhead).
    d. leakage at the foundation wall conduit hole.

172. If, when looking at a slate roof, you see ribbons, you should tell your client that
    a. these may be weak areas and the slate is not high quality.
    b. these are signs of particularly good, strong slates.
    c. these slates are rare and tend to be more expensive.
    d. these slates have changed color because of air pollution.

173. If you mix convectors and radiators, the convector-heated rooms will
    a. overheat when the boiler is running.
    b. be too cool when the boiler is running.
    c. cause air to be trapped in the radiators.
    d. cause air trapping to occur in the convectors.

174. Common shower stall problems include all of the following *EXCEPT*
    a. slow drains.
    b. rust.
    c. water damage around sills and thresholds.
    d. missing overflows.

175. A skylight has been added to a roof framed with rafters and ceiling joists. Three rafters are cut to make the opening. Which of the following statements are true?
    a. A single header should be installed to transfer the load from the cut rafters to the next full rafter.
    b. A single header and a double trimmer are required.
    c. A single trimmer and a double header are required.
    d. A double header and a double trimmer are required.

176. Common switch problems include all of the following *EXCEPT*
    a. damaged switches.
    b. inoperative switches.
    c. dimmer switches with a positive shut off.
    d. switches for garbage disposals on the front of base cabinets.

177. Which of the following is a common problem with exterior window drip caps (cap flashings)?
    a. Installed too high
    b. Installed too low
    c. Missing drip caps
    d. Made of metal

178. A guideline for the appropriate slope of a lot away from a house is
    a. one inch over six feet.
    b. one inch over ten feet.
    c. one inch per foot for two feet.
    d. one inch per foot for six feet.

179. Which single-ply roofing system typically uses a base sheet and cap sheet?
    a. PVC
    b. Metal
    c. Mod bit
    d. Roll roofing

180. All of the following functions are performed by trusses *EXCEPT*
    a. support for live and dead loads.
    b. lateral support for exterior walls.
    c. lateral support for masonry chimney.
    d. creation of attic space and ventilation space.

181. A copper #6-gauge cable has supplied a subpanel. The cable is protected by 60-amp breakers at the main panel. You should make sure that
    a. the cable is protected in a ventilated metal raceway.
    b. the cable is in rigid conduit.
    c. the cable is no longer than three feet.
    d. the subpanel is rated to handle at least 60 amps.

182. The purpose of the gravel on a built-up tar and gravel roof is to
    a. provide ballast to help hold the roof membrane down.
    b. prevent delamination of the plies.
    c. protect the membrane from ultraviolet light.
    d. do both a and c.

183. Reports can be released to people other than your client
    a. if they are the owner of the property at the time of the inspection.
    b. if they were either the selling or listing real estate agent involved in the transaction.
    c. only with the approval of the client.
    d. if the recipients have signed a third-party liability waiver.

184. All of the following are evidence of possible erosion on ravine lots *EXCEPT*
    a. evidence of chronic water problems in the basement.
    b. a lack of vegetation.
    c. bands of freshly exposed topsoil.
    d. tree trunks significantly off vertical.

185. A house has service entrance conductors designed for 100 amps and a main disconnect rated at 100 amps. Which of these conditions is unsafe?
    a. The service box is rated at 125 amps.
    b. The service box is rated at 75 amps.
    c. The distribution panel is rated at 125 amps.
    d. The distribution panel is rated at 200 amps.

186. A common problem with skylights in cold climates is
    a. reduced visibility and light entry due to snow covering.
    b. cool drafts on people sitting below skylights.
    c. ice dams.
    d. poor operability.

187. A subpanel is supplying a three-ton air conditioner (running load amps = 18A) and an electric dryer (5,000W). The 10-gauge copper subpanel feed wire is connected to a 60A breaker in the main panel. You should
    a. report the installation as okay.
    b. recommend changing the size of the feed wire to match the breaker.
    c. recommend changing the size of the breaker to match the feed wire.
    d. recommend switching to a gas dryer.

188. Which of these statements about rot is *FALSE?*
    a. Rot is actually a fungus.
    b. Wood above 20 percent moisture content is vulnerable to rot.
    c. Wood below 40°F is vulnerable to rot.
    d. End grains of wood are more susceptible to rot.

189. If there is no water in the boiler, the low water cutout prevents the
    a. circulator from operating.
    b. burner from firing.
    c. pressure reducer from adding water.
    d. entrapment of air in the air separator.

190. Two reasons for dedicated circuits are that
    a. the circuit uses so much electricity, and the circuit is so important.
    b. the circuit is so important, and you can't hook high-demand circuits up in series.
    c. we want to avoid nuisance tripping, and the appliances are near a wet location.
    d. the high start-up surge is a problem, and the high operating temperatures of furnaces and boilers may overheat the wire.

191. A clue that a new built-up roof was applied over the old flat roof is
    a. usually there is no gravel because of the additional weight.
    b. there are two layers of drip edge flashings.
    c. the felts are delaminating at the edges.
    d. both layers would be visible if you were to look down the roof drain.

192. All of the following contain condition statements *EXCEPT*
    a. the overhead service entrance conductors are aluminum and rated for 100 amps.
    b. the garage door operator should be adjusted to reverse when hitting an obstruction as it closes.
    c. missing chimney flashings should be provided.
    d. the inoperative ground fault circuit interrupter should be replaced to improve electrical safety.

193. The most important implication of cracked or broken walkways is
    a. water in the basement.
    b. difficulty in snow removal.
    c. a trip hazard.
    d. water ponding on the walkway.

194. During an inspection you find 20 blown 15-amp fuses beside the panel. You might tell your client that
    a. there must have been several defective fuses purchased, perhaps from one bad lot.
    b. the 15-amp fuses should be replaced with a larger fuse size that will not blow.
    c. it's likely that there is a least one overloaded circuit in the panel.
    d. it's likely that there is a defect in the panel.

195. Common thermostat problems include all of the following *EXCEPT*
    a. poor location.
    b. not level.
    c. looseness.
    d. wrong size.

196. Which one of the following statements about retaining wall drainage is *FALSE?*
    a. Drainage is important.
    b. Soils that drain well, such as clay, should be used behind retaining walls.
    c. A weeping tile or drainage holes are often recommended.
    d. Tied-back walls do not usually require drain holes.

197. If a metal roof seems to have many leaks (but no specific leakage area) and it only leaks in the winter, you should consider which of the following?
    a. Ice damming
    b. No cant strip at the roof wall intersection
    c. Condensation on the underside of the metal
    d. Chimney flashing failure

198. All of the following are priority statements, *EXCEPT* that
    a. the electrical cleanup work should be done immediately.
    b. prompt repairs to the gutters and downspouts will help prevent wet basement problems.
    c. the asphalt shingle roofing has a remaining life of 10 to 15 years.
    d. the fireplace chimney should be swept before using the fireplace.

199. Which of the following supply piping materials cannot be used on a hot water system in modern construction?
    a. Copper
    b. Polyethylene
    c. Polybutylene
    d. CPVC

200. The pressure-reducing valve
    a. reduces plumbing water pressure to boiler pressure.
    b. reduces boiler water pressure to plumbing pressure.
    c. reduces the pressure in the radiator to atmospheric pressure.
    d. prevents overheating.

SAMPLE EXAM ANSWERS AND EXPLANATIONS

1. **c.** You have to report anything that you would usually inspect but didn't and to say in your report why you didn't inspect it.

2. **d.** Replacing 50 feet of 100-foot pipe will make the same positive difference no matter which 50-feet of pipe is replaced.

3. **a.** Knob-and-tube wiring was commonly used from 1920 to 1950.

4. **a.** Slate lasts the longest of the materials listed.

5. **b.** Leaking is a common flow control valve problem.

6. **c.** You can't predict future settlement from a single visit.

7. **a.** A Freon leak is typically identified as an oil stain.

8. **b.** Bridging is not typically a part of a wood frame wall assembly.

9. **d.** Resloping the cap is not a common approach to improving chimney draft.

10. **c.** Vertical shear is not associated with shrinkage cracks.

11. **c.** A pressure regulator is not usually found on private water supply systems because water pressures are usually not in excess of 80 psi.

12. **c.** Central air-conditioning systems have two fans.

13. **c.** Insulated metal exterior doors with storm doors may overheat.

14. **c.** Unplugging the washing machine will ensure that your tester doesn't read a false ground connection through the washing machine.

15. **a.** Home inspectors must disclose an interest in a business that may affect their client.

16. **c.** Excessive drafts usually result in lower humidity levels.

17. **c.** The common temperature rise is 70°F to 100°F.

18. **b.** If the wall has moved inward, the cracks are typically wider on the inside face.

19. **b.** On most steep roofs, exposed fasteners are a sign of poor installation.

20. **d.** An undersized expansion tank is not a common problem.

21. **c.** Only two-pipe steam systems are commonly converted to hot water systems.

22. **c.** There is no such thing as an inverted slab.

23. **b.** Masonry chimneys should have a 2-inch clearance from combustible framing members.

24. **b.** Mounting the light on a wall above the door in a closet is not a problem.

25. **b.** The combustion and dilution air requirements are about 2 square inches of net vent space for each 1,000 BTU per hour input.

26. **a.** Efflorescence is a result of water moving through masonry or concrete walls.

27. **a.** The high-pressure side of an air-conditioning system is between the compressor and the metering device.

28. **b.** If the red and black wires are connected to the same bus, the white wire will see 22 amps. This is an unsafe condition on 14-gauge wire.

29. **d.** You can find step flashing by lifting the shingles adjacent to the chimney or wall in most cases.

30. **d.** Fiberglass is not an air barrier.

31. **b.** Basements are common in cold climates because we have to dig down below the frost line for the footings anyway.

32. **b.** Most inspectors do not charge a premium for allowing clients to attend.

33. **a.** If the flame touches the heat exchanger when the blower is running, the blower is probably pushing the flame over. This means the heat exchanger is probably cracked.

34. **d.** Cut trusses need evaluation by specialists. Sistering is not necessarily adequate.

35. **b.** An oversized cap is not a common problem.

36. **b.** CPVC water pipe may not be used for hot and cold supply lines in multifamily residences. Combustible piping material is not allowed to run from one dwelling to another, typically.

37. **a.** A seven-inch step down into the garage is a good thing, not a problem.

38. **c.** The current in the water heater is 12.5 amps ($P = V \times I$, $I = P/V$, $I = 3,000/240$).

39. **d.** Uniform settlement may stress utility pipes.

40. **a.** Foundation irrigation is a method of stabilizing expansive soils.

41. **c.** A horizontal fracture in the foundation weakens the foundation. It won't be able to resist soil pressure as it could originally.

42. **c.** A 175-amp service is not common.

43. **c.** The condenser coil dissipates heat from the Freon downstream of the compressor.

44. **b.** The condensate lines are probably blocked.

45. **b.** Using 12-inch vertical extensions at the end of supply lines can help solve or reduce water hammer.

46. **c.** Piers may move because soil below is disturbed.

47. **a.** Insulation too close to chimneys does not result in the insulation being wet.

48. **d.** Caulking is not a common roof patching material and is not in the same category as the other materials in this list that are asphalt based.

49. **d.** The finish coat on EIFS is thinner than with traditional stucco.

50. **c.** An improperly supported service drop may result in the drip loop disappearing under tension.

51. **a.** Heat recovery ventilators do not have burners.

52. **a.** The introductory discussion should set goals for your inspection.

53. **b.** The steady state efficiency is 80 percent if the input is 100,000 Btu and the output is 80,000 Btu.

54. **c.** Rising damp is capillary wicking of water into masonry units. It can rise a great distance up through the masonry.

55. **b.** The upper element on an electric water heater usually comes on second. The lower element sees the cold water being let into the heater as the hot water is drawn off the top. It's the lower element that sees the cold water first and responds first.

56. **b.** Houses are blown off of foundations most often during construction.

57. **b.** In an asphalt shingle roof you would typically go through two layers of shingles.

58. **b.** Indoor swimming pool enclosures can be corrosive because of the chemicals. Watch for more than the usual amount of rusting.

59. **d.** Inadequate height is not the result of an offset problem.

60. **b.** Most concrete foundation cracks occur at window corners.

61. **c.** Leakage is a common problem with water-cooled coils.

62. **d.** Columns see mostly compression loads.

63. **d.** A home inspection is not an appraisal inspection.

64. **b.** Hardboard is combustible.

65. **c.** Clamp-on amp meters are used to check that all of the furnace elements are working.

66. **a.** Columns may settle because the footing for them is too small.

67. **b.** A chimney protruding through a valley flashing obstructs valley drainage and therefore has great potential for leakage.

68. **c.** Exhaust flues on gas-fired or oil-fired water heaters should have a slope of ¼-inch per foot.

69. **b.** In the United States, a 100-amp service must have 4-gauge wire.

70. **d.** Rot is the most serious implication of insulation problems.

71. **b.** The top of the column should be as wide as the beam that it supports.

72. **b.** Your liability is greater if the buyer's expectations are unrealistic.

73. **c.** Beams transfer loads directly from floors to columns.

74. **c.** The condensate drain pan is located below the evaporator coil.

75. **c.** To look for a loose connection, look for signs of overheating near the end of the wire and/or at the connection point.

76. **c.** A leaking humidifier may rust out the heat exchanger.

77. **b.** Painting is one way to protect galvanized steel roofing.

78. **b.** A barometric damper that is stuck closed will not allow an oil smell into the house.

79. **c.** Trying to avoid letting agents talk because they may show you up should not be an issue.

80. **a.** Joists are like small beams.

81. **c.** You should report that the main service fuse rating was not determinable if you can't read the fuse labels.

82. **c.** Fiber cement shingles are lighter than slate.

83. **b.** An electric baseboard heater should get warm within one minute of turning it on.

84. **b.** Crawl space floors that are insulated often result in the floor above feeling cool.

85. **a.** Probing the ends of beams with a screwdriver is a good way to check for rot.

86. **d.** Home inspectors cannot accept or pay commissions.

87. **b.** Overlapping joists that extend 12 inches past the support beam may cause a hump in the floor as the end of the joist kicks up when the center part of the joist on the other side of the beam is loaded.

88. **c.** An auxiliary drain pan is needed when leakage in the primary pan may damage interior finishes.

89. **d.** Engineered wood often needs larger end bearing than conventional joists.

90. **a.** The flame sensor ensures that the pilot or burner is on.

91. **d.** The total wattage in the circuit is 240 + 360 = 600. These are 120 volt appliances. P = VI, I = P/V, I = 600/120 = 5 amps. V = IR, R = V/I, R = 120/5 = 24.

92. **c.** Irregular cracks on young asphalt shingle roofs indicate a manufacturing defect and possible shortening of the life expectancy.

93. **a.** Power-vented or fan-assisted water heaters do not have clogged condensation collection system problems because they are not condensing units.

94. **c.** Clay or slate will not buckle.

95. **b.** Walls should not support masonry chimneys in most cases.

96. **d.** The closing discussion is a brief summary of key points that can be held in front agents and the seller if that is satisfactory to your client.

97. **a.** Exposed fasteners are acceptable on metal roofing.

98. **c.** Copper tube boilers have a life expectancy of 15 to 25 years.

99. **b.** Masonry walls may lean outward if the wall extends higher than the ceiling joists. This is usually a result of roof rafters pushing out on the wall.

100. **a.** Creosote should be no thicker than ¼-inch before it is removed.

101. **c.** Three prong plugs became standard in all branch circuits in the early 1960s.

102. **d.** Spalling and mortar damage near the bottom of a masonry column outside the home are usually the result of freeze/thaw cycles.

103. **d.** Gas water heaters do not have a barometric damper.

104. **e.** Flow measuring stations on warm-side ducts are appropriate.

105. **a.** Caulking is not an appropriate repair for brickwork.

106. **c.** Squeaking subflooring usually indicates poor fastening of the subfloors.

107. **c.** Obsolete service boxes typically have exposed terminals.

108. **d.** When you see roofing cement on a chimney like this, you typically won't know if proper step flashings were installed. The roofing cement is only a temporary repair. This is definitely not good building practice.

109. **d.** Slopes of ¼-inch to ½-inch per foot are desirable on horizontal drain pipes, not a problem.

110. **c.** Cedar is not a common structural wood because it is relatively weak.

111. **d.** A high-efficiency gas furnace in old ductwork may have higher maintenance requirements, is likely to have excess temperature rise across the heat exchanger, and, as a result, a shorter life span.

112. **d.** Refrigerant lines being too far from each other is not a common problem.

113. **a.** A landing may not be needed for exterior steps if they lead to a secondary entrance and there are three or fewer risers.

114. **c.** This service is probably too small and you should be recommending upgrading.

115. **c.** If the backup heat system is a gas furnace, the indoor coil must be downstream of the furnace heat exchanger.

116. **a.** Jack studs support lintels.

117. **b.** Double tapping is a term for attaching two wires to a single fuse or breaker. It is poor practice and not allowed in most cases.

118. **d.** Wood deterioration is discovered by probing and looking.

119. **d.** Wood siding should stop at least 8 inches above grade.

120. **b.** Common and dangerous cracks in the hearth are often found at the joint between the hearth and the hearth extension.

121. **b.** Galvanized-iron or galvanized-steel drain piping should not be installed in the ground.

122. **b.** In this case the roofer should have installed new flashings.

123. **d.** Masonry veneer walls are brittle.

124. **b.** Grinding noises indicate bearings in distress in the induced-draft fan.

125. **b.** The best way to check the thickness of the subflooring and flooring is to lift out a heat register.

126. **b.** When you see a wooden post supporting the service drop, you should check for rot, damage, or movement.

127. **b.** Rope wicks are often used in place of weep holes.

128. **c.** Third-party liability is where people rely on your report that you did not intend. If your client gives your report to some else, that is a third party. You may be liable to them for the contents of your report even though you never met them unless you disclaim third party liability in the report itself.

129. **d.** Wood lintels need 1½ -inches of end bearing.

130. **b.** Hot-dipped, galvanized nails are acceptable deck fasteners.

131. **b.** A trap primer requires an air gap or backflow prevention device.

132. **b.** You should sight along the underside of the length of a beam to see if it is sagging.

133. **d.** The evaporator fan may be adjacent to the expansion device.

134. **c.** Heat circulators for fireplaces may use fans to promote air flow.

135. **b.** Wood siding at wall flashings should be cut back one to two inches above the roof.

136. **a.** Home inspectors should not avoid lifting the tiles just because they can be difficult to get back in.

137. **d.** Neutral and ground wires should be connected at the main panel and separated at subpanels.

138. **a.** Turn up the thermostat and check for spillage.

139. **a.** The span here is four feet. The spans are interrupted by the end of the rafters, the peak, and the collar ties.

140. **b.** The service entrance conductors belong on the "line" side of the main switch.

141. **a.** Most radiant-heating systems are located in the ceiling.

142. **a.**   The main difference between laundry tub pumps and sump pumps are that laundry tub pumps can handle lint.

143. **a.**   Metal ductwork from a forced-air heating system passing through a garage should be insulated.

144. **c.**   Concentrated loads of snow drifting on a lower roof when it's adjacent to a wall can cause truss members to sag or break.

145. **a.**   Piers and columns are vertical compression members. Trusses are typically horizontal members that see bending forces and shear forces.

146. **d.**   Abandoned wires should be removed.

147. **b.**   The minimum stair headroom is roughly 80 inches.

148. **b.**   Where steep roofs meet lower sloped roofs at a valley, the valley is especially vulnerable to water penetration under the shingles on the lower side.

149. **b.**   Gravity, warm-air furnaces do not have a high temperature limit switch.

150. **d.**   If you are going to talk about changes, do so away from the seller, who may be upset by the buyer's plans for the home.

151. **b.**   Excess pressure is not a common problem with sinks and basins.

152. **a.**   Soffits pulling away from the house wall suggests rafter spread.

153. **d.**   Freon leaks are not the result of a dirty evaporator fan.

154. **d.**   You should be looking for melting, charring, or damage to the wire insulation.

155. **a.**   Pyrolysis is a phenomenon where the auto-ignition temperature of the wood is reduced.

156. **c.**   You should never stand on the glazed section of a skylight.

157. **a.**   Bare wires at the splice between the service drop and service entrance are a safety hazard.

158. **b.**   Sweating toilets are worse if the toilet runs continuously.

159. **c.**   The heat pump in the defrost cycle may have the system operating in a cooling mode.

160. **b.**   Neither holes nor notches are permitted in trusses.

161. **c.**   Home inspectors normally use a visual examination to check the exterior grading.

162. **b.**   You should be looking for pooling oil in the firepot. You should not reset the primary control. This may contribute to flooding the firepot.

163. **c.**   Solariums in areas of high humidity such as kitchens are prone to condensation.

164. **b.**   Flashlights can help identify wall irregularities if you shine the beam parallel to the wall.

165. **b.**   The most common cross connection on a bathtub is a tub fill spout below the tub flood rim.

166. **b.**   Whole-house fans should not be operated during the winter months if there are combustion appliances in the house.

167. **d.**   An aluminum wire receptacle with an electric baseboard heater plugged in is most likely to overheat.

168. **b.**   It is a mistake to never admit that there is a problem with the home; there often is a problem.

169. **d.**   Headers are used to transfer loads to the trimmers.

170. **b.**   We should always test for spillage at the draft hood.

171. **d.**   This water is probably a result of leakage at the foundation wall conduit hole.

172. **a.**   Ribbons in slate are weak areas, indicating that the slate is not of high quality.

173. **a.**   Mixing convectors and radiators is a problem because the convector-heated rooms will be too hot when the boiler is running and will be unable to maintain the same water temperature as the radiator-heated rooms. This means that they will cool off more quickly than the rooms with radiators.

174. **d.**   Slow drains, rust, and water damage around sills and thresholds are all common shower stall problems.

175. **d.**   When cutting three rafters, a double header and a double trimmer are required.

176. **c.** Dimmer switches with a positive shut off are not a problem.

177. **c.** Missing drip caps are the most common problem.

178. **d.** A good slope is one inch per foot for at least six feet.

179. **c.** Mod bit may have a base sheet and a cap sheet.

180. **c.** Trusses do not support masonry chimneys.

181. **d.** You should check if sub panel is rated for 60 Amps.

182. **d.** Gravel on a built-up roof provides ballast to help hold the membrane down, and protects against UV light.

183. **c.** We can only release reports with the approval of the client. It is the client who actually owns the report.

184. **a.** Chronic water problems in the basement are not necessarily related to erosion. All of the other items on this list are definitely erosion related.

185. **b.** A service box rated at 75 amps is not adequate for 100-amp service.

186. **c.** Ice dams are a common problem with skylights in cold climates.

187. **b.** The breaker size and the feed wire size should be a match. Alternatively, the wire amp capacity should be greater than the breaker rating. The 10-gauge copper wire can safely carry 30 amps.

188. **c.** Wood below 40°F is not vulnerable to rot.

189. **b.** If there is no water in the boiler, the low water cutout prevents the burner from firing.

190. **a.** You might want a dedicated circuit, because the circuit uses a lot of electricity, or because the circuit is very important (a furnace or freezer circuit, for example).

191. **b.** Two layers of drip edge flashings suggest two layers of roofing.

192. **a.** The statement about the service conductors is descriptive only. It provides no insight as to what condition the service is in.

193. **c.** Cracked or broken walkways can be trip hazards.

194. **c.** All of these blown fuses tell you that there is at least one overloaded circuit that continually blows fuses.

195. **d.** Incorrect size is not a common thermostat problem.

196. **b.** Clay is not a good draining soil.

197. **c.** Condensation on the underside of the metal roof may be the culprit.

198. **c.** The shingle roofing statement is not a priority statement because no specific action is recommended and the time frame is a span of five years.

199. **b.** Polyethylene pipe cannot be used on a hot water system.

200. **a.** Pressure reducing valves reduce the house plumbing water pressure to about 12 psi.